INSIDE JOB

National decline is typically blamed on special interests from the demand side of politics corrupting a country's institutions. The usual demand-side suspects include crony capitalists, consumer activists, economic elites, and labor unions. Less attention is given to government insiders on the supply side of politics – rulers, elected officials, bureaucrats, and public employees. In autocracies and democracies, government insiders have the motive, means, and opportunity to co-opt political power for their benefit and at the expense of national well-being. Many storied empires have succumbed to such inside jobs. Today, they imperil countries as different as China and the United States. Democracy, government by the people, does not ensure government for the people. Understanding how government insiders use their power to subvert the public interest – and how these negative consequences can be mitigated – is the topic of this book by Mark A. Zupan.

Mark A. Zupan is President of Alfred University, New York. He holds a B.A. from Harvard University and a Ph.D. in economics from the Massachusetts Institute of Technology (MIT) and has won several teaching awards. He has served on the boards of several for-profit companies, including Constellation Brands, PAETEC Holdings, Northern Trust, HNP Capital, iVEDiX, and Stocker Yale, as well as nonprofits such as the United Way, the Harley School, GMAC, and AACSB. His previous book, *Microeconomics: Theory and Applications*, co-authored with Edgar Browning, is currently in its twelfth edition. Zupan has published in the *Wall Street Journal, New York Times, LA Times, Bloomberg Businessweek, Huffington Post, Kiplingers,* and *Financial Times.*

Inside Job

How Government Insiders Subvert the Public Interest

MARK A. ZUPAN

President, Alfred University, NY, USA

CAMBRIDGE
UNIVERSITY PRESS

University Printing House, Cambridge CB2 8BS, United Kingdom

One Liberty Plaza, 20th Floor, New York, NY 10006, USA

477 Williamstown Road, Port Melbourne, VIC 3207, Australia

4843/24, 2nd Floor, Ansari Road, Daryaganj, Delhi – 110002, India

79 Anson Road, #06–04/06, Singapore 079906

Cambridge University Press is part of the University of Cambridge.

It furthers the University's mission by disseminating knowledge in the pursuit of education, learning, and research at the highest international levels of excellence.

www.cambridge.org
Information on this title: www.cambridge.org/9781107153738
DOI: 10.1017/9781316599983

© Mark A. Zupan 2017

First published 2017

Printed in the United States of America by Sheridan Books, Inc.

A catalogue record for this publication is available from the British Library.

Library of Congress Cataloging-in-Publication Data
Names: Zupan, Mark A., author.
Title: Inside job : how government insiders subvert the public interest / Mark A. Zupan.
Description: Cambridge, United Kingdom ; New York, NY : Cambridge University Press, 2017.
Identifiers: LCCN 2016044124| ISBN 9781107153738 (hardback) | ISBN 9781316607770 (paperback)
Subjects: LCSH: Public interest. | Political corruption. | Public officers. | Civil service.
Classification: LCC JC330.15 .Z87 2017 | DDC 320.101–dc23
LC record available at https://lccn.loc.gov/2016044124

ISBN 978-1-107-15373-8 Hardback
ISBN 978-1-316-60777-0 Paperback

Contents

Preface

The book is targeted, first and foremost, at scholars and students of political economy. While the economic model of politics that has been developed over the last fifty years has helped us to better explain and predict policy outcomes, the model has even greater potency than has been realized. By "economic model of politics," I mean the market-based framework wherein public officials are the sellers of wealth transfers through their policy actions so that interest groups must compete for favorable wealth transfers by offering support to public officials in return. The expanded potency of the model comes through relying on insights from disciplines such as history, political science, sociology, and psychology while applying the model broadly over time and across autocracies and democracies. Along the way, I pry open what has typically been treated, at least by most economists, as a black box on the supply side of politics. By doing so, a key insight that emerges is the extent to which government insiders can subvert the public interest. Taking this insight and coupling it with lessons from historical or present-day cases of the political system being captured by government insiders allows us to better conceptualize what can be done to mitigate the potential of such capture.

Too little attention has been paid to the supply side of political markets populated by rulers, elected officials, bureaucrats, and public employees and the extent to which such government insiders can profit at the expense of the public interest. Existing explanations for national decline focus on capture of the state by special interests operating on the demand side of politics, such as businesses, consumer activists, crony capitalists, trade unions, industry cartels, economic elites, and so on. Government insiders have the motive, means, and opportunity that investigators focus on when seeking to identify the perpetrator of a crime.

Looking across the broad expanse of time and around the globe, inside jobs have led to the decline of both autocracies and democracies. At the present time, they threaten both the world's largest democratic economy, the United States, and the world's largest autocracy, China. In the United States, the danger from inside jobs is posed by congressional representatives who have grown increasingly insulated from electoral competition; a K-12 public education sector whose supply side has become increasingly monopolized over the past fifty years; and rising public sector unionization. The last of these trends has resulted in mushrooming unfunded pension and health care liabilities for public workers that now represent the second-largest fiscal challenge for the country (larger than Social Security but not as large as Medicare/Medicaid/ObamaCare) and have produced budgetary crises in locations such as Detroit, Puerto Rico, Chicago, Philadelphia, Illinois, and Rhode Island. In China, inside jobs and the extent to which the ruling class has a vested interest in preserving its wealth and political power threaten to diminish the high GDP growth rates resulting from Deng Xiaoping's economic reforms.

Historical cases of inside jobs bringing down nations include the New Kingdom of Egypt, the Ottoman Empire, France under the Bourbon kings Louis XIV through Louis XVI, and China under certain emperors of the Ming dynasty. Modern examples of government insiders subverting the public interest can be found in the news on a daily basis and range from autocracies such as Venezuela, North Korea, Cuba, Russia, Zaire, and Iran to democracies such as Brazil, Turkey, Argentina, India, Malaysia, Greece, Italy, and the European Union. Inside jobs diminish a nation's prosperity, curtail citizens' political rights and civil liberties, erode citizens' trust in their government, dissipate resources through efforts to capture the rents associated with political power, and promote conflict both within a nation and between nations.

Particularly in democracies that provide more opportunity for demand-side interests to operate, capture of the state often involves a symbiotic relationship between demand-side and supply-side interests. This symbiotic capture is akin to how cancer, a leading cause of death in humans, involves a defect in the genetic code that leads to over-replication of cells to the detriment of the host organism. In our genetic code, the nucleotide base guanine, in one strand of DNA's double helix, always bonds with cytosine in the other strand, while adenine always bonds with thymine. Thus, whenever there is an incorrect nucleotide base on one strand of our DNA, it is also paired with an incorrect base on the other strand. This serves to amplify the damage done to the human body through cellular over-replication, or cancer. Analogously, any co-opting of the state by demand-side special interests is likely to be associated with government insiders who simultaneously benefit and thus serve to encrust the political outcome. Such symbiotic capture of the political process underscores why, according to Milton and Rose Friedman, "there is nothing so permanent as a temporary government program."

The book provides a simple equation ($P = G \times S \times I$) explaining how the magnitude by which government insiders profit at the expense of the public interest (P) is determined by three factors: the prospective gains from such capture (G), which depend in a positive fashion on the size of government in a society; the slack between citizens and their public officials (S); and the interest of public officials in exploiting any such slack for their benefit (I). Various chapters explore the determinants of these factors and how they either increase or diminish the possibility of inside jobs and the damage to a nation from government self-capture.

The book helps to explain the movement toward democracy and away from autocracy over the last two centuries through the operation of a quasi-market in politics. Such a market responds to changes in the costs associated with autocracy, albeit often accompanied by violence in the course of changes in political power. The costs associated with autocracy have grown over the last two centuries on account of factors such as specialization, education, and trade.

Relying on Transparency International measures of public sector integrity, this book is the first to show that democracy represents an improvement, on average, over autocracies. This is presumably due to the lower slack (S) between citizens and their public officials in democracies versus autocracies. While there are some notable exceptions such as Singapore, the UAE, and Botswana, the public sector tends to be more corrupt in autocracies than in democracies. That said, democracy, or government *by* the people, is not sufficient to ensure government *for* the people. Over a quarter of the world's democracies, for example, have a lower Transparency International rating for public sector integrity than does the average autocracy. And fewer than half of the world's democracies score higher than 50, the midpoint of the 0–100 Transparency International scale for public sector integrity, where 100 represents a perfectly clean public sector.

The book perhaps helps to explain the success of certain US presidential candidates such as Donald Trump and Bernie Sanders in the 2016 electoral season. Both Trump and Sanders railed against the extent to which government insiders have co-opted the political system to their benefit and at the expense of our nation's citizens.

The book's insights also are germane to broader audiences interested in what determines organizational success – whether such organizations are for-profit firms or nonprofit churches, hospitals, and universities. While there are more ample curbs against inside jobs in nonpolitical settings, the restraints are imperfect. So long as there are prospective gains to be realized (G), slack between managers and owners (S), and interest on the part of managers to co-opt the organization for their benefit (I), there is the possibility of an inside job and its associated destructive consequences. Witness the shenanigans at FIFA, soccer's international governing body, or the damage done during the Middle Ages by corruption within the Catholic Church's ecclesiastical ranks all the way up, at times, to the Pope. Or recall how the vested film interests within Kodak impeded the move toward digital products and thus ultimately resulted in that iconic firm's bankruptcy.

While this book has only one figure, one equation, and two tables, it is my fond hope that, through illustrating the importance of the supply side of the political marketplace, it will add to our understanding of why nations succeed or fail – whether the nations are autocracies or democracies. Government *by* the people, that is, is not sufficient to ensure government *for* the people. Democracy by itself cannot be the socioeconomic terminus if we seek to promote national well-being. Further attention has to be given to the supply side of political markets and how we can better ensure the accountability of rulers, elected officials, bureaucrats, and public employees to the public interest.

Acknowledgments

Paul Kalnithi's poignant recent memoir, *When Breath Becomes Air*, reminds us of the briefness of each of our individual interludes on this earth. In light of the brevity, one can question the wisdom of devoting a year or more of one's existence to writing a book. Yet, as Matt Ridley so eloquently notes in *The Rational Optimist: How Prosperity Evolves*, the defining and ennobling characteristic of the human species is our capacity to promote the "sex of ideas." Through language, stories, and scholarship we have developed the capacity to retain and build upon the knowledge that we have collectively accumulated in the past and thereby to create a better future for our species. The ability of universities to foster such a capacity for retaining and building upon knowledge helps explain the durability of our institutions of higher education. Whereas only one of the twelve companies comprising the initial Dow Jones Industrial Average in 1896 survives to this day (General Electric), virtually all of the top universities in existence 120 years ago continue to flourish and contribute to our nation's socioeconomic development.

In writing this book, I have benefited from the wisdom and insights of numerous historians, sociologists, psychologists, political scientists, philosophers, and economists. Many have educated me through their writings – Robert Caro, Francis Fukuyama, Paul Kennedy, Ibn Khaldun, and Max Weber, to name but a few. I have been privileged to meet and directly learn from others such as Tom Borcherding, Edgar Browning, Ronald Coase, Carolyn Minter Hoxby, Paul Joskow, Gary Libecap, Deirdre McCloskey, Terry Moe, Robert Nozick, Sam Peltzman, Richard Schmalensee, Robert Solow, George Stigler, Stephan Thernstrom, Gordon Tullock, and James Q. Wilson. Among those who comprise the latter category, I owe the deepest debt to Joe Kalt. As a freshly hired professor at Harvard, Joe first inspired me to study economics and then taught me how to do scholarship in the field of political economy.

The two papers that I was fortunate enough to co-author with Joe Kalt roughly three decades ago on the determinants of legislator voting behavior in representative democracies planted the seeds for this book. In effect, the papers showed, contrary to our own priors going into the research endeavor, that there was considerable slack between citizens and their public officials in a representative democracy such as the United States. On account of the slack, senators had latitude to pursue their worldviews or ideologies when casting roll-call votes. Contrary to the emerging economic model of politics, in other words, elected public officials in democracies did not appear to be perfectly accountable to their citizens and to how the interests of those citizens were manifest on the demand side of the political marketplace. The interests of the public officials operating on the supply side of politics mattered when it came to explaining and predicting political outcomes.

I am grateful to the University of Rochester's Simon Business School for providing a sabbatical that gave me the gift of time to write this book. The administrative experiences as a dean at Simon and prior to that as a dean at the University of Arizona's Eller College of Management and associate dean at USC's Marshall School of Business also afforded valuable insights as to how the central arguments of this book also can be applied to organizational settings outside of the political arena.

During my sabbatical, Jim Dorn generously provided an office at the Cato Institute in Washington, D.C., where I could reflect and write. He regularly pointed me to books and articles that were instrumental to sharpening my thinking. Colleagues and/or alums at the University of Rochester, such as Mark Ain, Jim Brickley, Richard Couch, Ray Dorsey, Chris Dunstan, Ron Hansen, Dennis Kessler, David Primo, Eric Rubin, Mike Ryan, Alex Sukhoy, Janice Willett, and Jerry Zimmerman, offered constructive suggestions and valued encouragement. So did seminar participants at the Cato Institute, CEMA, Clemson, Florida Atlantic, George Mason, Georgia Tech, and Johns Hopkins.

The editorial insights provided at different stages of the project by Margo Beth Fleming, Teresa Hartnett, and Janice Willett profoundly improved the final product, while Edie Trimble, my administrative assistant at Simon, supplied countless hours of dedicated help. Karen Maloney, the economics editor at Cambridge University Press, deserves the credit for coming up with the catchy title, *Inside Job*, for the book. Karen her Cambridge University Press team and Puviarassy Kalieperumal also have my thanks for adroitly handling the final production process.

Family members were both understanding and helpful. My mom read every draft chapter, consistently catching typos and grammatical errors while offering suggestions to improve the manuscript's readability. My sons, Will and Walker, came up with ideas to illustrate the book's arguments from their respective experiences in Argentina and from watching the Netflix series, *House of Cards*. My partner, Mary Gail, was steadfast with her support and love.

This book is dedicated in memory of my younger brother, Andy, who positively impacted so many of us through his wide-ranging intellect, good cheer, committed service as a pediatrician, love for his family, and noble spirit. With each passing day, I treasure his example while wishing that I still had the opportunity to discuss the ideas that follow with him.

1

Government for the People?

In a memorable address at Gettysburg in 1863, President Abraham Lincoln exhorted his fellow citizens to recommit themselves to the American democratic experiment – government of, by, and for the people. Under Lincoln's leadership, the Union survived the great test of the Civil War and, soon after, experienced a new birth of freedom. Meanwhile, the concept of government of and by the people began to transform into something quite different. As noted by filmmaker Ken Burns in his poignant film documentary on the Civil War, one of the changes wrought by the conflict is that when referring to the "the" in "the United States of America," Americans took the definite article to refer to the singular "United States" after the conflict versus the plural prior to the conflict. The change was tectonic not editorial. It has, as natural human behaviors have played out over time, set the stage for a replay of a historic phenomenon that threatens the heart of the Union Lincoln fought to preserve.

As in many other countries around the globe, the role of government in the United States has grown, changing markedly in the short arc of time since Lincoln delivered his Gettysburg address. Beyond expanding the size of the military, the Civil War precipitated the nation's first income tax, which Congress passed to help pay for the army. Paper currency, no longer backed by gold, was issued to finance the war effort.[1]

A Department of Agriculture was launched to assist farmers as the United States industrialized and urbanized. A Bureau of Pensions was established to aid wounded soldiers and the families of dead ones. One of the country's first social welfare programs, the bureau grew appreciably following the war and became a central part of the Veterans Administration instituted in 1930.

---

[1] Bensel (1990) details how the Civil War spurred a reconceptualization of the US government.

1

Congress enacted land grants for public universities, western settlers, and a transcontinental railroad. Federal protection of civil liberties was increased with the postwar passage of three Constitutional amendments that abolished slavery, guaranteed equal protection, and extended voting rights to African-Americans.

In less than a century, subsequent tectonic shifts further remade the political-economic landscape. The United States grew emboldened by the spirit of Manifest Destiny; saw the rise of big business; and encountered world wars, the Great Depression, and the Cold War. Each of these events influenced and enhanced the state's role in American society. While liberties were compromised at times (for example, the Japanese internment camps during World War II), progress was made in terms of advancing the rights of minorities, women, gays, and immigrants.

Outside the United States, the same period has been characterized by increasing democratization. Two world wars reduced the number of monarchies and the extent of colonial holdings by established powers. The end of the Cold War further diminished, although by no means depleted, the ranks of autocratic states. This trend prompted political theorist Francis Fukuyama to argue that the world was approaching a sociocultural terminus: "the universalization of Western liberal democracy as the final form of human government."[2] Sparked by the Jasmine Revolution of 2010 in Tunisia, the Arab Spring fanned hopes for the demise of entrenched autocracies in the Middle East.

NAGGING QUESTIONS

Yet, despite the progress toward government by the people, a nagging question remains. That is, does the trend toward democratically elected rulers ensure that a government operates for its people?

This question is readily apparent outside the United States. Autocratic rule remains all too common, but even many democracies are dysfunctional and deliver meager results when it comes to creating jobs and promoting economic prosperity. Some politically repressive governments, such as those in China and Singapore, have been outpacing more liberal states in growing gross domestic product (GDP).

Celebrations of new democracy movements often have proved premature. The Arab Spring has produced precious few democratic blossoms.

---

[2] Fukuyama (1992). However, in more recent work, Fukuyama (2014) has become less optimistic about an inevitable global march to democracy.

Instead, its failure to launch confirms autocracy's staying power. It fuels the theory by political scientists that over 75 percent of autocratic regimes, once overthrown, are replaced by another autocracy (or something worse) rather than by democracy.[3] Witness the reversion to military-autocratic rule in Egypt; the destruction Bashar al-Assad continues to levy on Syria so as to retain power; the spread and savagery of ISIS; and the lawlessness in Libya, Yemen, and large parts of Iraq. The manner in which the Arab Spring has played out forces to the fore questions about what makes a government seemingly by the people strong enough to endure for the people.

These questions span far beyond the Arab Spring. Political and economic freedoms have declined in democratic Turkey, Thailand, and Nicaragua, as well as in many of the autocratic USSR's former republics. Venezuela provides a prime example of why government by the people does not necessarily result in government for the people.

Largely freed of colonial rule, sub-Saharan Africa remains the poster child for autocracy and its debilitating effects. While failure is a proverbial orphan, many parents have been blamed for the struggling progeny where such autocracies continue to fail their citizens. Chief among the suspected parents in sub-Saharan Africa are culture; an unconstrained geography allowing for greater tribal mobility, thus impeding the precolonial development of effective states; colonization on the cheap by Europeans who invested little in building political institutions while undermining traditional sources of authority; excessive postcolonial foreign aid keeping despots in power; and ignorance.[4] It is frequently presumed that the last of these causes of hardship – ignorance – can be alleviated by the enlightened advice of development economists and the attention of music and movie icons. Although well intentioned, the advice and attention has, at least so far, largely failed to ameliorate the damage done by Africa's autocrats.

In democracies, questions keep arising over the extent to which government *by* the people operates *for* the people. Argentina provides an enigma in this regard. Having been a New World economic beacon, Argentina rivaled the United States in the early part of the twentieth century in terms of both growth and per capita income. From being richer than Switzerland and Canada, Argentina began a relative slide in the 1930s to where it now has no more than one-third the per capita

---

[3] See Geddes, Wright, and Frantz (2014) on the durability of autocracies.
[4] See, for example, Acemoglu and Robinson (2012) and Fukuyama (2014).

incomes of these two countries. From its high standing in First World wealth not quite a century ago, Argentina has declined to become a persistent member of the Latin American sovereign debt default club, perpetually trying to extricate itself from the clutches of the latest round of spurned financial creditors.[5] This ostensibly democratic government by the people shows evidence of failure to work for the greater good of its people.

Japan likewise has fallen from the economic heavens. It has gone through a lost generation of slow to no growth. Its public debt now totals nearly 250 percent of GDP. Its Nikkei stock market remains mired at half the peak it attained in 1989. The Land of the Rising Sun represents another democracy where the government's ability to deliver well-being, let alone prosperity, has waned over the arc of relatively few years.

Europe, particularly Portugal, Italy, Greece, and Spain, amply illustrates democracy failing to deliver the economic goods. Often portrayed as having been turned into a museum, Venice may portend the future for all of Europe. Political economy scholars Daron Acemoglu and James Robinson claim that Venice has been reduced to a historical relic, living off its charms for tourists, by the Republic's *Serrata*, or the economic and political closure that began in 1297.[6] Far more recently, much of Europe now similarly relies evermore on past grandeur and tourism as increasingly entrenched structural economic features inhibit innovation and job formation.

Look beyond Venice and consider all of Italy, the birthplace of the Renaissance. Italy is a democracy that routinely earns the highest possible Freedom House scores for civil liberties and political rights.[7] Italy also is hypercompetitive when it comes to its political leadership, having had forty-four different prime ministers since World War II and, so, offering its citizens appreciable electoral choice. Yet, notwithstanding the apparent full-blown government by the people, Italy's policy makers by and large have failed to deliver the economic goods for the people. The country has averaged a meager annual GDP growth rate of 0.62 percent since 1960, and that rate has turned negative in recent years. Per capita GDP has declined by 7 percent since 2000. Italy's economic freedom ratings also are nothing to brag about. They parallel Italy's anemic productivity and both run counter to the country's political openness.

---

[5] Acemoglu and Robinson (2012) and Fukuyama (2014).
[6] Acemoglu and Robinson (2012).
[7] Freedom House annually rates nations on a 1–7 scale.

Italy's Index of Economic Freedom score typically places it barely above the "Mostly Unfree" category.[8]

Closer to home, the United States has rebounded from the 2007–2009 financial market meltdown. However, the rebound has been tepid when measured against other economic recoveries and against expectations raised as the government engaged in highly stimulative fiscal and monetary policies and the world market saw the halving of oil prices over 2014–2015. While some would argue over the degree, most would agree that the United States remains a stable government by the people. Yet, even against this political backdrop and ample resources, the United States appears unable to recharge the dynamism of its citizens' economic opportunities and wealth.

The lethargic US economic recovery actually is not as puzzling as it may seem at first. The trend here correlates with the trends that scholars have observed about economic performance across many countries.[9] Similar to Italy, over the last decade, the United States has maintained high Freedom House marks for the civil liberties and political rights of its citizens. However, the Index of Economic Freedom score for the United States has declined in eight of the ten years from 2006 to 2016, through two presidential administrations, and across an arc of time spanning both major parties.

How a decline in economic freedom affects the very real tepid recovery following the US financial market meltdown has been hotly debated in the media and policy arena. But generally, indices of economic freedom, such as the Index of Economic Freedom and Economic Freedom of the World, are consistently and positively related to a nation's economic performance. By contrast, the relationship between indices of political freedom (for example, Freedom House and Polity) and a nation's economic performance is less consistent, and less clear. The idea that economic freedom has a positive impact on economic performance does, at least, dovetail with research showing that economic freedom matters more than political freedom when it comes to determining the wealth of nations.

Americans seem to agree. Studies indicate that talk of increasing income and wealth inequality has failed to spark Americans' support for redistribution.[10] Their focus remains on more and not less economic freedom. Americans are more concerned about growing the economic pie than over how the pie is divided.

---

[8] See Miller, Kim, and Holmes (2015). The Index of Economic Freedom rates nations annually on a 0–100 scale for the extent of their economic freedom.

[9] See Zupan (2015a) for a summary.   [10] See, for example, Kuziemko et al. (2015).

POLITICAL OUTCOMES AND THE PUBLIC INTEREST

As Americans focus on more and not less freedom of any kind, including economic freedom, the inevitable issue is the power of choice by individuals that reduces the power of the government to choose for the collective. Usually, this balance is debated in terms of trading off individual good for public good, and vice versa. The debate assumes that political outcomes are crafted in the public interest, for which individuals cede power over their choices. This book challenges that assumption.

That is, to what extent does government actually operate on behalf of its citizens? To what extent is it reasonable, even safe, to assume that as individuals cede some degree of freedom to government, what the public gets in return are political outcomes that serve all or most individuals?

Political ideologies have been founded on the answer to such a question, but to avoid slipping into their assumptions this book will look broadly across the globe and through history for examples of a striking trend that is lost when our focus is trained narrowly on our own nation in our own era. Perhaps most surprisingly, we will look across democracies and autocracies to find valuable perspectives gained by applying a model of politics spanning both.[11] Guiding learning across centuries, this principle bears repeating here: by exploring the broad course of human history seeking insights we need today, we avail ourselves of a dispassionate lens which makes it easier to see where we are now. Poet T.S. Eliot aptly notes the virtues of traveling and questioning across time and place: "we shall not cease from exploration, and the end of all our exploring will be to arrive where we started and know the place for the first time."[12]

Examining diverse policies across time and place will not allow us, in inductive fashion, to conclusively determine the state's appropriate role in society. The answer to this question surely varies by circumstance of location and time. At least after the fact, we can identify policies serving the public interest as well as ones that do not. For example, my birthplace of Rochester became an entrepreneurial hotbed when the Erie Canal's construction in the 1820s lowered the cost of transporting goods across

---

[11] Bueno de Mesquita and Smith (2011) note that classifying governance forms as being either democracies or autocracies can be overly simplistic and that it may be more important to focus on three dimensions spanning all political systems: the nominal selectorate or interchangeables, individuals who at least have some legal say in choosing their nation's leader; the real selectorate, or influentials, individuals whose support is critical to electing a nation's leader; and the winning coalition, or essentials, individual supporters without whom a leader would be unable to retain power.

[12] Eliot (1943).

the State of New York by over 90 percent. The enhanced commercial activity easily justified the public investment, and the tolls collected in just two years recouped the state outlays.[13]

While the Erie Canal's net benefits are clear, it is harder to ascertain the effect of other policies on the public interest, especially those associated with significant non-pecuniary benefits and costs which are hard to measure, such as those dealing with divisive ideological issues like abortion and affirmative action. So, even though I look at particular policies in this book, my focus is not on definitively proving the appropriate role of the state in society. Rather, policies are chosen for their power to illustrate the extent to which government, any government in any place and at any time, has proven capable of serving the public interest.

That is not to say that the extent to which government serves the public interest can be settled deductively. It cannot. Economists argue that state intervention is justified for so-called public goods benefiting multiple parties and for which it is prohibitively costly to exclude individual parties from realizing benefits. However, there is no consensus over which specific goods are public, and this disagreement limits our ability to deduce the state's appropriate role in society. Whereas most economists agree that national defense, an effective system of property rights, fire protection, and perhaps parks and transportation infrastructure are public goods, debate persists over classifying other programs such as education, social security, health care, welfare, and basic research. For example, Thomas Piketty marshals considerable data favoring progressive global income taxation so as to promote greater equality and what is often termed "social peace." Other economists, however, dispute Piketty's data, methodology, and policy proposals.[14]

Neither starting, deductively, with a guiding principle about the appropriate role of the state, nor building up, inductively, from examples of policies that appear to serve the public interest, this book will nonetheless explore whether government has promoted social well-being across time and around the globe, particularly in instances where governments become players in their own policy actions.

THE ECONOMIC MODEL OF POLITICS AND ITS POTENCY

In the process of revealing what has happened across nations and centuries when public officials assume roles in the policies they devise, this

[13] Bernstein (2005).
[14] Piketty (2014). For a critique, see Acemoglu and Robinson (2015).

book will show that the economic model of politics has greater potency than has generally been realized. By "economic model of politics," I mean the market-based framework wherein public officials are the sellers of wealth transfers through their policy actions so that interest groups must compete for favorable wealth transfers by offering support to public officials in return. By "potency," I mean the economic model's ability to explain and predict policy outcomes, thereby allowing us to determine the extent to which government operates for the people – and to apply these lessons to current situations. By "government," I mean individuals who serve as rulers, elected officials, or public employees and have some ability to influence policy outcomes on account of their positions. By "public interest," I mean the maximum outcome for a society's total net economic benefits (pecuniary as well as non-pecuniary) based on an initial distribution of resources.[15]

While the economic model will be applied to governments from many eras and regions, what we know from behavioral economics is that reference points matter.[16] With this in mind, the relative youth and focus of the economic model of politics is notable. Birthed over the last fifty years, the economic model thus far has been applied principally to democracies – governments characterized, to different degrees, by electoral competition, rule of law, and accountability.[17] So, it is not surprising that democracies have fared badly in scholarly examinations of why political-economic institutions may not serve the public interest, and that voters have formed something akin to the demand side of the political marketplace, seeking favorable wealth transfers. In that scenario, it generally has been presumed that untoward outcomes must result from some demand-side interest groups co-opting the apparatus of the state for their benefit and at the expense of the general citizenry. The flaw, it would seem, is in fragmenting constituency and in interest groups hijacking the political process at the expense of the public good – not in government itself.

As shown in the Figure 1.1 depiction of the economic model of the political marketplace, the list of such co-opting "demand-side groups" in democracies has varied and grown over time. Depending on the varying outcomes scholars have sought to explain, the culprits have included producers, capitalists, economic elites, one-percenters, consumer activists, labor unions, industry cartels, and ideologically oriented environmentalists. Domestic-producer

---

[15] Becker (1983), Peltzman (1976), Posner (1974), and Stigler (1971) provide foundational pillars for the economic model of politics.
[16] See, for example, Kahneman (2011).   [17] Fukuyama (2011, 2014).

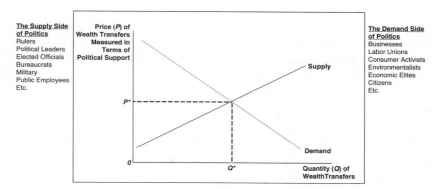

Figure 1.1 The political marketplace

interests are the suspects when it comes to trade restrictions. Consumer interests bear responsibility for rent control or price ceilings on pharmaceutical drugs. Economic elites, or one-percenters, are blamed for the government bailout of financial institutions following the downturn of 2007–2009. The list of particular policies as demand-side capture stories goes on.

Yet other political outcomes are tougher to explain through a capture story which features a culprit drawn solely from the demand side of politics. The phenomenon of tyrannical governments turning on their own people, or acting against voters' greater will, is sadly commonplace, such as with Hitler and his henchmen in 1930s Germany, or Japanese rulers' moving toward militarism in the 1920s–1930s.

Government policies running counter to popular will, of course, have not always furthered harmful ends, such as with Peter the Great's modernizing influence on Russia in the early eighteenth century, or Mustafa Kemal Ataturk's drive to create a secular, progressive Turkey at the same time that Germany was shifting under Hitler's control and Japan was moving toward militarism. As president, Ataturk effected a separation of government and religion, abolished the caliphate and religious Sharia courts, instituted free and compulsory public education, granted women equal civil and political rights, replaced Arabic script with a Latinate alphabet, promoted Western dress, and liberalized culture and the arts.[18]

---

[18] See Kissinger (2014) on the role played by military and political leaders in Japan's turn toward militarism in the 1920s–1930s. For a leading biography on Ataturk, see Kinross (2001).

Even when government officials did not act in unison, there are many instances where policy outcomes were captured by someone other than those on the demand side of politics, thus leaving a lasting imprint on history. The French politician Talleyrand, whose name is synonymous with craftiness and self-interested diplomacy, survived Bourbon kings, the French Revolutionaries, and Napoleon as advisor to all, often pressing for peace where his rulers sought vainglory and expansion with a citizenry agitated and ready for battle and conquest.

Where an individual managed to capture a policy outcome without any mandate from the demand side of the political marketplace is illustrated with particular clarity through the public works projects championed by "master builder" Robert Moses in New York City in the middle of the twentieth century. New York still has a greater proportion of public benefit corporations than any other US state. Yet, the public authorities Moses established or led provided the means to limit citizen input, to issue bonds to underwrite infrastructure ventures with minimal legislative oversight, and to generate sizable revenues from tolls and other fees to finance his largely autonomous empire, lifestyle, and, most importantly, influence.[19] In other words, Moses created public works with public authority to advance his own power as a government insider.

Without Moses' forceful leadership it is hard to imagine New York City having the public benefit of its extensive parkway system, the United Nations headquarters, Lincoln Center, the Triborough Bridge, and the iconic Tavern on the Green restaurant in Central Park. Favoring cars over buses, Moses also managed to leave a lasting signature in New York City's preponderance of highways over public transit, creating a dearth to this day of public transit options between LaGuardia Airport and Manhattan. The same can be said of New York's large urban renewal projects which reflect Moses' personal policy preferences regarding public housing. By seeking to co-locate area professional sports teams in Flushing Meadows, Moses drove the Brooklyn Dodgers off to a new city, Los Angeles, and the New York Giants to San Francisco. While the individual or cumulative public benefit of Robert Moses' policies is debatable, his ability to capture and control political outcomes without benefit of the demand side of the economic model is clear.

Robert Moses and Talleyrand illustrate what I will call "government insiders," who, as opposed to members of demand-side special-interest groups, are hard to ignore when it comes to influencing political outcomes

---

[19] Caro (1974).

in autocracies and democracies. Consider the origins of World War I and the failures of public K-12 education in the United States. As documented by historians, certain ministers and military commanders in Austria-Hungary, France, Germany, and Russia played pivotal roles in precipitating World War I. Whereas Kaiser Wilhelm II was reluctant to mobilize troops after the assassination of Archduke Francis Ferdinand in Sarajevo in 1914, General Moltke and other generals and diplomats hastened Germany's move toward war.[20]

From a distinctly different era, place, and policy, government insiders play a pivotal role in undermining the public good in public education. Few dispute that student outcomes from K-12 public education in the United States are dismal. Yet, despite the woeful student outcomes, notably in major urban settings, America's K-12 public school system appears impervious to reform. The level of state funding fails to explain the phenomenon; spending per pupil, in real terms, has tripled since 1960. Moreover, it is hard to relate the status quo to the lobbying efforts of parents and/or general taxpayers. Rather, as we will see in later chapters, the results are attributable to concentrated and influential teachers' unions operating from within government – or, government insiders, from the supply side of politics – acting similarly to those who hijacked what would have been resistance to war with a process of escalation in pre–World War I Europe.[21]

The foregoing examples of apparent capture of the political process by non-demand-side interests are drawn largely from the last century. When looking back further in time, we find even more frequent cases of the political process being co-opted by government insiders. Indeed, the world pre-1900 had little by way of a demand side to politics. The landscape was dominated by autocracies, notably monarchies. The state and its citizens were, if anything, viewed as the property of rulers, often by divine right. King Louis XIV of France could exclaim without much question, "It is legal because I wish it" and "L'état c'est moi" [I am the state]. The public good would have been defined more likely as what was good for the ruling class, the nobility, or the military which supported the state. In these circumstances, government insiders have greater opportunity and means to capture political outcomes operating on the supply side of politics, nevertheless working against what was arguably the greater public good – and, as with Louis XIV, often leading to disaster.

---

[20] Fukuyama (2014) and MacMillan (2014).
[21] Hoxby (1996, 2000) and Moe (2009, 2011, 2015).

Exploring history with this new lens, looking at how government insiders operate from the supply side of politics in an economic model, we begin to see that the collapse of nations has been due more often than not to an "inside job." The lavish excesses of the Bourbon monarchy during the Ancien Regime of France led to the French Revolution, which by the way interjected the demand side of politics into the history of France. The building of pyramids and other self-glorifying monuments drained the coffers of the pharaohs of Ancient Egypt, ultimately leaving a collapsed body politic. The resistance to change by the rulers and civil servants of several Chinese dynasties built to a crescendo of misery that fueled political and economic instability and led to Mao's ascent to power. The examples are many, including the collective chokehold exercised by the elite Janissary fighting force, public scribes, and sultans on the Ottoman Empire, which eventually crumbled.

Criminal investigators know that identifying the perpetrator requires focusing on who has the motive, means, and opportunity. Thus, to find the real culprit in crimes against the public interest, we need to pay attention to the supply side of politics. Government insiders – whether monarchs, royal advisors, revolutionaries, elected representatives, or public-sector workers – consistently have proven that they have the impulse and ability to capture the machinery of the state to promote their own objectives, often to the detriment of the public good. What results is akin to how cancer hijacks the body's own biological machinery to grow, like a parasite, at its expense. Appropriately guarding against our political "guardians" is thus of paramount importance when seeking to promote national well-being.

Vigilance against the possibility of an inside job, however, neither denies nor denigrates the noble motives that government insiders have and their potential for entrepreneurship and sacrifice on behalf of the public good. Ataturk ended the second caliphate and brought Turkey into the twentieth century. Public employees in America today participate in many important programs to advance the public good. Singapore still enjoys an economic miracle created by former prime minister Lee Kuan Yew. While these examples have significant qualifiers, they are still inside jobs advancing the public good and illustrating that individuals on the supply side of politics come from the same genus and species as those on the demand side. They too have the same capacity for virtue and vice.

Nothing that follows is intended to cast aspersions on public employees. To do so would be like castigating business people for behaving self-interestedly when analyzing the supply side of private markets. My goal, rather, is to better understand the workings of political markets in terms of the two sides of any market – supply and demand. This model involves an economics point of view, so I will ask why political markets may not promote the public interest. What we learn by exploring how political markets work will provide lessons to better ensure that such markets serve the public good. Whether autocratic or democratic, governments seeking to promote the public good can become better immunized against inside jobs, where an insider hijacks the state's resources for narrow purposes and thus increases the likelihood of a nation's instability and collapse.

PRYING OPEN THE BLACK BOX

This book pries open the supply side of politics, which has heretofore largely been treated, at least by economists, as a black box. Doing so, it will show the explanatory power of the economic model of politics and even ways it may be enhanced in the study of policy outcomes. As mentioned, to date the economic model has focused more on when and where it has been developed – a time and place more heavily populated by democracies characterized by demand-side politics. Indeed, whenever outcomes which are inconsistent with the public interest are observed, more attention has been focused on the state being captured by demand-side interest groups than on internal interests at work in government. Findings of historians, political scientists, and sociologists, regarding the independent role that those within government play in shaping policy outcomes, largely have been neglected.[22] Doubt has instead been cast on the ability of democracies, characterized by electoral competition, to promote the public interest.

Yet, competition has a salutary role to play in politics. Whenever perfect competition prevails in a market – be it economic or political – the interests

---

[22] Notable exceptions include Acemoglu, Reed, and Robinson (2014); Acemoglu and Robinson (2012); Anzia and Moe (2015); Buchanan and Tullock (1977); Chayes (2015); Cost (2015); Diermeier, Keane, and Merlo (2005); DiSalvo (2015); Fiorina and Noll (1978); Holcombe (2012, 2015); Hubbard and Kane (2013); Johnson and Libecap (1994); Kalt and Zupan (1984, 1990); Kau and Rubin (1979); Keech and Munger (2015); Levitt (1996); McChesney (1997); McKean (1965); Bueno de Mesquita and Smith (2011); Moe (2006, 2011, 2015); Niskanen (1971); Persson and Tabellini (2003); Posner (1977); Rodrik (2014); Schuck (2014); Schweitzer (2013, 2015); Shleifer and Vishny (1998); and Walters (2014). While Moe (2011, 2015) notes how reluctant scholars have been to look, for a variety of reasons, at vested interests on the supply side of politics when it comes to the K-12 US public school system, it is somewhat ironic to see how his own influential analysis of the system has evolved. Contrast, for instance, the focus on organizational architecture in Chubb and Moe (1990) versus the more extensive attention paid to the influence of teachers' unions in Moe (2011, 2015).

of suppliers are aligned with those who create demand. This is because any suppliers failing to be hyper-attentive to the interests of consumers, who demand their goods and services, will find themselves out of a job. Inattentive suppliers will lose business to other suppliers who seek to profit by staying more attuned to consumer interests and focus on satisfying demand. Such is the nature of competition. It promotes supplier account-ability to consumer interests and purges the market of insiders who would otherwise hijack the machinery to produce for their benefit and at the expense of the public.

To the degree that competition and accountability do not weed out inattentive producers on the supply side of politics, government insiders will be less likely to promote the public good. Of course, many government insiders still may be committed to serving the public good over their own independent and personal interests. Democracies and some autocracies work on such a presumption, which represents an admirable, normative wish. We certainly learned it in high school civics classes and it is con-sistent with the Great Man theory of history that was in vogue in the nineteenth century through World War II.[23] That said, presuming that government insiders are motivated only to advance the public interest rather than their own interests (pecuniary or ideological) runs counter to well-documented social science explanations of what drives human behavior.

Government insiders do not work alone but often rely on the symbiotic relationship between supply- and demand-side interests in profiting at the public expense. The strength of this symbiosis helps explain the tyranny of the political status quo. When government insiders have "skin in the game," added resistance to policy change is introduced. Unlike demand-side interests, supply-side interests have and use the power to write and enforce the rules. The power represents both the means and the opportu-nity. The benefits government insiders can appropriate are the motive. The potent mix ossifies political outcomes. As Milton and Rose Friedman wryly observed, "Nothing is so permanent as a temporary government program."[24]

The impact of symbiotic coupling of supply- and demand-side political interests can be likened to what happens to an organism's DNA when

---

[23] On the Great Man theory, see Carlyle (1841) and Nietzsche (1909). Pfeffer (2015) notes an analogue to the theory in managerial settings where business leaders tend to be viewed as heroes during good economic times and as goats during economic downturns.

[24] Friedman and Friedman (1984).

cancerous gene mutation leads to cell over-replication. In the case of DNA and its four component nucleobases, guanine (G) always pairs with cytosine (C) while adenine (A) always couples with thymine (T). Thus, when cancer leads to an improper sequence of nucleobases on one of the two strands of DNA's double helix, it also tends to be associated with an incorrect nucleobase sequence on the other strand. Analogously, we can expect any demand-side co-opting of the political process to be intertwined with supply-side capture, thereby further locking in a political outcome while amplifying the damage done to the body politic by demand-side special interests. To play off the explanation offered by Mancur Olson for economic arteriosclerosis in Western Europe, the arteries of the body politic become even more hardened when one accounts for supply-side capture by government insiders interlocking with the co-opting damage done by demand-side special interests.[25]

In this dynamic hidden in the black box that has characterized the supply side of politics in the economic model, government insiders act not as one would wish in the Great Man theory but rather on the basis of self-interest – and thus like any other human beings studied by social scientists. The insiders may view their behavior as being based on a blend of self-interest and public-spiritedness, or they may not. The reality is that, whether in a democracy or autocracy, government insiders benefit from imperfect competition and, so, an imperfect accountability on the supply side of politics. Here the black box reveals its secret, explaining and predicting public policy outcomes – that is, government insiders acting in their own interests which may or may not align with the public good.[26]

The arc of this book will be to rely on the economic model to seek, identify, and disarm this powerful culprit behind the decline of nations and, closer to home, the dysfunction of government programs. To paraphrase political scientist Harold Lasswell, politics can be defined as "Who Gets What, How, Why, When, and Where."[27] Chapters 2 through 7 rely on this definition to frame our thinking about government insiders: who they are; what their hijacking of the political apparatus involves; how their influence can grow in autocracies as well as in democracies; why they are difficult to restrain; and when and where they have led to the decline of

---

[25] Olson (1982).

[26] Empirical evidence on the imperfect accountability of legislators to their constituents when casting roll-call votes in a representative democracy is provided by Kalt and Zupan (1984, 1990); Kau and Rubin (1979); and Levitt (1996), among others.

[27] Lasswell (1936).

nations. Examples of government insiders subverting the public interest range from historical cases such as Egypt's New Kingdom, China's Han dynasty, and the Roman and Ottoman empires to modern settings such as Venezuela, North Korea, and individual US states and cities.

Chapters 4 through 7 explore nuances regarding inside jobs. That is, government insiders do not usually act alone. For example, especially in democracies, political outcomes at odds with the public interest may involve symbiotic capture by interest groups from both the demand and supply sides of politics. And history is replete with examples from autocracies and democracies of government insiders simultaneously benefiting, along with demand-side special interests, from extractive institutions at the expense of the public good.

Trade between Spain and its New World colonies was cartelized by King Ferdinand and Queen Isabella through a merchants' guild in return for a flow of gold and silver to the royals. The British Crown enriched its coffers with revenue, prior to the Glorious Revolution, from state-conferred monopolies. In the Congo, Les Grosses Legumes (the Big Vegetables) profited from exclusive licenses issued by President Mobutu in the second half of the twentieth century in return for enriching him. US city leaders granted exclusive cable television franchises in return for non-price concessions such as franchise fees and televised city council meetings.[28] To some these were mere business exchanges, but on deeper exploration we see that they involved the supply side of politics advancing its interests at the expense of the greater public good.

Chapters 8 and 9 focus on the two nations most likely to shape the twenty-first century in which we live. Chapter 8 explores the inside job at work in autocratic China and why that country's growth prospects are likely to dim, much as the Japanese economic miracle has ground to a halt since 1990. China has been growing rapidly since Deng Xiaoping and the ruling Communist Party began ushering in market reforms in the late 1970s. However, this trajectory will be unsustainable without increased accountability on the supply side of politics through stronger curbs on government insiders. Anticorruption campaigns, such as the one now being led by President Xi Jinping, may be cosmetically beneficial and ultimately driven by the desire to solidify political power. But they will not overcome the underlying drag that a monopolistic state exerts on economic performance.

---

[28] Acemoglu and Robinson (2012); Fukuyama (2011, 2014); Hubbard and Kane (2013); Shleifer and Vishny (1998); and Zupan (1989).

Chapter 9 turns to the United States, where various factors contribute to the inside job at work here. Members of Congress and in other public roles enjoy an increasingly heightened insulation from the demand side of politics. Unfunded pension and health care liabilities of public workers are growing to a dangerous crescendo, placing public funding at odds with private resources. And K-12 education exemplifies the negative effects of government insiders on the public interest, with debilitating impacts on our nation's workforce and wealth. If not addressed, these and other detrimental effects of insulated government imperil America's future.

More fundamentally, the situation in America highlights that democracy, or government *by* the people, is not sufficient to guarantee government *for* the people. With a government elected *by* them, the citizens of democracies are even more responsible than those in autocracies to demand that their government works *for* them – and to remain vigilant against an inside job. Moreover, the larger the role that government plays, the greater is the need for vigilance against government being hijacked by government insiders in a democratic society.

Keeping government insiders from subverting the public interest was a core concern to the Founders when constructing the constitutional foundations of the United States. And, as spelled out in the ensuing chapters, government insiders remain a clear and present danger to the success of countries around the globe – be they brutal dictatorships such as Syria's, relatively new nation-states in Africa, well-established European and Latin American polities generating anemic economic growth, or major economies such as Japan, China, and the United States. In today's developed nations, total government outlays average more than 50 percent of GDP while public-sector employment averages more than 28 percent (it exceeds 50 percent in some countries such as China). That's a lot of treasure, which provides a lot of motive to a growing number of government insiders who are less and less accountable to the public whom they ostensibly serve.

As noted, and as will be seen in the ensuing pages, nations decline often due to inside jobs – whether the nations are autocracies or democracies. So, this exploration of inside jobs over time and around the globe offers many valuable lessons. Among these lessons are that the capture of the state by government insiders is not inevitable, and there are some important ways to mitigate the circumstances that give rise to the inside job. Building on the curbs identified in an earlier chapter, the book's closing chapter, Chapter 10, offers suggestions for restraining government insiders and thereby promoting the public interest.

While difficult to restrain, capture of the political process is not inevitable. Nor is it immutable. Friedrich Hayek penned *The Road to Serfdom* not to argue that totalitarianism was inexorable and irreversible but to caution readers about the dangers to liberty posed by central planning.[29] Analogously, this book's intent is not to spread paralytic gloom but to be a cautionary tale about the danger to the public interest from government insiders and what can be done to guard against their acquisition and exercise of unaccountable power and the decline of our nation.

---

[29] Hayek (1944).

2

Why Worry about Government Insiders and Their Profits?

The idea of a government insider contradicts the ideal on which people most often support their government as an agent who serves to promote the public good. History argues against the ideal, by offering many examples in which government insiders have benefited, in a myriad of ways, from hijacking political authority at the expense of those they are supposed to serve. Indeed, *kleptocracy*, that is (deriving from the Greek), "rule by thieves," is a common phenomenon in not only autocracies but also democracies. How power is hijacked may vary by era and form of government, but the ways insiders profit from co-opting the political machine are fairly constant across time and geographic locale. The apparently irascible human impulse to succumb to the temptations of power seems subject only to measures of accountability on the supply side of politics. Before delving into the mechanisms through which government insiders may be held more accountable, however, let's first look at the ways they can personally profit at the public's expense.

Quantitatively, relatively contemporary national leaders reveal the self-enriching benefit of their positions in sheer dollar wealth, measured in today's dollars: former Libyan dictator Muammar Gaddafi, $200 billion; former Egyptian president Hosni Mubarak, $70 billion; former Indonesian president Suharto, $35 billion; former Philippine president Ferdinand and First Lady Imelda Marcos, $5–10 billion; former Palestine Liberation Organization chair Yasser Arafat, $4.5–6.3 billion; former Congolese dictator Mobutu Sese Seko, $5 billion; and former generalissimo Francisco Franco of Spain, $2.2–$3.5 billion. The amount pilfered by Malaysian prime minister Najib Razak and his family is still being tabulated but is likely to run into the billions. The wealth of Russian president Vladimir Putin is estimated to be as high as

$200 billion.[1] The recent Panama Papers leak provides a treasure trove of information regarding the wealth that twelve of the world's political leaders have been able to amass and shield through the off-shore tax havens managed by Panama-headquartered law firm Mossack Fonseca – leaders including Putin; Mubarak; the prime minister of Pakistan, Nawaz Sharif; and the former prime minister of Iraq, Ayad Allawi.[2]

Whole cultures have designated the names of national leaders as cultural icons for amassing great wealth while the fate of their countries floundered. In the early sixth century BC, the very name of Croesus, the Greek king, became synonymous with possessing astounding wealth – which, in the case of Croesus, was a precursor to the destruction of a great empire. Even now, people may be referred to as "richer than Croesus." King Solomon is renowned for having lost his spiritual way in the pursuit of wealth and worldly pleasure, only to end his life disaffected and with his kingdom in peril. Similarly, from humble guard of the gate to the Forbidden City in the eighteenth century BC, Henshen exploited favor as counsel for the Emperor to become known in China to this very day as the most corrupt official of all time.

The ways different leaders shared – or did not share – the benefits associated with their power vary, too. In the early fourteenth century BC, the ruler of Mali, Mansa Musa, destabilized economies across Africa and parts of the Middle East as his enormous entourage spent abundant gold while making a pilgrimage to Mecca; Musa remained so rich that he was able to buy gold back from the devastated areas.[3] Nicholas II began his reign as the last of the Romanov tsars at the peak of imperial power but, after bloody wars and internal strife, led Russia into complete economic, military, and political collapse, ushering in the still bloodier Soviet era.

Even closer to our day, consider two autocrats who ruled during roughly the same time period. The thirty-year reign of Mir Osman Ali Khan Bahadur in the state of Hyderabad saw him become the undisputed richest man in the world while under British colonial rule, with some estimates placing his wealth at 2 percent of the US GDP.[4] While Mir Osman promoted infrastructure and education during his reign, he largely is remembered for amassing great wealth and seeing his state

---

[1] See, for example, Browder (2015); Bueno de Mesquita and Smith (2011); and "1MDB Probe Shows Malaysian Leader Najib Spent Millions on Luxury Goods," *Wall Street Journal*, March 21, 2016.

[2] "What Are the Panama Papers?: A Guide to History's Biggest Data Leak," *The Guardian*, April 5, 2016.

[3] Goodwin (1957).   [4] "India: The Nizam's Daughter," *Time*, January 19, 1959.

conquered – and coffers tapped – by India. His personal wealth failed to enrich his nation and was instead whittled away by warring progeny. During roughly the same time period, Rafael Leonidas Trujillo Molina, known as El Jefe, wielded absolute power in the Dominican Republic through what is considered to be the bloodiest reign in the Americas. While his advocates argue that he created stability for the country, by the end of Trujillo's regime his family's fortune equaled 100 percent of the country's GDP and 60 percent of the country's labor force owed its living, directly or indirectly, to him.[5]

Beyond the pecuniary benefits derived by autocratic leaders, who are the most obvious examples of government insiders, the license to pursue a specific worldview or ideology is commonplace in history. Ideologies are a key aspect of the political arena for which government insiders have many different ways to develop and promote so as to attain power and achieve certain policy outcomes – benefiting those who favor the ideology. Not all ideologies pursued by government insiders diminish the public interest in the way, for example, that Hitler and his Nazi coterie did. By contrast, Lee Kuan Yew, Singapore's founding prime minister, asserted a worldview, comprising economic reforms and an anticorruption campaign, which largely enhanced his country's well-being.[6]

Despite some rulers' benevolent intentions, there remains an inherent danger when ideological goals are pursued by government insiders. When mixed with the state's coercive power, ideology can become a potent brew that reverses the relationship between citizens and their public agents or "servants." Citizens can end up becoming the servants of political principals and the subjects of their rulers' ideological principles. Just as pecuniary gains tend to insulate rulers from the struggles of those whom they rule, ideology has a history of blinding those in power to the hardships of those without access to state power. As the eighteenth-century German Romantic poet Friedrich Holderlin observed: "What has always made the state a hell on earth has been precisely that man has tried to make it his heaven."[7]

It is not just political leaders, whether ideological or simply greedy, who are capable of subverting the public interest for the sake of their own

---

[5] Acemoglu, Robinson, and Verdier (2004).

[6] Among the studies highlighting the salience of ideological goals to politicians and the latitude that they have, even in democracies, to pursue such goals are Diermeier, Keane, and Merlo (2005); Kalt and Zupan (1984, 1990); Kau and Rubin (1979); Levitt (1996); Rodrik (2014); and Zhang (2015).

[7] Holderlin (2008). Moe (2006) notes the ability of bureaucrats and public employees to control their principals.

objectives. Clustered around rulers in history are cases of other government insiders benefiting from their positions, including, for example, the barons, nobles, and knights in service of feudal European monarchies; ancient China's warrior-scholar-bureaucratic class; the vast priesthood on the pay-roll of ancient Egypt's pharaohs; the Roman Empire's Praetorian Guard; the *nomenklatura* in communist states, that is, senior political appointees who had access to special grocery stores, medical care, resorts, clubs, and other privileges unavailable to general citizens; or the thousands of committeemen supporting Boss Tweed and Tammany Hall in New York City (Tweed ultimately was convicted of diverting $200 million in public funds, the equivalent of $4.5 billion in today's dollars).[8]

Indeed, office for profit is a cultural norm in the government system that most influenced the design of our own. The old British title for a civil servant was "an office for profit under the Crown." In the seventeenth century, when parliamentary positions afforded little power, honor, and pay, members were prohibited from leaving their posts for more lucrative Crown employ. Public offices were viewed as private property with remuneration being unrelated to effort or duty. Succession was by heredity or sale, the latter to those who typically viewed the purchase as a financial investment.[9]

REASONS TO WORRY

When government insiders profit from their power, they harm their nations in various ways. For one, inside jobs diminish national prosperity. In *The Rise and Fall of Great Powers*, historian Paul Kennedy focuses on 1500 AD, the year many scholars use to divide modern from premodern times. The leading world powers at that time were China's Ming dynasty and the Ottoman Empire. According to Kennedy, both declined in the ensuing centuries largely due to inside jobs.[10]

In the early 1400s, China's population numbered 100–130 million versus Europe's 50–55 million. It had a sophisticated canal and agricultural irrigation system and a coherent and well-educated Confucian bureaucracy. China's technological advances included movable type (as of the eleventh century), books, substantial libraries, gunpowder, paper money,

---

[8] Ackerman (2011).   [9] Thomas (2015).

[10] Kennedy (1987). Other scholars who note the role played by government insiders in the decline of these two powers include Acemoglu and Robinson (2012); Fukuyama (2011); and Hubbard and Kane (2013).

canons, the magnetic compass, naval and commercial vessels that exceeded later Spanish galleons in size and displacement and promoted exploration and commerce, and extensive iron production (125,000 tons per year as of the eleventh century, far larger than the total in Britain at the start of the Industrial Revolution seven centuries later).[11]

Notwithstanding the prosperity, China began to turn its back on the world due to certain Ming dynasty emperors. Kennedy notes (p. 7):

An imperial edict [in 1433] banned the construction of . . . ships; later . . . a specific order forbade . . . ships with more than two masts . . . [admiral] Cheng Ho's great warships were laid up and rotted away.

Beyond Ming emperors, China's retreat resulted from the power and conservatism of the Confucian bureaucracy that was suspicious of the military, overseas expansion, commerce, and traders (p. 8):

The accumulation of private capital, the practice of buying cheap and selling dear, the ostentation of the *nouveaux riche* merchant, all offended the . . . bureaucrats . . . While not wishing to bring the entire market economy to a halt, the mandarins often intervened against . . . merchants . . . confiscating their property or banning their business.

Due to the influence and conservatism of the elite, scholarly bureaucrats (p. 8):

the canals were permitted to decay, the army was . . . starved of new equipment, the astronomical clocks . . . were disregarded, the ironworks . . . fell into desuetude . . . Printing was restricted to scholarly works and not employed for the widespread dissemination of practical knowledge, much less for social criticism. The use of paper currency was discontinued . . . the banning of overseas trade and fishing took away another potential stimulus to sustained economic expansion.

China under the Ming dynasty became less vibrant than it had been under the Sung dynasty four centuries prior.

Kennedy similarly recounts the splendor of the Ottoman Empire at the peak of a flourishing economy and society. Constantinople, with over 500,000 inhabitants in 1600, had a larger population than any European city. The empire's total population was 14 million versus 5 million in Spain and 2.5 million in Britain. It boasted a formidable navy; a dedicated, elite army of Janissaries composed of the most able conscripted Christian youth; and a unifying, single official language, faith, and culture spanning over an area larger than the Roman Empire. The Ottoman Empire's stability and splendor could be seen in its

---

[11] Kennedy (1987).

tolerance for other races and religions along with well-lit and well-drained cities, and leading libraries and universities. The Ottomans had generated important advances in astronomy, architecture, mathematics, cartography, medicine, industry, navigation, and science. The seeds of the empire's own destruction, however, might be noted in its strong and expansive bureaucracy.

As with the Ming dynasty, the Ottoman Empire's decline came from within, principally at the hands of despotic and conservative government insiders. These insiders stifled dissent and entrepreneurial activity (pp. 11–12):

> An idiot sultan could paralyze the Ottoman Empire in a way that a pope or Holy Roman emperor could never do for all of Europe. Without clear directives from above, the arteries of the bureaucracy hardened . . . Merchants and entrepreneurs (nearly all of whom were foreigners), who earlier had been encouraged, now found themselves subject to unpredictable taxes and outright seizures of property. Ever higher dues ruined trade and depopulated towns.

Exports were forbidden, religious criticism of traders increased, and European ideas, on topics ranging from weaponry to plague containment, were shunned. Disorder grew.

Soldiers and other officials turned to plunder, demanding bribes and confiscating the property of peasants. The Janissary army saw its ranks and clout swell, thus becoming a fixed power base and key impediment to reform. Their elite positions even became hereditary and no longer merit-based. They were able to secure better salaries, pensions, educational opportunities, and benefits for their families, while countering efforts to limit their perks and influence. The indomitable power of the Janissaries is seen in their murder of two reform-minded sultans – Osman II in 1622 and Selim III in 1807.

Different powerful parties unified to restrict free thought; certain sultans, state-sponsored clerics, and a sizable group of public scribes stood to lose their jobs from advances like public criticism spread by the printing press. Sultan Bayezid II outlawed printing in Arabic in 1485. Not until 1727 was the first printing press even permitted, but any book had to be approved by a religious panel. The consequences of these restrictions to preserve power further weakened the empire more broadly by suppressing literacy rates, innovativeness, and economic growth. The literacy rate in 1800 was 2–3 percent in the Ottoman Empire versus over 50 percent in England, Germany, and Holland.[12] The once preeminent empire became Europe's "Sick Man."

---

[12] Acemoglu and Robinson (2012).

Beyond diminishing prosperity, when government insiders hijack the state they do so often by infringing on citizens' political rights and civil liberties. Literacy, free thought and speech, and other personal freedoms are subjugated to the state's control, therefore to those who control the state. This was true during the declines of both the Ming dynasty and the Ottoman Empire. It was true under Nicholas II, under the Soviet government that followed, and under Mir Osman Ali Khan Bahadur and Rafael Leonidas Trujillo Molina. It was true of the Armenian genocide carried out by the Ottoman Empire in the early twentieth century, when between 800,000 and 1,500,000 Armenians were killed in an atrocity Turkey still remains unwilling to officially acknowledge.[13]

In addition, powerful government insiders erode citizens' trust in their government. Trust is a key element of social capital. The decline of trust has a broad negative impact by undermining government performance and impairing the ease and efficacy of economic and social interactions. Overall, it is yet another way that an inside job corrodes its host nation and diminishes national well-being.[14]

Striking trends over the last half century in the United States as well as in other Western democracies have been the decline of trust in government and the growth of those governments. As government in these democracies has grown, those by whom the government officials are elected trust their elected officials less. For example, the Pew Research Center reports that respondents in the United States who indicate that they trust government "most of the time" or "just about always" has fallen from 77 percent in 1966 to 19 percent in 2015.[15] Studies indicate that across all countries, trust improves with growth in the economy, investment, and entrepreneurship. By contrast, mistrust of government hinges on factors such as special interests being too influential, misconduct by politicians, and government inefficiency. In other words, governments are trusted by the people when they are perceived of as working for the benefit of the people and not for their own ends.

Another way government insiders harm their host nation is by undermining security and peace. In *Thieves of State*, Sarah Chayes, a former US military adviser and head of an Afghan-based charity, argues that the injustice of government corruption enrages people and leads to violent extremism and international conflict.[16]

---

[13] Ferguson (2006) and Winter (2003).

[14] See, for example, Aghion et al. (2010); Garen and Clark (2015); Grief (1994); Knack and Keefer (1997); McCloskey (2010); and Pharr and Putnam (2000).

[15] www.people-press.org/2015/11/23/public-trust-in-government/.   [16] Chayes (2015).

Experiments with "ultimatum games" support Chayes' claim. In the experiments, a first player (the proposer) is asked to divide a given sum of money with a second player (the responder). If the responder accepts the proposer's offer, the deal goes through. If the responder rejects the offer, both parties get nothing. Researchers find that half of all responders in ultimatum games reject offers lower than 20 percent of the total sum. This persists even when the stakes are sizable (a month's salary) and rationality dictates accepting 20 percent of the total versus nothing at all. The desire to be treated fairly triggers seemingly irrational behavior – walking away from the experiment empty-handed.[17]

Based on her experiences with the Karzai family that ruled Afghanistan, Chayes asserts that US efforts to establish sustainable democracies in Iraq and Afghanistan have been hindered most by governments rigged for the benefit of those in power. Moreover, countries like Afghanistan operating for the benefit of government insiders while preying on the general citizenry prove to be ripe breeding grounds for ideologically based groups that offer greater purity and succor to citizens at the expense of fostering instability within their home countries and violence across national borders. ISIS, the Taliban, al-Qaeda, Boko Haram, and Jemaah Islamiah exemplify this effect.

Many in the West seek to spread democracy as an antidote to the negative effects of autocratic rule, which is faulted for its tendency toward an inside job. Yet, democracy does not guarantee peace. Political scientist Patrick McDonald analyzes international conflicts over the past two centuries and argues that a laissez-faire attitude with regard to international trade better predicts peace than the practice of democracy. This is because democracies still can have poorly defined property rights in which special interests, whether from the demand or supply side of politics, seek to profit at the public's expense.[18] In other words, democracy can be more vulnerable to an inside job than is participation in the economic benefits of the global economy. For insiders faced with dwindling benefits in an economy constrained by corruption, waging war against other nations is an extension of such a negative-sum redistributive mentality.

A final reason to worry about government insiders profiting from their positions involves their incentive to spend time, money, and other valuable resources to acquire or maintain power. These resources are drawn away from serving the public good. Economists term such dissipative activity

---

[17] See, for example, Camerer (1983).   [18] McDonald (2009).

"rent-seeking."[19] The focus vis-à-vis rent-seeking generally has been on the demand side of politics, that is, the costs associated with interest groups seeking special privileges from government. Yet, the concept also applies to the supply side.

The costs to a country from rent-seeking on the supply side of politics can be monumental. In autocracies where rival internal factions fight quite literally to the death for access to the benefits of holding power, we witness nations falling into utter chaos, such as in Somalia, Yemen, Sudan, Lebanon, Sri Lanka, Rwanda, and Angola. Supply-side rent-seeking costs, however, are present in democracies as well. Sarah Chayes notes that Nigerian politics have become a blood sport given that the annual salary of a democratically elected senator exceeds $1 million and the positions afford the further opportunity to feed at the trough through the government's control over oil revenues.[20] Even in the United States, the resources devoted to securing office are rising in real terms. In 2015, for example, Freedom Partners, the political organization supported by the multibillionaires David and Charles Koch, announced that it was budgeting nearly $900 million toward the 2016 US presidential contest versus $240 million in 2012.[21] The cost for influence rises with the degree of influence one seeks to win.

There are good reasons to worry about the impact on a host nation when government insiders, in tandem with demand-side special interests or not, hijack the political process. When government insiders profit from power, the adverse consequences include declines in prosperity, restrictions of citizens' liberties, erosion of trust in government, violence within and between nations, and the dissipative use of resources to acquire or maintain power. We will return to this disturbing theme in later chapters. Chapter 7 will add historical cases to show how government insiders have created such untoward outcomes. Chapters 8 and 9 will focus on how government insiders are presently imperiling the two largest economies in the world – China and the United States. First, the remainder of this chapter will further illustrate how, apart from China and the United States, government insiders are undermining the public interest, thus underscoring why it is important to worry about inside jobs under way around the world today.

---

[19] Krueger (1974) and Tullock (1967).   [20] Chayes (2015).
[21] "Koch Brothers' Budget of $889 Million Is on Par with Both Parties' Spending," *New York Times*, January 26, 2015.

GOVERNMENT INSIDERS AND MODERN AUTOCRACIES

Most current autocracies operate to the benefit of their rulers and at the expense of average citizens. North Korea provides a telling case study. Its recent international actions have been erratic and provocative, for example, creating its own time zone; developing nuclear weapons; sinking warships and shelling islands belonging to South Korea; issuing belligerent threats against neighboring countries and the United States; and firing submarine-launched ballistic missiles capable of hitting long-range targets.[22]

Three generations of repressive rule of North Korea by the Kim family have exacted a sizable toll. South Koreans now earn more than fifteen times per capita and live an average ten years longer than their North Korean counterparts. No such differences existed prior to when the Kim family and the Communist Party came to power in 1947. Moreover, the failing indicators in North Korea have emerged notwithstanding over $60 billion (in today's dollars) in foreign aid from China and the USSR over that same time period. The contrast extends even into outer space, where nighttime satellite photos show a largely dark land north of the 38th parallel while its southern neighbor is awash in light.[23]

While the average North Korean confronts regular famines and a low standard of living, the lifestyle of the ruling elites is a different matter. The present ruler, Kim Jong-un, disappeared from public view in mid-2014 due to treatment for gout, the so-called disease of kings. The malady was caused by his eating and drinking habits, including a taste for cheese acquired when he was in college in Switzerland. Large quantities of Emmental cheese are procured for him from overseas although foreign imports for average citizens are banned. Kim's father and grandfather sated their own predilections while in power. Kim Jong-un's father, Kim Jong-il, was Hennessy's largest cognac customer (over $1 million in annual purchases) and maintained a "joy brigade" of prostitutes to serve him and his ruling elite.[24]

---

[22] See, for example, "North Korea to Move 30 Minutes Backward to Create Its Own Time Zone," *New York Times*, August 7, 2015.

[23] Acemoglu and Robinson (2012); Ridley (2010); and Nicholas Eberstadt, "How North Korea Became the World's Worst Economy," *Wall Street Journal*, December 30, 2015, p. A13.

[24] See, for example, "Mystery Surrounds Kim Jong-il," CNN.com, October 9, 2006; "Kim Jong-il's Hennessy Thirst Cost $1 Million Per Year," www.inquisitr.com, July 7, 2013; and "Kim Jong-un in Hiding Due to Emmental Cheese Addiction," Metro.co.uk, September 29, 2014.

Russia provides another prime example of government insiders hijacking national and international well-being. Under Putin's effective rule since 2000, Russia has become increasingly dominated by state-owned and state-supported companies run by "pitertsy," or St. Petersburg boys. The pitertsy have ties to Putin from either childhood days or from working with him when he was with the head state security unit of the USSR and municipal administration in St. Petersburg.[25]

In Russia, the symbiosis between supply-side and demand-side co-opting of the state is personified by pitertsy government insiders working with crony capitalists outside the government. The symbiosis has created such an entrenched power base that it has led to an extremely unequal distribution of wealth. According to a 2013 Credit Suisse report, 110 individuals own 35 percent of Russia's wealth, the highest level of inequality in the world.[26] How this power elite functions is worth exploring more deeply.

The head of state-run oil giant Rosneft, Igor Sechin, worked with Putin in the St. Petersburg mayor's office. So did Alexei Miller, the head of the government natural gas monopoly Gazprom. The Kovalchuk and Yakunin families, who helped build a gated community in St. Petersburg with Putin, run, between them, the National Media Group conglomerate and the state's electricity export monopoly, nuclear energy research center, and railroad monopoly.[27]

Another state monopoly, Rosspirtprom, over the production of vodka and other spirits, was established by one of Putin's first decrees. The monopoly was awarded to the Rotenberg brothers, Putin's boyhood martial arts sparring partners from St. Petersburg. Putin issued the decree without consulting his economic team – a group inherited from his predecessor Boris Yeltsin which was intent on promoting the rule of law, competition, and transparency. Chief Economic Advisor Andrei Illarianov resigned due to the decree. The Rotenberg brothers continued to benefit from their childhood friendship with Putin. Their construction companies benefited from patronage, gaining major deals with Gazprom as well as $7 billion in contracts related to the 2014 Winter Olympic Games in Sochi.[28]

Putin's patronage affected Russian banking as well. Following Russia's annexation of Crimea and the imposition, in 2014, of US sanctions on

---

[25] "Putin's Powerful Friends Rally Around Russian President," Time.com, March 27, 2014.
[26] "Russia's Wealth Inequality One of Highest in the World," *The Huffington Post*, October 9, 2013.
[27] "Putin's Powerful Friends Rally Around Russian President," Time.com, March 27, 2014.
[28] Ibid.

Bank Rossiya, a smaller bank owned and used by Putin's St. Petersburg friends, several state agencies shifted their business to the bank so as to provide assistance. For example, the Market Council, the regulatory board overseeing Russia's wholesale electricity market, moved its accounts and the associated fees to Bank Rossiya. The fees total $100 million per year given that the wholesale electricity market equals 2 percent of Russia's GDP.[29]

As with other inside jobs across history, while Putin's policies have allowed him and his friends to amass great wealth, the average Russian has seen more limited gains. GDP grew by only 1.3 percent in 2013, considerably lower than the 7 percent annual rate prevailing prior to the economic downturn of 2007–2009 and fueled by then rising energy exports. The rate turned negative in 2014 and has remained so through 2016. The downturn is due to falling oil prices and energy exports; the imposition of sanctions by the United States and the European Union in the wake of Russia's annexation of Crimea and downing of a commercial airliner over Ukrainian airspace; a declining population driven by factors such as violence and the emigration of educated workers; and the economy's structural non-competitiveness.[30] Indeed, in keeping with the insights of Sarah Chayes, Russia's invasion of Ukraine and threatening actions toward other neighbors can be viewed as a natural outcome of government insiders running out of internal spoils – embarking on bellicose international forays as a way to deal with rising discontent among domestic citizens outside of the power elite.[31]

Meanwhile, the social strain on the nation that hosts this parasitic insider group is evident in basic measures of instability beyond the international acts of aggression. Russia's homicide rate is over double that of the United States – 9.2 versus 4.7 per 100,000 citizens.[32] The repressiveness of the Russian regime and its pattern of disposing of individuals such as Sergei Magnitsky, Anna Politkovskaya, and Boris Nemtsov, daring to stand in the way, contribute to the violence.[33]

Of Russian university students responding to a 2013 survey, 45 percent intend to move to a country outside of the former USSR. Russia's own

[29] See, for example, "Private Bank Fuels Fortunes of Putin's Inner Circle," *New York Times*, September 27, 2014.
[30] See, for example, Ariel Cohen, Ivan Benovic, and James Roberts, "Russia's Avoidable Economic Decline," Special Report #154 on Russia and Asia, heritage.org, September 27, 2014; and "Russia Overview," worldbank.org, April 17, 2015.
[31] Chayes (2015).   [32] United Nations Office on Drugs and Crime (2014).
[33] Browder (2015).

Ministry of Economic Development estimates that nearly 25 percent of the labor force works in the underground economy, driven there by government corruption and high payroll taxes. Another 20–25 percent works for small and mid-size private enterprises that account for only 15–25 percent of Russia's overall GDP (versus 40–50 percent in developed countries around the globe). The structural problems resulting from Russia's policies are hobbling the country's competitiveness.[34]

Iran is our next revealing autocratic stop. Here measures of strain and misery in the host country indict the ruling elite. Like North Korea, Iran has embarked on a path of coercion and belligerence, developing nuclear weapons, acting aggressively toward near neighbors, fomenting rebellion, most recently in Yemen, repressing its own citizens, and rating poorly for government integrity. In 2015, out of 168 countries and territories whose public sectors were evaluated by Transparency International on a 0 (highly corrupt) to 100 scale (very clean), Iran scored 27, tying five other nations for 130th place. Russia was only slightly less corrupt with a score of 29 and tied with three other countries for 119th place. North Korea scored 8, tying Somalia for last place.[35]

In Iran, the Islamic Revolutionary Guards Corps (IRGC) was set up after the 1979 overthrow of the Shah to defend the nation's Islamic system and to uphold the authority of the Supreme Ayatollah. Enterprises owned by the IRGC account for over a third of Iran's GDP, and they are heavily engaged in black-market profiteering. IRGC ventures include the nation's telecommunications monopoly, Tehran's airport and subway system, major oil and gas fields, banks, water and electrical power systems, and even car dealerships and laser eye clinics.[36]

Estimating the extent to which the IRGC controls Iran's economy is difficult due to the awarding of many no-bid government contracts to firms with opaque affiliations. In 2009, for example, three different firms, all of which were later identified as IRGC affiliates, collusively bid for the Mideast's largest lead and zinc mine located in Iran's Zanjan Province. Although the government placed the mine's value at $6 billion in 2007, the winning bid was less than $2 billion.[37]

---

[34] Ariel Cohen, Ivan Benovic, and James Roberts, "Russia's Avoidable Economic Decline," Special Report #154 on Russia and Asia, heritage.org, September 27, 2014.

[35] Transparency International (2015).

[36] See, for example, "Elite Guard in Iran Tightens Grip with Media Move," *New York Times*, October 9, 2009.

[37] Ibid.

While the elite prosper, the average Iranian confronts harsh economic conditions such as an annual GDP growth rate that averaged −2.5 percent over 2012–2016, while the annual inflation rate averaged over 20 percent over the same time period. Yet, the government retains a strong hold on power and is rife with nepotism, cronyism, and graft. The tight web of the powerful can be glimpsed in some prosecutions for graft. For example, a former president's son and mentor to the current president Hassan Rouhani, Mehdi Hashemi Rafsanjani, was tried in 2015 for receiving alleged kickbacks from international oil firms while serving another former president, Mohammad Khatami. Or, Mohammad Reza Rahimi, who served as the first vice president and head of an anticorruption agency under former president Mahmoud Ahmadinejad, was sentenced to five years in prison earlier in 2015 for "acquiring wealth through illegal means."[38]

General Iranian citizens, struggling with the adverse consequences associated with their government being hijacked by insiders, sometimes express their discontent. One such instance occurred in early 2015 in the wake of the crash in Tehran of a high-end Porsche claiming the lives of a leading ayatollah's grandson and a young woman. The anger among general Iranians stemmed less from the fact that the grandson was engaged to a different woman and Islamic law requires unmarried young men and women to be segregated. Rather, it was based on the pervasive self-enrichment by those who are either part of or tied to the state. One indication of this pervasiveness is that 25,000 luxury cars are imported into Iran annually despite a tax of 140 percent. The tax ensures that a Porsche such as the one involved in the fatal Tehran car wreck and selling for $78,000 in the United States costs at least $178,000 in Iran.[39]

Venezuela, tied with Haiti for the poorest public-sector integrity rating in the Western Hemisphere, completes our global autocratic tour. It scored 17 on the 0–100 Transparency International scale, tying for 158th out of 168 countries and territories rated in 2015. Venezuela's rating has declined markedly since the (democratic) election of President Hugo Chavez in 1998. After being elected by the people, Chavez illegally convened a constituent assembly, packed it with loyalists, and gave it absolute power to rewrite the constitution. The assembly dissolved Congress and dismissed

---

[38] See, for example, "Iran's President Rouhani Warns Against Corruption," BBC.com, December 8, 2014; and "Iran's Former Vice President Jailed for Corruption," theguardian .com, February 15, 2015.

[39] "In Iran, Fatal Porsche Crash Unleashes Middle-Class Anger at Elites," *New York Times*, April 30, 2015.

the Supreme Court, the attorney general, and most of the country's judges, replacing them with so-called Chavistas.[40]

Beyond the constitutional rewrite and the wholesale changes in those holding legislative and judicial offices, Chavez altered his country's official name to the Bolivarian Republic of Venezuela in honor of Simon Bolivar, the revolutionary responsible for the nation's independence. Venezuela's democratic government had been hijacked, leaving Chavez free to forge closer ties with Russia, China, Iran, Cuba, Iraq, and Libya. At one point Chavez hinted that such connections could facilitate Venezuela's nuclear ambitions.[41]

This government, which had been elected by the people but was no longer controlled by the people, was making radical changes in disregard of the welfare of the people. Large swaths of the economy were nationalized. Despite state spending restrictions and campaign claims by Chavez that he would get rid of all government aircraft, an Airbus 319 was purchased for $65 million for his travels. As the ultimate insider in Venezuela consolidated his power, Chavez's whim became national policy. An extra star was added to the country's flag; Venezuela's time zone was shifted by 30 minutes; and even the national coat of arms was altered at the suggestion of Chavez's then nine-year-old daughter.[42]

The inside job in Venezuela drained resources from the country. Despite Venezuela's state-owned oil company generating $1 trillion in export revenues from 2000 to 2015, government debt exploded and infrastructure atrophied. Lights on billboards went out after dark due to a crumbling electricity grid. In April 2016, the workweek for public employees was first shortened to four days (from five days) and then further to two days (Monday and Tuesday) to save on energy and electricity.[43] The water system faltered despite $10 billion in investment over the past decade.[44] The annual inflation rate was over 140 percent as of 2015. Shortages of food, clothing, and medicine were acute and getting worse. The International Monetary Fund expected the inflation rate to spike to 720 percent in 2016 and the GDP to shrink by 8 percent after

[40] Gustavo Coronel, "The Corruption of Democracy in Venezuela," *USA Today Magazine*, March 2008.

[41] Ted Galen Carpenter, "Venezuela's Obnoxious Regime Is Not a Security Threat," *National Interest*, March 12, 2015.

[42] See, for example, Francisco Toro, "Chavez Wasn't Just a Zany Buffoon, He Was an Oppressive Autocrat," theatlantic.com, March 5, 2013.

[43] "Venezuela Declares a 2-Day Workweek Because of Dire Energy Shortages," *Washington Post*, April 27, 2016.

[44] "Water Shortage Is Latest Venezuela Hardship," *Wall Street Journal*, April 4, 2016, p. A20.

contracting 10 percent in 2015.[45] Political repression increased to suppress challenges to those who hold power. Signs of social instability abound. The country now has one of the world's highest murder rates. In 2014, more than 24,000 citizens were murdered and Caracas, the capital, averaged thirty-five murders per day.[46]

After being briefly unseated by a coup in 2002, Chavez intensified his juggernaut of power by relying more on trusted military officials to fill public posts. His handpicked successor Nicolas Maduro has followed in Chavez's footsteps after coming to power in 2013. A consequence has been that elements of the National Guard, known as the Cartel of the Suns, have gained a license for lucrative extralegal activity, becoming heavily involved in drug trafficking. The nation's largest illegal and legal industries – narcotics and oil, respectively – thus are both state-run. The narcotics-based link between the National Guard and organized crime has contributed to violence in Venezuela and elsewhere. In 2008, a drugs-for-weapons deal was uncovered between high-level Venezuelan military personnel and communist rebels in neighboring Colombia.[47]

North Korea, Russia, Iran, and Venezuela are four autocracies that fit all too well the popular image of the state hijacked by a small elite who consolidates power over increasingly powerless and victimized populations. They also illustrate the symbiotic capture of the state by interests from the demand side and lesser-known supply side of politics, the latter comprised by government insiders operating for their own benefit and at the expense of the public good.

GOVERNMENT INSIDERS AND MODERN DEMOCRACIES

Less obvious and perhaps more surprising is the fact that it is not only in autocracies where government insiders profit from their positions. India, the world's largest democracy, with one and a quarter billion citizens, is a disturbing example of government insiders profiting from their positions at the public's expense. While India is the world's seventh-largest economy as of 2016, the biggest risk to its ongoing development stems from its bureaucracy and government corruption. In 2015, India scored only 38 on the 100-point Transparency International measure for

---

[45] "The Endgame in Venezuela," *The Economist*, February 6, 2016, p. 34.
[46] "Corruption, Falling Oil Prices, and Talk of a Coup: The End of Chavez's Socialist Dream in Venezuela," independent.co.uk, February 20, 2015.
[47] "Venezuela: Where the Mafia and the Military Come Together," latinofoxnews.com, February 7, 2014.

public-sector integrity, tying for 76th out of the 168 nations that were rated. The World Bank ranks India 134th out of 183 countries for "ease of doing business."[48]

By various other measures, the entrenched bureaucracy's power and profit can be seen. Building a Mumbai high-rise requires over sixty different state approvals and consequently takes up to a decade. In 2013, 54 percent of surveyed Indians reported having paid a bribe over the past year to access a public service or institution, double the global average of 27 percent.[49] Of India's 2014 electoral winners, 34 percent had criminal indictments pending against them at election time, according to political theorist Francis Fukuyama; these charges included those as serious as sexual assault, kidnapping, and murder.[50] One observation might be that those who pursue political office share a mindset with the criminal, considering the pending indictments and the fact that the winners in India's state elections realize an annual growth in their personal assets 3–5 percent higher than do runners-up. Asset appreciation is greater for electoral winners with greater incumbency and for those also holding ministerial positions.[51]

India's poor are harmed most by the graft, given that they are less able to pay the bribes associated with police and fire protection, clean water, and electricity. According to one survey, 75 percent of slum dwellers paid a bribe to obtain basic goods and services such as kerosene and medical care while 35 percent were denied service due to not being able to pay the required bribe.[52] The drain on social well-being stands in stark contrast to the estimated illegal financial sums which flow out of India – totaling nearly $100 billion annually, or over 5 percent of the country's GDP. The outflow exceeds what the national government budgets annually for health care and education.[53]

India's bureaucracy and corruption are rooted in the central planning instituted after national independence in 1947. The License or Permit Raj tied to such a system spawned an extensive array of regulations and rules, giving public officials wide latitude to extract benefits at the expense of general citizens. But India's bureaucracy and corruption can be traced further back to the colonial system which the British used to govern the subcontinent and, further still, to factors which thwart entrepreneurial

---

[48] Silverstein et al. (2012).
[49] "Corruption Rate in India Is Double of Global Average," *The Times of India*, July 6, 2013.
[50] Fukuyama (2014).   [51] Fisman, Schulz, and Vig (2014).
[52] "How Will India Confront Its Corruption Crisis?" *Huffington Post*, April 27, 2013.
[53] Ibid.

activity such as the caste system, Hindu religious taboos militating against modernization, the independent authority of Brahmin priests, and even predatory Mogul rule. For example, according to historian Paul Kennedy, the Mogul court had such size and conspicuous consumption as to make Louis XIV's Versailles entourage look puny and restrained by contrast. Tax collectors preyed on peasant and merchant alike to cover the court's costs, and taxation was called "eating," given how little the general population received in return.[54] The norms of one corrupted government have a way of perpetuating themselves through culture as subsequent governments come to power.

India is not the only democracy where the political machine has been hijacked by insiders. Argentina is a large democracy, presently ranked among the top twenty-five nations of the world in terms of GDP, where the well-being of the nation has been compromised by government insiders concerned with their own benefits. According to the latest Transparency International rating, Argentina scores 32 on the 0–100 scale. It ranks 107th overall in the world for public-sector integrity and eighth lowest in the Western Hemisphere – ahead of countries such as Guatemala (28), Nicaragua (27), and Venezuela (17), but behind Peru (36) and Cuba (47).

The Index of Economic Freedom categorizes Argentina as "Repressed" and rates its economy as being the 169th freest in the world as of 2015, that is, prior to the election of a reformist president, Mauricio Macri. Argentina's economic freedom score fell markedly under the leadership of the democratically elected Kirchners – Nestor from 2003 until 2007, followed by his wife, Cristina, from 2007 until 2015. Their personality-based politics was founded in the 1940s by Juan and Evita Peron, of the Peronist party, that the Kirchners headed. These two long-ruling couples illustrate how insider groups can gain and maintain power for long periods of time even in democratic settings.

The ability of the Kirchners to impose their leftist-populist ideology through hijacking a democratic government exemplifies how pecuniary and non-pecuniary benefits are intertwined in insider jobs. The Kirchners materially benefited as they nationalized private pension funds, an airline, and a major oil company; expanded government spending from 22 percent to 44 percent of GDP; set price controls on food and electricity; imposed export taxes; enacted controls on the amount of pesos that could be exchanged for more stable currencies such as dollars at the government-regulated exchange rate; reneged on contracts with foreign companies and

---

[54] Kennedy (1987). See also Fukuyama (2011).

debt holders; and printed money to finance the higher public spending.[55] Each of these policies undermined public well-being even as it enriched the power elite.

Argentinians suffered economically. Although the officially reported inflation rate was 5–11 percent per year under the Kirchners, independent economists, surveys of inflation expectations, and provincial statistical offices all indicated that the rate was at least two to four times the official number. Such alternative data sources were rare, however, because the Argentine government under the Kirchners prosecuted and fined anyone independently publishing inflation rate estimates.[56] It went so far as to pressure McDonald's restaurants to price their Big Mac burger at low levels. This faked price manipulated the value of Argentina's currency as reflected by the Big Mac index annually compiled across countries by *The Economist*.[57]

Try as the government might to portray a different reality, the facts could not be ignored in most Argentinians' daily lives. GDP per capita, adjusted for inflation, fell from 2013 to 2015, continuing a persistent pattern of relative decline. The contrast is staggering for a country that, just a century prior, in 1914 ranked as one of the ten richest in the world – ahead of France, Germany, and Italy. Indeed, Argentina at that time was a country rapidly climbing the world's relative wealth ladder. In the forty-three years before 1914, Argentina averaged a 6 percent annual growth rate, the longest and most sustained growth spurt recorded by any country up to that point in time. Its per capita income was 92 percent of the average across the sixteen richest countries in 1914. Today, its per capita income is only 43 percent of the average across the world's sixteen richest countries.[58] The contrast provides, sadly, a striking example of what an inside job, as the political cancer that it is, can do to a host country.

While the well-being of Argentina has suffered, the officially declared Kirchner wealth grew from $2.3 million to $21 million during their administrations – even though neither Nestor nor Cristina had jobs outside of politics. To amass and hide wealth they depended on cronies to help them tap into politically established revenue streams and then shield most of the derived funds from public view. For example, in 2014, businessman and family friend Lazaro Baez came under investigation for attempting to

[55] Ian Vasquez, "Argentina's Luck Is Finally Running Out," Forbes.com, January 31, 2014.
[56] "Don't Lie to Me, Argentina," *The Economist*, February 25, 2012.
[57] "Argentina's Big Mac Attack," *New York Times*, November 24, 2011.
[58] See, for example, Acemoglu and Robinson (2012); Fukuyama (2014); and "A Century of Decline," *The Economist*, February 15, 2014.

launder $65 million through a global network of shell companies on behalf of the Kirchners. The prosecutor charging Baez alleged that the money was diverted from a government fund earmarked for public works. Like Putin's pitertsy, Baez hails from the same province, Santa Cruz, as the Kirchners, and after the Kirchners came to power his construction firm became the province's largest employer by receiving massive public works contracts.[59]

Politicians and parties top the list of public institutions deemed by Argentines to be the most corrupt. Of surveyed respondents, 70 percent believe published allegations of corruption by public officials. They point to Amado Boudou, Cristina Kirchner's vice president, who was charged in both 2012 and 2014 for influence peddling and bribery, and to a former transportation head being charged in 2014 for illicit enrichment, with little expectation of justice to be served by the courts. Only 14 percent think that convictions will follow.[60] This is because the inside job under the Kirchners also diminished the independence and integrity of Argentina's judicial system, which long has been compromised.

Argentina's high courts and constitutional law were corrupted by Juan and Evita Peron and their personality-based Peronist party. After being elected president in 1946, Juan Peron worked with supportive legislators to launch impeachment proceedings that ended up removing four of the five Supreme Court justices. Later in the century, President Carlos Menem succeeded in expanding the size of the Supreme Court with four additional justices he selected. Menem also had the constitution re-written to permit him – and those who were his cronies – to benefit from being able to hold onto office longer than the previously mandated one-term limit on presidential tenure. He then came close to further revising the constitution so as to remove a two-term limit.[61]

Even where corruption is prosecuted in Argentina, it takes fourteen years on average for cases to be resolved and only two percent result in convictions. Manuel Garrido, Argentina's chief corruption prosecutor, resigned in 2009 after filing 100 cases and failing to win a single conviction in five years. He was replaced by a Kirchner family friend who had previously organized weekend soccer matches at the presidential mansion.[62] Judicial integrity was further hijacked by the inside elite,

---

[59] "Argentine Corruption: Business as Usual?" ft.com, April 22, 2013; and "In Argentina, Mix of Politics Stirs Intrigue Around Kirchner," *Wall Street Journal*, July 28, 2014.

[60] "Argentine Corruption: Business as Usual?" ft.com, April 22, 2013; and "Argentina's Vice President Charged in Corruption Case," *New York Times*, June 28, 2014.

[61] Acemoglu and Robinson (2012).

[62] "U.S. Embassy: Corruption Unpunished in Argentina," *Seattle Times*, February 9, 2011.

which many believed proved its determination to hold onto power by any means possible. In January 2015, federal prosecutor Alberto Nisman was found dead in his bathroom from a gunshot wound to the head just hours before he was slated to testify before Congress. Nisman intended to accuse Cristina Kirchner and other officials of covering up Iranian complicity in the 1994 bombing of a Jewish center in Buenos Aires that killed eighty-six people and injured hundreds.

As the Kirchner government protected its grip on power, so it protected the wealth that it was plundering. Cristina Kirchner decried American investors as "vultures" for refusing her government's offer to repay 25 percent of the $95 billion in outstanding debt from a 2001 default. She offered high praise for Vladimir Putin's willingness in 2014 to write off 90 percent of the $32 billion owed by Cuba to Russia, calling Putin's largesse worth imitating. Yet the Kirchner government declined to show similar largesse by refusing to write off any of the debt owed to Argentina by Cuba ($8–11 billion) and Paraguay ($18 billion), prompting a leading Paraguayan newspaper to note the irony and accuse Kirchner of "acting like a vulture."[63]

A last example of democratic politics being hijacked by government insiders involves Greece at the point after the Treaty of Maastricht of 1992 established the European Union and led to a common currency, the euro. In this case, a democratic federation of equal and democratic nations was from its inception created to favor policymakers at the core of the organization. This played out as the euro's advent induced huge capital flows from the euro-zone core to the periphery, triggering an inflationary credit bubble in the periphery but not in the EU core. The bubble was further fueled by banking provisions and expectations promoted by EU policymakers. These policies led to excessive private debt in countries such as Ireland and Spain, and they managed to relax the constraint of interest payments on outstanding public debt in periphery countries, where funds were, in turn, freed up for expanding state payrolls, thus growing financial liabilities to large groups on both the demand side and the supply side of politics. The economic and social well-being in the periphery countries grew increasingly unstable, undermining their long-run competitive position among nations.[64]

In particular, in Greece and Portugal the credit and state spending latitude were used primarily to pay higher salaries to public employees. Over the period between 2000 and 2008, public employees' salaries

---

[63] See, for example, "Now It's Argentina's Turn to Be the Debt Bully," bloomberg.com, May 18, 2015.

[64] Sinn (2014).

increased 80 percent in Greece and 30 percent in Portugal versus 10 percent in Germany and relative to a cumulative inflation rate of 15 percent. Moreover, public employment increased by 16 percent in Greece and 6 percent in Portugal versus a decline of 7 percent in Germany. The associated growth of public debt relative to GDP became a problem for southern European countries like Greece and Portugal with the recession of 2007–2009. It also threatened to unravel the European Union after the European Central Bank, contrary to provisions of the Maastricht Treaty, stepped in to supply $2 trillion in aid to crisis-stricken Greece and Portugal, along with Italy, Spain, Ireland, and Cyprus.[65]

Greece, democracy's birthplace, now reflects what happens when democracy is strapped by the cost of having been hijacked by government insiders. Greece found itself at the center of protracted negotiations in 2015 with a "Troika" of creditors consisting of the European Central Bank, European Commission, and International Monetary Fund (IMF). Greece's public debt – which some might define as a measure of the promises made to various interests by insiders seeking access to or the retention of power – to GDP ratio exceeds 160 percent and is the third-highest rate in the world after Japan and Zimbabwe. The country narrowly staved off an EU exit by accepting a new credit agreement in return for implementing austerity measures. Many structural problems, however, are likely to remain unaddressed by the socialist Syriza party that remains in power – thus hindering Greece's competitiveness.[66]

The extent to which Greece has been hijacked by government insiders also can be seen in the fact that its national debt averages out to over $250,000 for every working adult. This amount has grown in recent decades as public-sector employment has increased by nearly 4 percent per year since 1970. By contrast, private-sector employment grew by only 1 percent over the same time period. The average government job pays almost three times as much as the average private-sector job. Ostensibly to diminish patronage and nepotism, virtually iron-clad job protection for government workers has been enshrined in Greece's constitution since 1880. For every seven private-sector workers laid off in 2012 when unemployment hovered at 25 percent, only one had left the public sector.[67]

[65] Ibid.
[66] Holger Schmieding, "Debt Isn't Killing Greece. Its Leaders Are," *Wall Street Journal*, July 18–19, 2015.
[67] John Sfakianakis, "The Costs of Protecting Greece's Public Sector," *New York Times*, October 10, 2012; and "Greece Starts Firing Civil Servants for the First Time in a Century," csmonitor.com, April 26, 2013.

The average Greek citizen either holds a government job or has financially benefited in some way from those working in the public sector.

Since the public sector employs 29 percent of Greece's labor force in high-paying and virtually recession-proof jobs, it should come as no surprise that the government exercises formidable political muscle to preserve its size and benefits. In the 2015 debt restructuring, the Troika's efforts to promote lower public spending and public employee layoffs were resisted fiercely and successfully by the leftist Syriza party – to the detriment of the public good in Greece.

Michael Lewis, in *Boomerang*, describes the effect that public sector growth has had on trust in government and the Greek character (pp. 45–55):[68]

It is ... assumed that anyone ... working for the government is meant to be bribed ... Government officials are assumed to steal... [According to one tax collector, tax fraud has] "become a cultural trait." ... Greek people have a hard time saying a kind word about one another ... Everyone is pretty sure everyone is cheating on his taxes, or bribing politicians, or taking bribes, or lying about the value of his real estate. And this total absence of faith in one another is self-reinforcing. The epidemic of lying and stealing makes any sort of civic life impossible.

THE CENTRAL CONUNDRUM

As both democratic and autocratic examples show, an important conundrum lies at the heart of any effective government. Specifically, while political order is valuable and relies on centralized authority, centralized authority can lead to the monopolization of power and with it the potential for the political system to be co-opted by government insiders at the expense of the public interest, thus leading not to social well-being but instead to societal decay.

The conundrum resembles the natural monopoly problem in economics where economies of scale favor a single supplier for an entire market but the resulting (natural) monopoly position affords the sole supplier, if unchecked, the opportunity to profit at the expense of consumers, market output, and efficiency. Similarly, the many benefits derived by government insiders are incentive to obtain, exercise, and retain such monopoly power. The price of inside jobs is paid at the expense of the public interest through diminished prosperity, liberty, security, peace, and trust.

[68] Lewis (2011).

As we've seen in this chapter, the ways through which government insiders can benefit from co-opting the political process at the public's expense are manifold in both democracies and autocracies. The reason why they profit from power, either in pecuniary or non-pecuniary terms, is the subject of the next chapter.

3

How Do Government Insiders Profit
at the Public's Expense?

How do government insiders manage to divert resources from serving the welfare of the public to their own benefit seemingly without consequence? The answer to this question can be determined by more closely examining the circumstances in both democracies and autocracies that give rise to an inside job. What becomes apparent is that to whatever degree the supply side of politics is not perfectly accountable to a nation's citizens, government insiders can exploit the attendant slack for their own ends. Failure to hold officials accountable may be due to a lack of information, enfranchisement, constitutional or cultural checks, or even public will, but these and other factors, to the surprise of some readers, exist in both autocracies and democracies. To understand the complex of factors at work in this dynamic, let's introduce a straightforward formula.

The profits, P, to government insiders from an inside job – what economists call "rents" – can be expressed as follows:

$$P = G \times S \times I. \tag{3.1}$$

In this formula, G measures the potential gains to government insiders from their positions at the expense of the public interest, gains that are likely to be positively related to the size of the state in a society. The S term in the formula ranges in value between 0 and 1 and measures the slack or leeway in the relationship between citizens and their public "servants"; it thus also reflects the degree to which the public is able to, and chooses to, hold government insiders accountable for promoting the public interest. The formula's I term takes on a value between 0 and 1 and measures the extent to which government insiders are interested in exploiting any slack for their personal benefit; it is thus feasible, at least theoretically, that government insiders may have no oversight but still faithfully perform their duties to the public, without thought of self-interested alternatives.

In one set of extreme circumstances, where public officials are perfectly accountable, there is no slack in the relationship with their citizens ($S = 0$) and thus no profits accruing to government insiders ($P = 0$) since they are unable to hijack the political process for their benefit. No matter how great a value G or I may take on, P will remain equal to 0. No matter the prospective gains to tempt government insiders and no matter how great their interest in capturing those gains, the value of P remains 0 ($0 = G \times 0 \times I$).

At the opposite extreme, if public officials are entirely unaccountable, the slack in the relationship between them and their citizens is at a maximum ($S = 1$). Assuming that there are gains to be captured (G) and full interest in securing those gains ($I = 1$), the inside job will proceed unrestrained, with the profit extracted by government insiders limited only by the gains that can be extracted (G). In other words, where there is no degree of accountability ($S = 1$) government insiders take everything that is there as long as they are fully interested ($I = 1$). Hijacking of the state by government insiders will be total ($P = G$), provided they are fully willing to capture all the potential profit from their positions ($I = 1$) in other words, $P = G \times 1 \times 1$.

While exceedingly simple, the foregoing comparison highlights the central role played by imperfect accountability on the supply side of politics. Any slack in the relationship between citizens and their public officials increases the magnitude of political capture by government insiders. If citizens can perfectly police their public officials, the inside job ceases to become a danger. To the degree policing of public officials by their citizens is imperfect is the degree to which we need worry about the damage done by an inside job.

Something else happens as S (political slack) approaches a maximum value of 1. As the slack in the relationship between the public and its officials increases, citizens find themselves supplanted as the focus of government policy decisions. Citizens even find the principal–agent relationship between them and their officials will reverse. In examples across history, citizens have become the agents or servants of public officials who seek to maximize profit from their political power.[1] This is what analyst Sarah Chayes observed in Afghanistan, where money metaphorically defied the laws of gravity and flowed upward from citizens to the ruling

---

[1] Jensen and Meckling (1976) spell out the principal–agent problem. Moe (2006) notes the possibility of agents controlling their principals.

Karzai regime in order to forestall certain feared actions by the regime against its citizens.[2]

Between the two extremes this formula can reflect there are many subtleties for how government insiders hijack power to different degrees for personal profit. How the potential gains and interest in profit interplay with slack in the relationship between citizens and their public officials will be considered in the remainder of this chapter relying on the formula. Beyond that, subsequent chapters will explore the factors influencing the three key determinants of government insider profits. Chapter 4 examines factors driving government growth which increase the potential gains (G) that public officials can derive from their positions. Chapters 5 and 6 then investigate curbs on government growth and capture – curbs to mitigate the potential gains (G) government insiders can derive from co-opting the state, or to diminish the slack (S) between citizens and their public officials, or to decrease the interest (I) of officials in exercising any slack for their benefit and at the expense of citizens. However, as a preview of my closing remarks, the curbs prove to be imperfect, and so fail to prevent inside jobs completely. This is true for autocracies and democracies where the G, S, or I terms will never equal 0.

THE MANY PATHS TO PROFIT IN POLITICS

Let's review. If there is imperfect accountability on the supply side of politics ($S > 0$) and government insiders are willing to capitalize on the slack ($I > 0$), then government insiders will be free to convert at least some of the potential gains (G) from their positions into actual profit (P). (If $S > 0$ and $I > 0$, then $P > 0$.)

The potential ways for government insiders to profit from their positions are almost endless. Financial benefits can be secured openly or in secret. Wealth can accrue from the diversion of public funds or from payments received from other sources, legal as well as illegal. Benefits can be related to politicians' visibility, status, and/or ability to influence policy outcomes. Remuneration can be channeled directly through salaries and benefits or indirectly through campaign contributions, honoraria, in-kind gifts, revolving-door positions in industry, and all range of benefits or payments to family members and businesses. The profits may be derived from relevant special-interest groups in return for promoting particular

---

[2] Chayes (2015).

policies, but they also may accrue from politicians threatening to undertake activities that will make an interest group worse off.[3]

Government insiders can also benefit from access to knowledge about prospective regulatory changes. For example, members of the US Congress have outperformed the stock market when it comes to picking stocks. Between 1985 and 2001, US senators saw their personal stock portfolios earn an average of 12.3 percentage points more per year than the market rate of return, and the portfolios of members of the House of Representatives beat the market by an average of 6 percentage points annually.[4] During that same time period, the financial sage of Omaha and head of Berkshire Hathaway, Warren Buffet, didn't come close to matching Capitol Hill's stock-picking acumen. The abnormally high returns prompted passage of the Stop Trading on Congressional Knowledge (STOCK) Act of 2012, which sought to curb the obvious by increasing financial reporting requirements for congressional members and top executive branch officials.

Public employees also benefit from what is a double level of power in their compensation and other benefits. They in general are insulated from competitive market forces because the government often is the sole supplier or has some monopoly power with respect to the provision of a good or service. In addition, as noted by economist Daniel DiSalvo, public employees effectively get "two bites at the apple" versus the one bite available to their private-sector counterparts. That is, not only can they organize and collectively bargain with their managers, as can private employees, they also participate in electing and otherwise managing the people who are supposed to be managing them.[5] In these two ways, those who are managed exercise power over those who manage them. Such "management in reverse" increases the risk of organizational dysfunction that Junius S. Morgan, father of John Pierpont Morgan, warned about in expressing some skepticism about public service at the end of the nineteenth century by saying, "I have no doubt that there is a satisfaction in doing one's duty even if it is spelled with a large D, but don't you think it is a word that can be made to conform to almost anything which one wants to do?"[6]

This is a potent brew: public positions insulated from competition, public employees' collective bargaining power and their ability to manage in reverse. It increases both the potential gains (G) from an inside job and

---

[3] See, for example, Cost (2015); McChesney (1997); and Schweizer (2011, 2015).
[4] Ziobrowski et al. (2004, 2011).   [5] DiSalvo (2015). See also Moe (2006).
[6] Strouse (1999), p. 121.

also magnifies the slack (*S*) in the relationship and accountability between citizens and their public officials. As a result, the profits to government insiders (*P*) multiply along with their collective power.

Wisconsin's governor Scott Walker learned how challenging it can be to try to curb the political power of state employees. After his election in 2010, Walker supported legislation limiting the collective bargaining rights of Wisconsin's public employees, which was either resisted or hailed as a first step to reducing benefits for government employees in line with private citizens. His actions led to widespread protests by public union members (and their supporters) and a hotly contested recall election in 2011 which Walker won based on a surge of public support for reducing the power of unelected officials.

Exercising such power, public officials gain materially, but they can also advance their ideologies to secure additional, non-pecuniary gains. Consider autocrats who rose to power promoting ideologies in the twentieth century only, such as Adolf Hitler of the Nazi Party in Germany, Mobutu Sese Seko of the Democratic Republic of the Congo, Josef Stalin as head of the Communist Party and the Soviet Union, Pol Pot, who led the Khmer Rouge in Kampuchia (Cambodia), Idi Amin Dada, who was president of Uganda, Chairman Mao Zedong of the Communist Party of China, and Papa and Baby Doc Duvalier of Haiti. The periods over which these auto-crats ruled were historic bloodbaths created by their own policies. Vast numbers of people under their rule died or otherwise suffered greatly serving the government's appetite for power, principles, and wealth.

It is not only autocrats who can promote their ideological interests, and it is not only diabolical historic leaders who impose their personal ideology using their public position of power. Research finds that in democracies, political leaders, legislators, judges, and bureaucrats have considerable leeway to promote their worldviews through their work without answering to – and at the expense of – the citizens who they ostensibly serve.[7] The leeway such government insiders enjoy in demo-cratic settings results from what can be significant slack (*S* > 0) between the public and its public servants. Both imperfect competition and policing on the supply side of politics lessen the accountability of government insiders, who thereby have greater latitude to promote their own ideologies at the expense of the well-being of the citizens in their communities.

---

[7] See, for example, Diermeier, Keane, and Merlo (2005); Kalt and Zupan (1984, 1990); Kau and Rubin (1979); Levitt (1996); Niskanen (1971); Posner (1977); and Wilson (1989).

Being a government insider provides in both autocracies and democracies a unique power perch from which to impose an ideology on a community, group, or the population at large. It is not surprising, then, that positions of political power tend to attract individuals with relatively intense interest in promoting ideological goals.[8] The state's coercive power is a far greater prize to hijack than the power earned even at the head of private firms and nonprofit organizations, where accountability to multiple stakeholders and the state itself is greater. As the fictitious character House Majority Whip Francis Underwood notes in the television series *House of Cards* about a former staff member turned lobbyist:

Such a waste of talent! He chose money over power. In this town [Washington, DC], a mistake nearly everyone makes. Money is the McMansion in Sarasota that starts falling apart after ten years. Power is the old stone building that stands for centuries. I cannot respect someone that doesn't see the difference.

Ideologues have a signature set of variables. They are drawn to the potential gains (G) from public positions but from a non-pecuniary ambition, and they are especially interested (I) in co-opting the state. Motivated, they are poised to exploit any leeway to promote their ideologies that public positions afford.

WHEN DOORS CLOSE, INSIDERS SEEK OPEN WINDOWS

Efforts to promote the accountability of government insiders and decrease the slack in the government self-capture equation – and to impose new levels of accountability – must take into account the capacity of insiders to circumvent those efforts. In other words, efforts to decrease S are likely to meet with an increase in motivation to resist among government insiders, even a spike in I.

Consider how efforts to promote a level playing field for financial market investors simply created new avenues to leverage insider advantages. High-frequency traders found ways to undermine these regulatory efforts by paying fees to the firms running so-called dark pools in return for tips about large forthcoming institutional trades. In *Flash Boys*, Michael Lewis describes how high-frequency traders profit at the expense of institutional investors through such an early warning system.[9]

Likewise, in the political arena, efforts to reduce undue influence by donors on government have included legislated limits on contributions to

---

[8] Cowen and Sutter (1997); and Kalt and Zupan (1984).   [9] Lewis (2014).

candidates for US federal office. That legislation has been circumvented by the creative invention of super PACs (political action committees). Super PACs can accept unlimited funds from individuals, companies, and unions, offering an indirect way legally to spend an unrestricted amount in support of individual candidates.

The finances of two top 2016 US presidential candidates, Marco Rubio and Hillary Clinton, further highlight politicians' creativity, even in democracies, when they seek to circumvent accountability, that is, when they seek to preserve a greater level of S in the face of efforts to reduce S. In 2008, Republican Marco Rubio reported $8,000 in net worth upon leaving Florida's House of Representatives. His ascent to the US Senate and subsequent presidential run were fueled by $10 million from Norman Braman, a billionaire Miami auto dealer. Braman paid for Rubio's book that laid out a conservative vision for Florida; covered Rubio's $100,000 instructor salary at Florida International University; employed Rubio as a lawyer for his company during Rubio's Senate run; hired Rubio's wife to run his philanthropic foundation; and provided Rubio access to his private jet.[10] These were all legally permitted actions. For his part, Rubio championed $5 million in state funding for a Miami cancer institute bearing the Braman name and $80 million for a genomics institute at the University of Miami, another top Braman cause. Rubio claimed that his support was merit-based and not due to Braman's financial help, but the benefit Braman's money generated for Rubio is obvious.[11]

Questionable accountability is not limited to either major political party. Democrat Hillary Clinton and husband Bill have earned over $150 million in speaking fees since leaving the White House in 2000 in a financial circumstance described by Hillary Clinton in her now famous "dead broke" characterization.[12] Organizations based in the United States and paying up to $500,000 per talk have included financial and pharmaceutical firms, medical groups, and real estate associations. The fees to domestic organizations have averaged twice the going rate for other high-profile politicians. To many ordinary citizens, they convey the impression of a symbiotic relationship between the supply and demand sides of US politics.[13]

The symbiotic relationship can include international players on the demand side of politics with an interest in US policy outcomes. While

---

[10] "Billionaire Lifts Marco Rubio, Politically and Personally," *New York Times*, May 9, 2015.
[11] Ibid.   [12] Schweizer (2015).
[13] Nick Morgan, "How Much Can You Charge for Speaking?" Forbes.com, November 14, 2013.

foreign nationals are forbidden from donating to US political campaigns, there are no restrictions on paying a candidate's spouse for a speech, even though Hillary arguably benefits from Bill's wealth. Neither are foreign nationals prohibited from making contributions through a vehicle such as the Clinton Foundation and its affiliates operating outside of the United States – affiliates subject to less stringent reporting requirements than the parent foundation.

Over the years, significant revenue has flowed, albeit indirectly, into Hillary Clinton's life. Bill Clinton has been paid significant speaking fees. The Clinton family's foundation and its affiliates have accepted substantial sums of money from foreign governments, firms, and individuals. These contributions were legal and accepted even when Hillary Clinton, as a US senator and then secretary of state, was involved in policy matters germane to the foreign donors. The magnitude and temporal pattern of the wealth transfer were uncommon for a couple after leaving the White House. While the speaking fees of former presidents decline the longer they have been out of office, Bill's honoraria have risen. Although Hillary's intention to run for the office of president after Barack Obama's second term was no secret, Bill's three top earning years, in terms of speaking fees, occurred from 2009 to 2011 when his wife was secretary of state.[14]

Consider one case in point to illustrate how the interest (I) of a government insider can respond to the potential gain (G). In 2008, Canada's TD Bank was the largest owner of the Keystone pipeline project, which was seeking US government approval to transport oil from Alberta's oil sands to the Gulf Coast of Texas. Prior to the news that Hillary would be President Obama's choice to head up the State Department, TD Bank never invited Bill Clinton to speak nor paid him a fee. Following that announcement, TD Bank paid Bill over $1.5 million to give speeches, often closed to the public, in places such as Halifax, St. John, Calgary, Fredericton, Antigonish, and Abu Dhabi. After Bill began speaking on behalf of TD Bank, Hillary hinted that she would support Keystone. However, TD Bank's investment in Bill came to naught when President Obama postponed his decision on the project until after the 2012 elections – and Hillary left her leadership role at State in January 2013.[15] TD Bank has not invited Bill back as a speaker since.

In another episode, Canadian magnate Frank Giustra and his investing partners committed $145 million to the Clinton Foundation in two tranches. Giustra gave $31.3 million in 2007 after Bill introduced him to Kazakhstan's dictator Nursulan Nazarbayev and assisted Giustra's firm,

---

[14] Ibid.   [15] Ibid.

Uranium One, in acquiring uranium assets in Kazakhstan. Hillary, who at the time chaired a Senate subcommittee responsible for giving up to $110 million annually in nonproliferation program funds to Kazakhstan, provided useful pressure along the way to ensure that the Kazakh government was amenable to the deal. Additionally, the photo opportunities with and positive statements made by Bill allowed Nazarbayev to burnish his image domestically as well as on the global stage.[16]

Having had one successful interaction with the Clintons, in 2008, Giustra further committed $100 million and half of his company's future profits to the Clinton Foundation. The commitment paid off handsomely for all involved when Hillary Clinton, as secretary of state, approved the sale of Uranium One to the Russian government in 2010. Russia ended up owning 20 percent of America's uranium production capacity on top of similar mineral assets elsewhere around the globe – assets of interest to nations making or selling nuclear reactors or bombs. In the process, Russia's president, Vladimir Putin, won a valuable "reset" of relations with the United States. Giustra made $300 million on the sale. What the Clintons and their foundation earned has yet to be fully disclosed. In addition to the financial commitments to the foundation from Giustra and other Uranium One executives, Bill earned $500,000 for a single talk in Moscow in 2010. The talk, sponsored by an investment bank tied to Putin and his cronies, was given just prior to Hillary's decision to approve the Uranium One sale.[17]

Giustra also partnered with the Clintons from 2005 to 2012 on several Colombian deals. Through a relationship fostered by Bill Clinton between Giustra and Colombia's president, Alvaro Uribe, Giustra secured lucrative timber-cutting and oil drilling rights in Colombia. President Uribe and his government persuaded Hillary, as secretary of state, to champion a free trade agreement (thereby reversing her prior position on the matter) and the rapid expansion of energy and mining loans backed by the US government's Export-Import Bank and the Trade Development Agency. Among the Export-Import Bank's loans was $280 million to a Giustra company to transport liquid natural gas from Colombia to China.[18]

Surrounding these Colombian deals was a supporting cast of lesser known insiders who also profited. A South American business group

[16] Ibid.
[17] Ibid. See also "Fine Line for Clintons on Speaking Fees," *Wall Street Journal*, December 31, 2015, pp. A1 and A9.
[18] Ibid.

favoring the free trade agreement paid Bill $800,000 for four speeches in 2005; this fee went up once Hillary became secretary of state. The public relations firm run by Mark Penn, long-time Clinton advisor and Hillary's 2008 presidential campaign manager, was paid $300,000 to promote a lavish pro-Colombia dinner in New York. Bill received a "Colombia is Passion" award at the dinner and Uribe's praise for being the country's unofficial tourism minister. And the Colombian government put the lobbying firm run by Howard Wolfson, Hillary's campaign spokesperson, on a $40,000 monthly retainer.[19] These were all government insiders working across borders and crafting deals, but the question is for whose welfare: that of the public in the nations they represented or for themselves? And, are they even able to discern the difference?

Indeed, Hillary Clinton asserts that her policy stances regarding Kazakhstan, Russia, Colombia, and the Keystone pipeline were merit-based. She claims that her family's receipt of over $150 million directly or indirectly from individuals and organizations such as Frank Giustra of Uranium One, President Alvaro Uribe of Colombia, President Vladimir Putin of Russia, President Nursulan Nazarbayev of Kazakhstan, and TD Bank of Canada played no role in influencing her actions. She is quick to point out that nothing happened that ran counter to any US laws, including those designed to promote the accountability of government insiders. In other words, a high value of slack (S) can happen in plain view and be technically legal, but the lure of potential gains (G) and the drive of interest (I) have a way of motivating government insiders to circumvent efforts designed to reduce slack and impose accountability.

UNINTENDED CONSEQUENCES

Inside jobs can be an unintended consequence of policies with good intent. They also are not static at all. They change as the potential gains (G), slack (S), and interest (I) vary over time. For example, as the role of the state in a society grows, G is likely to increase. As the numbers of those benefiting from government positions grow, others gain interest in following suit. Also, it can take time for government interests to coalesce and, working together, subvert the public interest.

The growing influence of US federal employees as an interest group illustrates this last point.[20] Civil service reform that started in the late 1800s was based on a desire for a cleaner government and merit-based political

[19] Ibid.   [20] See, for example, Johnson and Libecap (1994).

appointments. It also stemmed from the growing size of the federal bureaucracy, which became increasingly difficult to manage for the president and Congress with their many other responsibilities. To accomplish the business of government was starting to require increasing levels of patronage beyond other sources of political support. So, efforts to reform the bureaucracy began. However, once time, as federal employees became more numerous, they also became more insulated, through civil service reforms, and unionized. Indeed, they became a vested interest with political clout within government but with very little of their work being accountable to voters. This scenario in American history is consistent with political economy scholar Mancur Olson's observation on the decline of certain Western democracies: it can take time for special interests to mobilize and thereby harden a nation's economic arteries.[21]

Political theorist Francis Fukuyama takes the point a step further, describing how policies designed to promote the public interest can end up subverting it instead. One case involves the Janissaries, the Ottoman Empire's elite fighting force mentioned earlier. Admission to the Janissaries was not based on kinship or on patronage. The Janissaries were intended to be strictly meritocratic and thus to run counter to the human tendency of favoring family and friends in government hiring. Scouts recruited only the most able-bodied young males, largely from Christian lands conquered by the Ottomans. While the Janissaries managed to remain a dynamic and powerful elite force, they initially helped the Ottoman Empire expand, but once their positions became hereditary and their numbers and influence grew, their own weakness corroded the entire empire's vitality.[22]

Similarly, the Kurdish Mamluks attained historic power based on meritocracy only to slowly give way to the phenomenon of the inside job, taking the fortunes of the kingdom that they protected with them. The Mamluk army appeared during the Kurdish Ayyubid dynasty, which ruled, during the twelfth and thirteenth centuries AD, much of the Middle East. The Ayyubid's most famous sultan was Saladin. The Ayyubid sultans recruited Mamluk slave soldiers from conquered lands. The Mamluks were conscripted based on physical prowess and came from various religious backgrounds. They were fused into a meritocratic, nonhereditary, and vaunted fighting force – indoctrinated in Islam, cut off from their families

---

[21] Olson (1982).

[22] Fukuyama (2011) attributes the tendency to hire family and friends to evolutionary biology factors such as reciprocal altruism and gene propagation.

and tribes, unsullied (through their slave status) by civilized life's temptations, limited in their access to female partners, educated by eunuchs so as to curtail homosexual liaisons, and trained to be loyal to their masters and each other.[23] They formed an elite army which many aspired to join, hoping to share in the acclaim and spoils of success in war. For example, in 1249, the Mamluks expelled the crusaders from Egypt. Along the way, they extracted a proverbial king's ransom, equal to then France's national product, for returning King Louis IX unharmed. Later, Mamluk troops saved Islam by fending off various Mongol invasions from 1260 to 1303.[24]

As the effectiveness, size, and influence of the Mamluk army grew, it usurped power, eventually taking over the state from the Ayyubid dynasty, which had been governing through loosely aligned principalities based on kinship. Initially, national stability was enhanced because of the centralized, professional manner in which the Mamluk army governed.[25] Over time, however, a reverse-agency problem set in similar to what would be observed centuries later under Karzai's Afghani government.[26] The army that had served the country began to expect the citizens of the country to serve its growing needs. This was exacerbated by the absence of a clearly defined leadership succession plan and the ensuing internal conflicts. Some Mamluk sultans sought to override the meritocracy at the heart of the Mamluks and instead to designate a son or relative as a successor, pitting their designs against rival army factions often powerful enough to veto the choice to preserve nonhereditary succession. Civilian control over the army might have curtailed infighting between Mamluk factions, but such control was lacking. The meritocratic, anti-hereditary rule, despite its early champions, eventually eroded as Mamluks devised ways to promote their families and friends and their clans' status and wealth. As the well-being of ruling Mamluk families eclipsed that of the country itself, the state grew even less effective than when ruled by the Ayyubids.

As the state functioned with decreasing effectiveness, Mamluk resources and ingenuity were being consumed internally and no longer focused on the prospect of external enemies – or opportunities. Portuguese forays into the Indian Ocean disrupting the spice trade proceeded unchecked, reducing the sultanate's revenues. To underwrite government operations as the spice trade was disrupted, the sultanate was forced to raise taxes on the population. The Mamluk government even resisted technological innovations such as firearms, overlooking their defensive military value while focusing on internal power grabs rather than external threats. It was no

---

[23] Ibid.   [24] Ibid.   [25] Ibid.   [26] Chayes (2015).

surprise that the Mamluk sultanate, resources exhausted by plundering government insiders, succumbed to the Ottomans in 1517.[27]

Examinations of how government insiders hijack the state show, like this chapter does, that the process of the inside job isn't necessarily top of mind for the insiders. They may not start out to plunder the full treasury. At times, it takes generations for incremental advances in the inside job before a country collapses from its parasitic effect. Often the focus is on the seemingly reasonable concern for the welfare of one's family, generation after generation, while losing sight of how that welfare is promoted at the expense of national well-being. There are exceptions, where ideology empowers its proponents with the vision and will to promote revolution – and not always at the expense of the public good.

GOVERNMENT INSIDERS CAN ADVANCE THE PUBLIC INTEREST

It is possible for the welfare of the public to align with the welfare of government insiders. The potential gains (G) in the government self-capture equation reflect the prospective rents that public officials can derive from their positions, but sometimes these gains are not at odds with the public interest. Even if there is slack in the relationship between citizens and their public officials ($S > 0$), it is possible for government insiders either faithfully to serve or meaningfully to advance the public interest. That is, the supply side of politics may profit from the same policies that advance the well-being of the demand side.

To understand how government insiders might advance the public interest, consider what is meant by the public interest. Promoting the public interest is generally assumed to mean maximizing a society's total net economic benefits, pecuniary as well as non-pecuniary, based on a given initial distribution of resources. The extent to which government insiders advance or diminish the public interest must be gauged against the status quo. Seen this way, it is possible for the benefits to government insiders to increase as the public interest is advanced. A wealthier nation, which generates greater wealth overall, offers more to be potentially appropriated by those on the supply side of politics.

The potential alignment of purposes can make government insiders quite useful to the state and its citizens. As articulated by economists Dani Rodrick and Weiying Zhang, government insiders are integral to

[27] Ibid.

the conceptualization and advocacy of ideas regarding how the state can best advance the public interest.[28] This is true in autocracies as well as democracies. Most of us, for example, would agree that the religious tolerance promoted by England's Queen Elizabeth I brought greater peace and prosperity to her realm. Likewise, the economic reforms and openness to foreign ideas fostered by Deng Xiaoping helped China make sizable developmental strides.

Nelson Mandela used his power as a government insider to advance the public interest in, many would say, opposition to the retribution it would have been reasonable for him to seek. His ability to forgive, despite having been jailed for twenty-seven years under apartheid, hastened reconciliation between whites and blacks after he was elected South Africa's president in 1994. Mandela took his national example into all public venues. He invited former jailers to his inaugural; asked the prosecutor who had attempted to impose the death penalty on him in 1963 to join him for lunch; and wore the jersey of the Springboks, the rugby team reviled by blacks for its close association with the former apartheid government, to the World Cup final in 1995. Mandela was fond of saying that "resentment is like drinking poison and then hoping it will kill your enemies."[29] But what he was doing was promoting his ideology of reconciliation seeking to draw his country's citizens through an era of anger into a functioning state that could advance the public good.

Another way that government insiders may further the public interest can seem ironic at first. One of the perhaps counterintuitive potential benefits of the ideologies advocated by political leaders is that they actually can decrease the need for material rewards and corruption to motivate bureaucrats and ruling party members. In other words, they reduce the relative pecuniary profits associated with political power. Political scientists James Hollyer and Leonard Wantchekon argue this point: the more compelling the ideology, the lower will be the petty corruption level, at least in autocratic regimes.[30] This is because an ideologically driven regime enjoys the loyalty of a broader segment of the populace, which shares its worldview. In this circumstance, material rewards are less necessary to motivate supporters and administrators. Hollyer and Wantchekon claim that one of the reasons that corruption has grown in post-Mao China is that the Communist Party is relying less on ideology as a means to legitimize its rule.

---

[28] Rodrik (2014) and Zhang (2015).   [29] Carlin (2009).
[30] Hollyer and Wantchekon (2015).

There is no guarantee, however, that the ideological and material interests of government insiders will dovetail with and advance the public interest when there is slack (S) in the relationship between citizens and their public officials. If anything, the historical and global trend toward reducing slack through mechanisms such as the rule of law and electoral competition suggests an ongoing need for accountability precisely because government insiders' interests do not consistently or ever completely align with or positively advance the public good. And, indeed, government insiders are prone, after securing some profit through their positions, to seek more.

IS PROFITING FROM POWER AN ACQUIRED OR LATENT TASTE?

How government insiders manage to hijack political power is the focus of this chapter, and how they become the insider willing to hijack power is part of that consideration. Do government insiders develop a penchant for profit while in office? Or is the proclivity something they are born with and is simply uncovered when they acquire power? With regard to our equation, does the interest (I) in profiting from power increase with an official's tenure or is it constant over time?

Lord Dalberg-Acton favored the former explanation, observing that "power tends to corrupt and absolute power corrupts absolutely."[31] Acton's observation is supported by the results of the well-known Stanford Prison Experiment conducted in 1971 by psychologist Philip Zimbardo.[32] In the experiment, twenty-four male student volunteers participated in the two-week paid simulation, with half randomly assigned to be prison guards and the other half prisoners. Zimbardo served as the superintendent. The prison guards were provided with suitable clothing and wooden batons to symbolize authority and mirrored sunglasses to limit eye contact. Prisoners were strip-searched, given uncomfortable clothes, identified only by number and not by name, and had a chain placed around one ankle.

Within two days, the prisoners began to "revolt," refusing to follow guards' instructions, not wearing their assigned clothing, and blockading their cell doors with their beds. To subdue the revolt, the guards used

---

[31] Dalberg-Acton (1907).

[32] Zimbardo (2007). Pfeffer (2015) also notes how different responsibilities alter individuals' behaviors.

progressively harsher tactics, including forcing the prisoners to repeatedly state only their assigned numbers, requiring them to engage in protracted physical exercise, taking away their mattresses, attacking them with fire extinguishers, mandating that they go to the bathroom only in a bucket inside their cell, moving the worst-behaving ones to solitary confinement in a closet, and even making some of the prisoners stand naked so as to mentally and emotionally degrade them. A third of the guards exhibited genuine sadistic behavior, to an extent that the experiment had to be terminated after only six days – to the dismay of all of the guards.

Zimbardo argues that both guards and prisoners internalized their respective identities. That is, position revealed the potential of each to react to their status. He testified before Congress following the Abu Ghraib military prison scandal in Iraq in 2004, asserting that the improper behavior could not be attributed to a few bad apples among the Abu Ghraib guards but rather to the overall incarceration system used by the US military occupying Iraq which fostered similar reactions in otherwise reputable troops.

Zimbardo's results comport with an earlier laboratory study by Yale psychologist Stanley Milgram, who found that 100 percent of male volunteers were willing to administer, on the orders of authority figures, electrical shocks to assigned "learners" when the learners answered questions incorrectly.[33] Of the volunteers, 65 percent were willing to administer shocks supposedly sufficient to kill the learner. Vested with power, the volunteers proved willing to exercise it to extremes that seemed unlikely prior to having power. With the new power amplified by symbols of authority, the volunteers proved even more inclined toward brutality. That is, the percentage willing to administer shocks increased with certain factors such as the physical proximity of the authority figure providing instructions, how "official" the attire of the authority figure appeared, and how imposing the building in which the experiment took place seemed.

By contrast, with the Zimbardo and Milgram research, a team of management scholars led by Katherine DeCelles argues that power reveals rather than alters individuals' underlying character or interest (I) in capitalizing on power.[34] Their findings are consistent with Abraham Lincoln's maxim that "nearly all men can stand adversity, but if you want to see a man's character, give him power."

To start, DeCelles and her colleagues asked a sample of working adults and undergraduates to rate how important it was to be "fair,"

---

[33] Milgram (1974).   [34] DeCelles et al. (2012).

"caring," "generous," and so on. Based on their responses, the participants were categorized as possessing either a high or low level of underlying moral identity. Various exercises then asked the participants to
recount a situation that primed them to feel either powerful or not. For
example, some of the participants were asked to write an essay about an
ordinary day, which presumably did not prime them to feel powerful.
Others were asked to recall an incident that made them feel powerful,
presumably contrary to an ordinary day without incident. A concluding
experiment then tested the extent to which the participants balanced
self-interest against the common good so as to determine the influence
of underlying character (as measured by the moral-identity categoriza-
tion) versus the possession of power (as accounted for by the priming
exercise).

Among the study's many insights, individuals with high moral-identity
scores and primed to think of themselves as being powerful were more
likely to take a broader communal perspective than similarly primed
individuals with low moral-identity scores. Also, working adults with
high moral-identity scores and primed to think of themselves as being
powerful were less likely to say that they had cheated their employer in the
previous week than assertively primed working adults with low moral-
identity scores. When individuals with high and low moral-identity scores
were primed by writing an essay about an ordinary day, they displayed no
difference in reported cheating. Thus, the absence of power appears to
make it harder to determine individuals' underlying character whereas
power reveals it.

The various findings regarding power and underlying character are not
readily reconciled. Some of power's corrupting influence observed by
Zimbardo and Milgram may reflect the so-called Hawthorne effect. This
phenomenon is named after the Hawthorne Works, a Chicago-area factory
where workers' productivity increased when they believed that they were
being observed more closely.[35] It's important to consider, however, that the
Hawthorne effect may operate to a greater extent in high moral-identity
individuals than in low moral-identity individuals and thus also may help
explain the findings by DeCelles and her colleagues.

In all likelihood, Abraham Lincoln is right. Power reveals character even
as it may corrupt it. These twin effects are worth noting when we explore
how government insiders have benefited over time at the expense of the
public interest. Proximity to power has proven and will continue to prove

---

[35] Landsberg (1958).

corrosive to many, even the most surprising people. Its potential for personal profit is hard to resist.

TRADE-OFFS

It is worth mentioning that government insiders face trade-offs when it comes to how they enjoy gains from hijacking political power. These are mitigating factors that keep the inside job in check to some degree and for some periods of time. For instance, by choosing not to exploit fully slack (S) in their relationship with citizens, government insiders may prolong their tenures and thereby profit more from retaining power for longer periods of time. Serving the public interest in some ways also may effectively diminish how closely government insiders are monitored by citizens and thereby enhance their latitude to shirk the public interest in other ways. In other words, government insiders sometimes have good reasons to act on a lower value interest (I) than they actually have in order to realize some compensating benefits in terms of higher values for the potential gains (G) from hijacking and the slack (S) in their relationship with the citizenry.

Similarly, government insiders might accept lower profit from power in order to hold power for a longer period of time as part of a coalition. The more broadly a coalition shares power, the longer it tends to remain in power, while profit must then be shared more broadly in smaller shares. This is particularly true in autocracies that face stronger opposition to their rule. Political scientists Andrea Kendall-Taylor and Erica Frantz argue that autocracies have become more resilient in recent decades because of their ability to mimic democracies.[36] In that sense, autocracies have expanded the coalition of power. Over 1946–1989, the average autocratic regime held power for twelve years. Since the Cold War's end, the average duration of autocratic regimes has nearly doubled to twenty years and has further increased to twenty-five years as of 2015.

The government self-capture equation helps explain this phenomenon. While regimes that are willing to enhance their accountability by adopting more (or seeming to adopt more) democratic institutions lower the value of the slack (S) and increase accountability, they likely realize higher potential gains (G) from remaining in power longer.

---

[36] Kendall-Taylor and Frantz (2015). See also Gandhi and Przeworski (2007); Zupan (2015b); and Sergei Guriev and Daniel Treisman, "The New Dictators Rule by Velvet Fist," *New York Times*, May 25, 2015.

Another mitigating factor in how much government insiders hijack political power is preserving potential gains. As the state's role in society grows, the potential gains (*G*) that power offers to public officials will increase – to a point. Beyond a certain point the growth tends to come at the expense of an economy's productivity on which government insider benefits depend. The negative effect of the inside job thus can sometimes limit its extent by constraining the magnitude of the potential gains (*G*) associated with such malignant activity.

The inside job can happen almost inadvertently, the collateral effect of families taking care of each other and triumphing over the public interest, with subsequent weakening of the state over the long run. The inside job might also happen quickly, most often as ideologues hijack power for revolutionary change. While it may be restrained by some mitigating factors, including the potential for the interests of public officials to be aligned with the public interest, the inside job corrodes its host country in addition to corrupting the character of those who hold power. The question remains whether there are factors that can fundamentally influence the magnitudes of the terms in the equation introduced in this chapter. The next three chapters will review potential gains (*G*), slack (*S*), and interest (*I*) in their turn.

4

What Do Government Insiders Stand to Gain?

$$P = \boldsymbol{G} \times S \times I$$

Up to this point, we've examined ways government insiders pursue opportunities for profit through their positions, and also how historically the process of hijacking power has taken root and progressed. As we have just seen in the impact of power on character, it becomes clear how government insiders may be drawn to profit from their positions at the expense of the public good; they find sharing in the treasure entrusted to them irresistible. More succinctly, asked why he robbed banks, Willie Sutton replied, "Because that is where the money is."

So it follows that anything which increases the state's role in society also adds to the lure for the government insider to take advantage – however small it may be to start – of the power and treasure in their trust. That is, a growing state amplifies the motive for an inside job. The balance in the government self-capture equation changes greatly as bigger government increases the potential for public officials to profit from power. Beyond driving the motive, government growth also enhances the means and opportunity for government insiders to hijack the state at the expense of its citizens.

The factors that contribute to the potential gains (G) available to public officials by increasing government size are the subject of this chapter. These factors work like incentives for public officials to subvert the public interest and are, contrary to certain popular claims, present in both autocracies and democracies. They are the perks of power; patronage and other political advantages associated with government provision of goods and services; bureaucratic growth goals; the transaction costs associated with government programs; special interests; the common-pool problem; and the political clout of public goods and services.

While all these factors are favored and many are driven by public officials involved on the supply side of politics, some of the factors behind government growth originate from the demand side of politics – such as agricultural interests seeking tariffs and quotas to shield them from foreign competition. In fact, scholars such as Robert Barro and Mancur Olson attribute the anemic growth, or economic arteriosclerosis, of modern democracies to demand-side special interests.[1] However, special-interest-group activity on the demand side of politics also enlarges government and thus the motive, means, and opportunity for an inside job. Public programs require supportive public officials who also profit from the outcome and thereby gain a vested interest in preserving political gridlock at the expense of national well-being. In this way, all factors, regardless of whether they operate on the supply or demand side of politics, drive government growth and thus fuel the supply side of politics, including increasing the likelihood of an inside job.

PERKS

The potential pecuniary and ideological gains (*G*) to government insiders from their public positions have been the primary focus of the book thus far. They have provided the motive for the insider job in examples from ancient Chinese dynasties, Western antiquity, African kingdoms, and modern societies on every continent – including the United States. In the process, like a natural life cycle, the inside job has historically expanded the size of government, because a larger government implies greater potential gains for those officials and also works to secure greater monopoly power over the perks that come with public office. The growing monopoly burdens the public and often leaves the host country existentially at risk – to the detriment of those in power. But monopoly political power and its perks tempt mightily.

Monopolizing and capturing the perks of power are typically associated with autocracies even at their inception. Mancur Olson notes how states are formed when a "roving bandit" sets up a dictatorship, creating a monopolization of power and the potential for the now "stationary bandit" to profit through levying taxes:[2]

Thus government ... arises, not because of social contracts or voluntary transactions ... but ... because of rational self-interest among those who can organize the greatest capacity for violence. These violent entrepreneurs ... do not

---

[1] Barro (1996) and Olson (1982). [2] Olson (1993), p. 568.

call themselves bandits but . . . give themselves and their descendants exalted titles. They sometimes even claim to rule by divine right. Autocrats of all kinds usually explain that their subjects want them to rule and . . . that government arose out of . . . voluntary choice.

As a step out of anarchy, the gains to both rulers and subjects can be substantial:[3]

The encompassing interest of the tax-collecting autocrat permits a considerable development of civilization. From . . . Sargon's conquests [that] created the empire of Akkad until . . . Louis XVI . . . there was an impressive development of civilization that occurred in large part under stationary banditry.

Yet, for the "stationary bandit," the monopolization of political power brings with it the appeal of perks of power for personal benefit. Here lies the potential for the inside job. Here, too, is the central conundrum noted in the relationship between public officials and the public whom they serve: whereas state formation may convey appreciable benefits to citizens, the public officials entrusted with power need to be prevented from exercising such monopoly power for their personal benefit at the expense of citizens. The timeless quality of this conundrum for every state and every governed people is why "guarding the guardians," which is a notion attributed to both Juvenal, the ancient Roman poet, and Plato, the Greek philosopher, has such staying power and relevance even today.[4]

Later we will consider various mechanisms societies have relied upon to guard their guardians. One of these worth mentioning here is observed when monopolies which are asserted by government insiders over the perks of power go unchecked. Built into the exercise of monopoly political power itself is a trigger that naturally counteracts the extent to which the guardians can profit as "bandits." Willie Sutton's bank robber runs out bank coffers to loot. As Olson observes just with respect to tax revenues:[5]

Though the subjects of the autocrat are better off than they would be under anarchy, they must endure taxes . . . so high that, if . . . [taxes] were increased further, income would fall by so much that even the autocrat, who absorbs only a portion of the fall in income in the form of lower tax collections, would be worse off.

The prevalence of insider monopolies over the perks of power is quite global. Economist Deirdre McCloskey estimates that 87 percent of humanity now lives under a corrupt government and notes that "Italians have a term for a thief government, that is *un governo ladro*; or as the Nigerians

---

[3] Ibid., p. 569.   [4] Hurwicz (2008).   [5] Ibid., p. 570.

say of their typical politician, ITT, 'international thief, thief' ... The very definition of a state, said [sociologist] Max Weber in 1919, is a monopoly of legitimate violence. The monopoly tempts mightily."[6] The problem's pervasiveness is driven home when one travels outside the United States. Indeed, when I was giving a talk on this book in Argentina, a prominent academic in attendance argued that the central hypothesis was obvious and that rather than nations such as his being anomalous, it is instead the United States that is the outlier when it comes to constraining government self-capture.

My colleague in Argentina makes a very good point. While there is no doubt that even well-established democracies must worry about inside jobs, there are differences with inside jobs in autocracies. One of these is that the pecuniary perks at the highest levels of government tend to be lower in democracies than in autocracies. Historian Robert Caro, for example, documents how Lyndon Johnson used his political clout to ensure that his wife's applications for a radio and a television station in Austin, Texas, were approved by the Federal Communications Commission. Through the influence that he then used to steer advertising to the stations held in his wife's name, Johnson amassed a personal fortune of $100 million.[7] While a tidy sum, Johnson's fortune still pales in comparison to the billions accumulated by autocrats such as Vladimir Putin and Muammar Gaddafi.

The ability of public officials in democracies to amass pecuniary perks is not limited to any one political party, nor is it limited to the top positions of executive power. From similarly modest roots, two Republicans who served as Speaker of the House of Representatives, Dennis Hastert and Newt Gingrich, accumulated substantial wealth through their political power. Hastert, a former high school teacher and wrestling coach, was worth $275,000 when he entered Congress in 1987. His fortune had increased to $17 million by the time he left Congress in 2007, thanks to a variety of government initiatives and earmarks benefiting his Illinois real estate holdings.[8] This wealth provided means for Hastert to pay hush money to a former student whom he had allegedly abused sexually.

Former Speaker of the House Newt Gingrich is worth $31 million, having made his fortune through book royalties, speaking honoraria, media commentary, video productions, and teaching. He has also benefited

---

[6] Deirdre N. McCloskey, "Two Cheers for Corruption," *Wall Street Journal*, February 28–March 1, 2015.
[7] Caro (2012).   [8] Schweizer (2011).

from ties with super PACs and think tanks as well as consulting roles for energy and health-care companies and the Federal Home Loan Mortgage Corporation (Freddie Mac). Seven years after leading the effort to unseat his Democrat predecessor Jim Wright on a lesser charge of failing to report $60,000 in income from the sales of a vanity book, Gingrich was fined $300,000 by the House Ethics Committee for laundering political donations through charities, the largest ethics fine ever imposed on a House Speaker.[9]

Across the proverbial pond, Tony Blair came from a modest family background but has accumulated over $150 million following his tenure as prime minister of Great Britain as a result of his political connections, knowledge, and influence. While in office, Blair's salary was, like for most modern prime ministers, lower than many top civil servants in government; he also did not collect his full pay. Blair's consulting clients have included wealthy autocratic rulers in Azerbaijan, Kazakhstan, Kuwait, Peru, Qatar, Saudi Arabia, and the United Arab Emirates, as well as companies such as British Petroleum and JPMorgan Chase.[10]

Here is just the beginning of manifold examples showing how much of the danger in democracies comes from government insiders who operate below the top rungs of power. On average across developed democracies, there is ample evidence that government is expanding. The public sector accounts for over 20 percent of total employment and 50 percent of GDP. Nearly one in six US employees works for state or local government and as a whole they account for 88 percent of public employment in the country. The unfunded pension and health-care liabilities for these workers equal $5 trillion, or 29 percent of the US GDP. That is, the sum of unfunded benefit liabilities for these public workers, for which general taxpayers are on the hook, equals 150 percent of the total annual state and local government revenue.[11] The unfunded benefit liabilities for all public workers (state, local, and federal) are the second-largest fiscal problem in the United States – larger than Social Security. Yet, there is also a worse one: Medicare/Medicaid/ObamaCare. While much of the social compact in modern democracies such as the United States is commonly viewed as providing a safety net and essential goods and services to citizens who are less well off, the extent to which government spending reflects the salaries and promised benefits of public employees administering government programs remains striking.

---

[9] Ibid.   [10] Ellison (2015).
[11] Novy-Marx and Rauh (2014a, 2014b); and DiSalvo (2015).

PATRONAGE AND OTHER BENEFITS
OF PUBLIC PROVISION

Beyond perks, government grows because such growth provides the political support necessary to secure and maintain power. Patronage represents the use of government resources to reward individuals for their political support. Examples of patronage, also known as clientelism, are present in both autocracies and democracies. Fukuyama asserts that patronage is more common in the early stages of democracy, prior to the development of expanded means of acquiring wealth through the private sector.[12]

Many forms of patronage are legal and well recognized, such as offering federal appointments and ambassadorships to major campaign contributors. President Abraham Lincoln was overwhelmed by the number of office and favor seekers clamoring for his attention. Once, indisposed with a bad cold, Lincoln jokingly instructed his secretary to be sure to let all the office seekers in since "he finally had something he wanted to give them."

Other patronage forms violate legal or ethical codes, such as when officials award noncompetitive state contracts to their relatives or friends or simply hire them outright. Indeed, Fukuyama argues that political institutions, if unchecked, revert toward nepotism on account of the evolutionary biology forces of kin selection and reciprocal altruism. The Mamluks and Janissaries both followed this trend, as have many other inside jobs considered by this book.

The operations of Louisiana governor Huey Long, Boston mayor James Michael Curley, the Perons and Kirchners in Argentina, and New York City's Tammany Hall exemplify patronage in epic proportions. For example, Tammany Hall was the legendary political organization that controlled New York City starting in the 1780s. For nearly 150 years, Tammany Hall influenced US presidential races from the time of Andrew Jackson until well into the twentieth century. At the apex of its power, under Boss Tweed in the 1860s and during the few decades beyond, Tammany had grown enormously, counting over 32,000 committeemen spread over five counties. Its patronage in 1888 over just Manhattan County and a part of the Bronx totaled 12,000 municipal jobs. Its $12 million annual payroll exceeded the payroll of Andrew Carnegie's iron and steel works. Boss Tweed, at the height of his influence, was the third-largest individual landowner in New York City. He also was a director of the Erie Railway, New York Printing Company, and Tenth National Bank, and the proprietor of the prominent Metropolitan Hotel.[13]

---

[12] Fukuyama (2011, 2014).　　[13] Ackerman (2011).

Economists Roland Hodler and Paul Raschky illuminate the extent to which political leaders rely on patronage. Congolese dictator Mobutu Sese Seko, for example, constructed a $100-million palace and related guest-houses in Gbadolite, his remote ancestral hometown. Despite other cities having far greater populations which could benefit from the favors, Gbadolite received the Congo's best supply of medical services, water, and electricity. It even had an airport capable of accommodating the Concorde jets that Mobutu rented from Air France, often for his wife's European shopping trips. Mobutu Sese Seko is no exception. Hodler and Raschky find that across 83,427 subnational regions in 126 countries between 1992 and 2009, a leader's birth region has a 4 percent higher nighttime light intensity and a 1 percent larger GDP than the rest of the nation. A leader's birthplace also benefits from greater foreign aid when the potential for the leader to exercise monopoly power on the supply side of politics is greater, as reflected by tenure in office, citizen ignorance, and the imperfectness of electoral accountability.[14]

A similar study on patronage examined Kenyan road building after the country's independence in 1963. Three factors were at play in this study. First, Kenya has significant ethnic segregation across political districts – an artifact of British colonial administration. Second, the Kenyan presidency has switched into and out of democracy. Last, roads have been the largest public spending category, representing 15 percent of total government spending since independence. The study found that during periods of autocratic rule, political districts sharing the ethnicity of Kenya's president received double the road expenditures and five times more paving (by road length) relative to other districts. Yet, these differences evaporated when Kenya was a democracy. Shifts from autocracy to democracy, in other words, increased the accountability of rulers to the public good and reduced patronage.[15]

Patronage generates political support through government spending, so it favors the public provision of goods and services which offers more opportunities for granting favors. From a pure economics perspective, public provision adds costs and is inefficient; providing individuals cash grants or vouchers for the direct purchase of a good or service is more efficient and less wasteful than the state adding a role for itself in the middle of the transaction. Indeed, individuals enjoy greater freedom and realize a greater economic benefit when they are given the latitude to spend cash as they deem useful rather than the state spending the cash for them on goods or services that the state deems meritorious for them.

---

[14] Hodler and Raschky (2014).   [15] Burgess et al. (2015).

Additionally, public provision increases production cost and lowers the innovation rate. This is because public provision – through monopoly, nonprofit means – suffers from a lack of competitive pressure as well as diminished incentives for economic profit from greater productive efficiency or innovativeness. Witness the slowness with which the US Postal Service decided to accept credit cards as a payment form or offer overnight delivery, to say nothing of the fact that labor costs are 50 percent lower on routes contracted out to private providers.[16] Economist Tom Borcherding suggests the "Bureaucratic Rule of Two" in light of cross-country evidence showing that moving an activity from private to government provision doubles unit production costs.[17]

Beyond the rationales for public provision offered by some scholars, it is not hard to understand why it is favored by government insiders: it gives public officials patronage credit from both the supply and demand sides of the market for the good or service being publicly provided.[18] Such double-sided patronage credit translates into greater political support and power. While the administrative costs of government programs grow, so do the political profit and power from patronage.

Take the case of education. When education is publicly provided, the teachers and staff are paid by and are accountable to the government. Working on the supply side of education, the teachers and staff attribute their livelihood to the beneficence of public officials backing public schools. Likewise, families, on the demand side of the education market, whose children – and home property values – benefit from local public schools, credit those same officials.[19] Government is the conduit for educational services to the demand side, leaving both the supply and demand sides of the education market grateful to government.

Contrast this approach with a different policy whereby government does not serve as the conduit for education services. Instead, families are given vouchers and are free to select the school their children attend. Now, these families can more directly hold teachers and staff accountable for their

---

[16] Merewitz and Zupan (1993).

[17] Borcherding (1977); and Borcherding, Pommerehne, and Schneider (1982).

[18] The rationales include indoctrination through education (Lott, 1987); ensuring a desired output in cases, such as defense in wartime, involving imperfect information and uncertainty (Weitzman, 1974); productivity and trust gains from relying on intrinsically motivated suppliers (Hansmann, 1986; Pink, 2011; Rose-Ackerman, 1986; and Sandel, 2012); and reduced monitoring costs (DiIulio, 2014).

[19] This discussion presumes that public schools provide appreciable benefits. If the educational services are shoddy, the politicians backing the public schools will reap some of the blame.

performance through how they choose to spend their vouchers. While the families, on the demand side of the education market, will appreciate the politicians supporting vouchers, the teachers and staff on education's supply side will attribute their livelihood more directly to parents and be less likely to credit politicians for their beneficence. This one-sided political credit reduces patronage value because teachers and staff are one step removed from politicians' voucher support.

Families receiving vouchers gain economic freedom when they possess decision rights over education. They no longer rely on the government to decide if the quality of education at any school merits their buying services there. When they enroll their children at a school, parents are credited by the school's faculty and staff for that decision. The politicians who are the underlying source of the voucher funding may garner some minimal appreciation from families, but the patronage value to them is reduced relative to the case where education is publicly provided. Furthermore, the faculty and staff are likely to credit their own hard work and service quality – not politicians' largesse – when they succeed at attracting voucher dollars to their school.

So, when public officials promote a policy that permits more economic freedom to the public, the prospective political gains (G) to the officials are reduced. The one-sided (at best) patronage credit that public officials derive when outsourcing the provision of a good or service is analogous to the political invisibility of the benefits of promoting free trade. As Milton Friedman observes:[20]

Steelworkers whose jobs are threatened by imports from Japan are highly visible. They . . . can see clearly the benefit to them from restricting imports . . . The cost is large but spread thinly. Tens of thousands of buyers of objects made with steel would pay a bit more because of the restriction. The Japanese would earn fewer dollars here and, as a result, purchase fewer U.S. goods. But that cost too is invisible. The man who might have had a job producing a product the Japanese would have purchased if they had been permitted to sell more steel here will have no way of knowing that he was hurt.

As Friedman notes, politicians promoting free trade are not appreciated by the domestic producers who would benefit from enhanced exports. Neither

---

[20] Milton Friedman, "In Defense of Dumping," *Newsweek*, February 20, 1978. The political invisibility of certain costs was highlighted by the controversial comments made about ObamaCare by MIT economist Jonathan Gruber in 2014. Gruber noted that the legislation passed because voters did not realize how tax incidence depends on the relative elasticity of supply and demand and not on whether the tax is collected from suppliers or consumers.

are free-trade advocates appreciated by the domestic producers who stand to gain from the consumer spending freed up by lower-priced imports. Because the causal chain is longer and less readily understood regarding trade's benefits, trade restraints are imposed to protect visibly affected special interests.

Likewise, when politicians outsource the provision of a good or service, it may seem that they could gain patronage credit from the demand side by regulating the prices charged by private providers. However, such credit from consumers is likely to be limited given that the government is not the conduit for providing the good or service. Moreover, on the supply side of the good or service, a regulated private utility views its public overseers as meddlesome irritants. The winning private bidder for a public contract tends to credit its own capabilities rather than the wisdom of public officials. Moreover, losing bidders blame the relevant officials. As Louis XIV noted: "Every time I appoint someone to a vacant position, I make a hundred unhappy and one ungrateful." While appointments to positions overseeing the public supply of a good or service also have such adverse consequences, they are muted to the extent that the appointment process is less competitive and visible.

Politicians exploit the potential for greater gains (G) through patronage when they grow the supply side of politics through public provision. Their gains are greater when their policies are more transparent, even if those policies diminish the public good. And, politicians are better appreciated for their interventionist policies because of information acquisition and processing costs – costs that make political outcomes opaque to certain citizens.[21] Behavioral economists also note that prospective losses are weighted more heavily than gains.[22] The preceding are among the many reasons that the incentive to support markets free of state intervention is lower than the incentive to rely on public provision, which fosters government growth and increases the potential for inside jobs.

BUREAUCRATIC MOTIVES

For reasons described above, once politicians decide what goods and services are to be produced through government spending and in what quantities, a public bureau typically channels the funding. This occurs

---

[21] For reasons such as ignorance and bounded rationality, see Caplan (2006) and Simon (1978).

[22] Kahneman (2011).

whether the goods and services are procured from the private sector or are publicly provided. Bureaucracies often are tasked with developing the regulations giving substance to laws passed by a legislature. The ability to define and even originate the rules can be substantial. For example, the European Commission and its 25,000 employees are "paid to think European." It is the only EU body capable of initiating legislation.[23]

External controls over bureaucracies tend to be weak, as are the internal incentives for efficiency and innovation within bureaucracies. The reasons for this are many. Measuring a bureau's quality and quantity of output is difficult, so performance improvements are hard to determine. Competition among different potential bureaus supplying a service is imperfect, so its salutary effects are lost. Oversight by politicians and citizens is patchy due to differing goals; for example, the chief executive's objectives may not align with those of legislators or citizens. There also are free-rider problems associated with supervising bureaus, with individual politicians not willing to sink their time and effort into policing an agency when the benefits from their efforts will be communally shared while other options add more directly to their political capital. Political representatives of high-demand users (special-interest groups) have disproportionate influence over bureaucracies, such as by populating legislative oversight committees; that is, through government insiders already holding entrenched positions. And, bureaus suffer from the absence of a profit motive.[24] So, they tend to be inefficient and resistant to innovation – while they expand under the eye of government insiders.

Consider now bureaucracy's goals. Economist William Niskanen argues that budget growth is a central goal for bureaucracy because it is positively related to salary, perks, reputation, power, patronage, and impact. While this also is often true in the private sector, bureaucrats have greater leeway to expand their budgets due to imperfect oversight. The situation unique to public bureaucracy fuels increases in government size, thus making inside jobs more likely.[25]

Niskanen suggests there are ways to mitigate bureaucratic growth, such as increasing competition through other bureaus and private market alternatives, or incorporating greater reliance in government goal-setting on profit motives. Political scientist James Q. Wilson further suggests clarifying the mission and culture of agencies; giving them greater freedom to achieve their goals through being able to negotiate constraints with their

---

[23] See, for example, Sinn (2014). [24] See Mueller (1979) and Niskanen (1971).
[25] Niskanen (1971).

political overseers; aligning decision rights with relevant information and accountability; and fostering experimentation coupled with rigorous measurement of results. Whether giving agencies more leeway would mitigate their growth, however, is debatable. Wilson admits that so long as there is government there will be the risks associated with governing – not just management problems, but also circumstances that tempt public officials to pursue potential gains (G) for themselves at the expense of public well-being.[26]

As government grows to offer more goods and services, the sheer number of individuals working for public agencies grows into a constituency itself. This group can be politically organized, lobby, and otherwise exercise political clout. As we will explore in greater detail in Chapter 9, public-sector unions are growing even as private-sector unions are waning. For example, while private-sector union membership in the nonagricultural sector of the United States has fallen from 38 percent in the early 1950s to less than 7 percent today, public-sector union membership has grown from 10 percent to 36 percent. A key factor driving this change has been the elimination, by many states, of laws proscribing public worker unionization, collective bargaining, and lobbying.

The benefits that public unions bestow on their members through collective bargaining and lobbying are significant and tend to be at the expense of the public. For one striking example, economist Daniel DiSalvo documents how unionized US public employees often can retire in their fifties with annual pension and medical benefits approaching $100,000. They are also paid appreciably more than their private-sector counterparts when all fringe benefits are taken into account.[27]

Political scientists Sarah Anzia and Terry Moe, analyzing US municipal finances over the period from 1992 to 2010, find that cities where public workers have collective bargaining rights spend 9–10 percent more on wages for police and firefighters and 21–25 percent more on health benefits. Every 10 percent increase in a state's public union membership increases per capita pension liabilities by $1,412, or the equivalent of 20 percent of the average state's per capita GDP.[28] Moe further argues that, in the case of K-12 public education in the United States, teachers unions have not only raised costs but retarded innovation and diminished student outcomes.[29] According to Moe, teachers unions have been the key impediment to improving the public K-12 educational system over the past half century.

---

[26] Wilson (1989).   [27] DiSalvo (2015).   [28] Anzia and Moe (2015).
[29] Moe (2011, 2015).

DiSalvo notes how legislative provisions promoted by public unions tend to insulate them against any downside from collective bargaining. For example, because of such provisions, New York City's unions allowed their contracts to expire during the last years of Bloomberg's mayoral term. Because they were protected against any downside in delayed arbitration, the unions reasoned that Bloomberg's successor would be more pro-union, since they would be instrumental in electing that official who then could be expected to be grateful for their support. Their strategy was validated by Bill de Blasio's election in 2013. De Blasio approved new contracts with a 4 percent retroactive raise, which cost taxpayers $3.6 billion. Teachers' base pay was increased 19.5 percent over five years. Other union members received annual pay increases of 1–3 percent.[30]

TRANSACTION COSTS

Public programs cost money to operate. As they grow, they cost more money. Public provision involves substantive, even staggering, operating costs. The US Department of Health and Human Services (HHS), for example, employs 80,000 people to administer $1 trillion in annual outlays on agencies such as the Food and Drug Administration, Medicare, Medicaid, and the National Institutes of Health. Conservatively assuming $65,000 in salary and benefits per HHS employee, at least $5 billion is spent each year on staffing the department.

Beyond the direct administrative costs, public policies also alter the incentives that market participants face and thus affect productivity more broadly in the economy. Consider the collateral damage from ObamaCare, which was enacted in 2010 and intended to expand health insurance coverage in the United States. The nonpartisan Congressional Budget Office (CBO) expects that, due to the manner in which the law's health insurance subsidy declines with median family income, a disincentive to work will be created, resulting in the equivalent of 2.3 million fewer Americans opting for full-time employment. The CBO estimate does not include any other collateral job losses resulting from the law's fee on insurers, its 2.3 percent excise tax on medical devices, and its taxes on the health industry. A further 500,000 jobs will likely be lost due to these other provisions.[31]

The administrative costs and costs resulting from distorted incentives which are associated with public programs are common in economic

---

[30] DiSalvo (2015).
[31] "ObamaCare Will Cost 2.9 Million or More Jobs a Year," Forbes.com, February 24, 2014.

study. Arthur Okun, the chair of President Lyndon Johnson's Council of Economic Advisors, coined the term "leaky bucket" to refer to these costs.[32] Other economists simply call them transaction costs.[33] They may be direct or indirect, but they are the costs of transacting public programs. Direct costs involve staff and other resources needed to operate public programs. Indirect costs consist of the incentive-distorting effects on citizens who are either contributing toward or benefiting from the programs. Direct costs enlarge government. Indirect costs, by diminishing productivity, increase the state's relative size. Whether they increase the state's size in absolute or relative terms, transaction costs enhance the incentive for inside jobs.

Based on empirical studies, economist Edgar Browning estimates the porousness of the leaky bucket associated with US programs that tax certain citizens and then transfer the funds generated to other citizens, such as Social Security or Medicaid beneficiaries. To acquire $1 to spend, an average $1.50 in costs is imposed on taxpayers. Of the $0.50 inefficiency, $0.10 reflects direct compliance costs while the remaining $0.40 is due to distorted incentives. In addition, per dollar spent on welfare programs, administrative costs account for $0.10. Of the remaining $0.90, the value to recipients averages only $0.60 due to the marginal tax rates implicit in welfare programs, coupled with restrictions on how the sums can be spent (in-kind programs rather than cash grants). Compliance costs for transfer recipients deduct a further $0.10. In sum, Browning estimates that government transfers cost taxpayers $1.50 while benefiting recipients by $0.50.[34] Two-thirds of the tax and transfer bucket leaks out due to direct and indirect costs.

Browning's estimate of the porousness of the leaky bucket reflects the waste and mismanagement associated with tax and transfer programs, including those involving capture by government insiders. Considering the magnitude of the transaction costs associated with tax and transfer programs, perhaps the greatest solace that can be taken is through remembering the quip made by humorist Will Rogers: "Be thankful we're not getting all the government we pay for."

Transaction costs are part of policies promoting efficiency or equity. Programs promoting equity, of course, typically reduce productivity. Economists Allan Meltzer and Scott Richard model the trade-off and show how expanded voting privileges alter the decisive voter's position regarding

---

[32] Okun (1975).   [33] See, for example, Coase (1937) and Williamson (1975).
[34] Browning (2008).

income distribution, government size, and economic productivity. When average income relative to the decisive voter's income increases, government grows due to a greater incentive for redistribution. Technological specialization widens the distribution of productivity and leads to higher tax rates, larger government, and reduced growth.[35]

Whether its causes are demand- or supply-side interests, whether efficiency enhancing or diminishing, whether equity promoting or not, public intervention involves transaction costs. As the state expands, so do these transaction costs. A growing state with more transaction costs increases the potential gains (G) to government insiders from co-opting the state.

SPECIAL INTERESTS

Special-interest groups' economic stakes in policy matters do not directly translate into political clout, because some groups mobilize more readily than others. Those special-interest groups whose members are more concentrated and have higher per capita stakes tend to mobilize more readily than diffuse groups with lower per capita incentives – even though the former may have fewer total dollars at stake. This differential in incentives is at the heart of special-interest-group politics. It explains the enactment of efficiency-decreasing policies that benefit particular special interests at the expense of public well-being – policies such as import quotas/tariffs, rent controls, agricultural price supports, home mortgage loan subsidies, and entry restrictions on municipal taxi services.[36]

Because the political arena responds to clout, special interests fuel government growth and thus the potential for inside jobs. Economic illiteracy on the part of citizens regarding the pernicious effects of special interests – whether it is based on ignorance or the pursuit of ideological interests such as xenophobia in the case of trade legislation – compounds the special-interest problem and how it fosters conditions for inside jobs.[37]

An illustration of the extent to which special interests appear to work at cross-purposes to the public good is found in US tax policy. Whereas surveys of citizens consistently indicate a preference for a progressive tax code that helps those who are less fortunate, economist Deirdre McCloskey estimates that only 1/16th of the dollars collected and distributed by the US federal government end up in the hands of individuals below the poverty line. To further reinforce this point, McCloskey notes that if 1/4th of the amount

---

[35] Meltzer and Richard (1981, 2014).
[36] See Olson (1971) on the logic of collective action.   [37] Caplan (2006).

that the federal government collects was allocated to less well-off citizens, the average family of four living below the poverty line in the United States would receive over \$120,000 annually. The fact that we don't observe such an outcome in reality suggests that our tax code does fairly little to promote equity and instead is more responsive to the activity of special interests representing relatively more affluent members of our society.[38]

Mancur Olson attributes the relative decline of many Western democracies in recent decades to economic arteriosclerosis resulting from special-interest-group activity. He argues that a hardening of commercial arteries becomes more likely the longer a nation enjoys political stability, because it takes time for special interests to coalesce and learn how to exert influence.[39]

Olson focuses on special interests which operate on the demand side of politics such as trade unions and corporate cartels. Of course, government insiders, operating from the supply side of politics, can also be a special interest contributing to economic arteriosclerosis. Whether it is special interests from the demand or supply side of politics, however, they both similarly wield influence based on clout. Like a cancer bringing down its host organism, special interests grow government the more influential they become, and they become more influential as government grows. Their clout heightens the potential gains (G) for public officials at the expense of the public interest.

An example of capture by supply-side special interests is seen in the rising public enactment and enforcement of laws against US companies. Law scholars Margaret Lemos and Max Minzner argue that the increase in such activity reflects public officials seeking resources, reputation, and clout:[40]

The incentives are strongest when enforcement agencies are permitted to retain all or some of the proceeds of enforcement – an institutional arrangement that is common at the state level and beginning to crop up in federal law.

The criminal penalties levied annually on US corporations now average over \$10 billion and can provide some appreciable resources to the relevant public officials. For instance, on account of settlements with three international banks, Manhattan district attorney Cyrus Vance secured \$808 million in 2015 to help underwrite his crime-fighting efforts. The significant sums involved can lead to clashes between different government levels as each seeks their "fair share." In 2014, an \$8.9 billion settlement between French

---

[38] McCloskey (2010).   [39] Olson (1982).   [40] Lemos and Minzner (2014), p. 854.

bank BNP Paribas and five different regulators was in the works over the circumvention of federal sanctions against Sudan and Iran. The settlement nearly ran aground when Governor Andrew Cuomo demanded a bigger share of the total offered sum, to multiple contending plaintiffs, for the State of New York.[41]

Private-sector producers or capitalists have been the focus of scholars as ideologically diverse as Gabriel Kolko, Karl Marx, and George Stigler for their efforts to profit from policies restricting rival firms.[42] The benefits to such demand-side special interests are patently obvious and examples are easy to provide. But the possibility that some of the gains, or rents, sought by demand-side special interests might end up in the hands of public officials on politics' supply side has received less attention and less scholarship. Yet, if the supply side is imperfectly accountable – which can occur, as noted earlier, in both democracies and autocracies – and political contributions are not outlawed, then some of the prospective gains (G) can be diverted to government insiders. This creates incentives on both the supply and demand sides of politics to increase the state's size and the ultimate profit (P) to public officials from inside jobs.

Economists Gary Becker and Donald Wittman argue that competition, at least in democracies, promotes efficient political outcomes. The competition occurs on the demand side between interest groups seeking wealth transfers as well on the supply side between politicians offering wealth transfers.[43] However, competition in the political arena is less than perfect in democracies as well as in autocracies. So, we can expect political outcomes to be inefficient. For one, on the demand side of politics, special interests can more readily mobilize and exercise political clout disproportionate to their economic stakes on policy issues, thereby leading to policy outcomes at odds with the public good.

On the supply side, politicians find it advantageous, at least when acquiring non-vote-related resources, to serve a smaller number of buyers of wealth transfers. As with almost any economic transfer, the 80/20 rule works for government insiders too. Much as a university or other nonprofit generates 80 percent of its philanthropic support from 20 percent of its donors and private companies generate 80 percent of their profit from 20 percent of their products, so too we can expect politicians to concentrate their scarce time and energy on securing the support of a relatively small

[41] Ibid. See also "A Mammoth Guilt Trip," *The Economist*, August 30, 2014.
[42] Kolko (1963); Marx ([1867] 2009); and Stigler (1971).
[43] Becker (1983) and Wittman (1989).

number of citizens offering the highest potential political gains (G). Given the cultivation time and effort required, it is easier for a politician to raise $50,000 from a single domestic producer protected from international competition by import quotas than a like amount from 1,000 consumers harmed by the quotas, for in the latter scenario the amount must be raised in increments of $50 per consumer, each of whom is likely to expect some attention or access.

Another way competition is less effective in the public sector than in the private sector involves the extent to which voluntary transactions are enforceable. In politics, government insiders, who are on one side of the transactions, have some leeway to interpret, enforce, and alter their commitments to the party on the other side of the transaction. The absence of an independent party with the means to enforce politicians' commitments limits the potential for mutually beneficial exchange to promote efficiency when it comes to political deals. Especially, given the incentive that government insiders have to alter their commitments in ways that will preserve their power and profits, the transactional risk to counter-parties is increased. This limits the willingness of such counter-parties to engage in political deals that offer, at least up-front, the prospect of mutual benefit.

This slack (S) or lack of accountability when political commitments cannot be independently enforced explains how the potential for public officials to profit has, in many political settings, led to spiraling public misery. Without accountability, autocrats can retain power in spite of highly inefficient policies which permit them to expropriate great wealth from citizens, and to use such funds for self-enrichment or glorification.[44] By threatening or cultivating the support of segments of their population, kleptocrats manage to extend their tenures. Moreover, political patronage can be facilitated by tax revenues, foreign aid, and natural resources. While scholars make these observations as they focus on explaining the persistence of inefficient autocracies, their research implications are relevant for democracies in which officials are imperfectly accountable to the public interest.

THE COMMON-POOL PROBLEM

Two factors, together, can exacerbate the already sizable adverse consequences of special interests. First, sometimes public officials are more

---

[44] See, for example, Acemoglu (2003); Acemoglu, Robinson, and Verdier (2004); and Buchanan (1972).

accountable to a subset of citizens. Second, sometimes the costs of any policies that they promote on behalf of this subset can be spread more broadly. When these factors coincide, a common-pool problem ensues: officials will "overfish" the broader tax base so as to benefit their client subset of citizens and themselves.

An example of a common-pool problem in democracies involves legislators who are elected to represent a particular district while the cost of public spending on any district tends to be spread across the entire nation. In these settings, the "law of $1/n$" applies: the more districts, n, into which a nation is divided, the greater the level of public spending.[45] It is more profitable for a district and its representative to seek (net) public spending, or so-called political bacon, the larger the number of districts into which a nation is divided. This is because other people's money will be relied upon more extensively the greater the number of districts. In addition, securing political bacon is more attractive to legislators than other activities: it is easier to take credit for and less controversial than engaging in policy debates on issues like abortion or gun control.

From a game-theoretic perspective, the preferred strategy for a district and its political representative in a common-pool setting is to engage in local benefit-seeking. This creates competition and even clashes between different interests, but the value of an action to the overall nation is not the relevant decision-making criteria. Instead, the optimal strategy in such a competition is to obtain one's "fair share" of the total (net) state spending pie. Failing to do so results in less bacon for one's district while not appreciably lowering the taxes/debt for which the districts' constituents are accountable. The game is to beat other districts and their political representatives who have the same incentive to "overfish" the common tax base.

Economist Russell Roberts likens the difficulty of a representative democracy in restraining spending to the case in which one's restaurant bill is spread evenly across 100 other diners. If you were responsible for your entire bill, you would spend only $20 on a meal and wouldn't splurge on a second drink and dessert. By contrast, adding $15 for a drink and dessert costs you only 15 cents when the bill is spread evenly over all 100 patrons of the restaurant:[46]

---

[45] See Berry (2009) and Zupan (1991b).
[46] Russell Roberts, "If You're Paying, I'll Have Top Sirloin," *Wall Street Journal*, May 18, 1995.

Splurging is easy to justify now. In fact, you won't just add a drink and dessert. You'll upgrade to the steak and add a bottle of wine. Suppose you and everyone else orders $75 worth of food. The [total] tab will be . . . $7,500. Divided by the 100 diners, your bill will be $75. While you'll get your "fair share" this outcome is a disaster . . . [Dining alone] you spent $20. The extra $55 of steak and other treats were not worth it. But in competition with the others, you chose a meal far out of your price range whose enjoyment fell far short of its cost.

Self-restraint goes unrewarded in such a setting:[47]

If you go back to ordering your $20 meal in hopes of saving money, your tab will be close to $75 anyway, unless the other 99 diners cut back also. The good citizen starts to feel like a chump. And so we read of the freshman Congressman eager to cut pork out of the budget but in trouble back home because local projects will also come under the knife. Instead of being proud to lead the way, he is forced to fight for the projects, to make sure that his district gets its "fair share."

The common-pool problem is aggravated if politicians are also rewarded by providing facilitation or ombudsperson services to the subset of citizens to which they are most closely tied. These services involve supportive intervention with other levels of government. In the United States, for example, members of Congress often help their constituents obtain expedited passports for overseas travel, ensure that Social Security checks are delivered on time, and put in a good word with relevant bureaucrats regarding Medicare funding for a particular medical procedure. Like bacon, facilitation services represent local benefit-seeking and offer similar advantages to the politicians providing them: they are noncontroversial and easy to take credit for, and their costs can be spread broadly.[48]

The common-pool problem afflicts representative democracies through more than just the incentive of districts and their legislators to engage in local benefit-seeking. Political scientist Christopher Berry notes how, at least in the United States, local public jurisdictions focusing on a single service such as education, fire protection, sanitation, or recreation are spreading. There are now nearly 90,000 total governments in the United States and a new one is created every eighteen hours. Most are single-function jurisdictions empowered to collect revenues from a common tax base. Because of their overlapping powers to tax, there is a new complexity in accountability, and meanwhile an incentive persists for all jurisdictions to overfish the common tax pool. This incentive is amplified because elections for the public positions, which are empowered to oversee the jurisdictions, are often not coordinated. As the electorate is fragmented,

[47] Ibid.   [48] Fiorina and Noll (1978).

the influence of special interests benefiting from the service provided by each jurisdiction is thereby enhanced.[49]

In 2008, for example, the total tax on sales in Chicago was 10.25 percent, the highest of any major US city. Sales taxes are imposed on Chicagoans by six different governments: state, city, county, transit authority, parks and recreation district, and water commission. Chicago achieved its 10.25 sales tax rate in 2008 due to a 0.25-percentage-point increase added by the regional transit authority and a 1-percentage-point increase mandated by Cook County for public safety and hospital services.[50] Chicagoans would have to go to the polls six different times every four years to vote for the seventy local officials that represent them with these various jurisdictions. This electoral fragmentation helps explain why voter turnout in single-function jurisdictions ranges between 2 and 10 percent. As slack (S) increases and accountability reduces, special interests acquire more influence, thus increasing the overfishing of the common tax base.

While democracies have been the focus of the study of the common-pool problem, autocracies are not immune in practice. So long as certain ministers, bureaucrats, or other officials are more closely tied to a particular subset of citizens and can benefit that subset at the expense of the broader public, a common-pool problem exists and leads to state growth even in autocracies. One way localized benefits can be used to foster government growth may involve facilitation services. In the Arab world, for example, sheikhs and emirs often hold public audiences so as to hear citizen petitions while enhancing their political support and legitimacy.

In both democracies and autocracies, the common-pool problem and the deleterious influence of special interests are exacerbated by the gerrymandering of political districts. Gerrymandering enhances the influence of special interests and the officials representing them. As gerrymandering grows, chances increase that other people's money will be used to fund the policies of special interest to subsets of citizens and their public officials who are advantaged through gerrymandering.[51]

PUBLIC GOODS' POLITICAL CLOUT

As noted in Chapter 1, public goods are a central justification for state intervention. This stems from two characteristics which define public goods. First, they benefit multiple consumers; and, second, preventing consumers from realizing the benefits from public goods is prohibitively

---

[49] Berry (2009).   [50] Ibid.   [51] Bueno de Mesquita and Smith (2011).

costly. On account of these very same characteristics, prospective beneficiaries have an incentive to hitch a free-ride as others make efforts to procure the public goods. Inherently conducive to promoting inside jobs, providing public goods through state intervention can end up subverting the public interest.

Some scholars argue that even with state intervention public goods will be underprovided. In their line of thinking, for example, voters may be more aware of the costs of a policy than its benefits. While consumer-voters are subject to intensive advertising from suppliers of private goods, there is little corresponding promotion of public goods. The beneficiaries of public goods are also likely to understate their value if they believe that they will be taxed accordingly, ultimately providing fewer goods than anticipated.[52]

Other scholars, by contrast, assert that public goods will be overprovided. In their view, voters suffering from "fiscal illusion" underestimate the tax cost of public services. Additionally, entrepreneurial public officials seeking political support have an incentive to propose new programs – especially those involving privately provided goods already familiar to citizens and whose underwriting can be taken over by the state. Public officials also have an incentive to propose modifications or extensions of existing programs for the same reason. Rising state involvement in the United States in health care and education are examples of this principle at work. Public goods are overprovided due to such political entrepreneurship.[53]

In either view, the suppliers and consumers of public goods have more concentrated benefits and political clout than do the taxpayers footing the bill. Due to the greater political clout of both suppliers and consumers than general taxpayers, we can expect public goods to be overprovided.[54]

Consider national defense, perhaps the archetypical public good. The political clout of the US military–industrial–government complex is evident when it comes to advocacy for new programs as well as for existing weapons systems and military bases. The F-35 and F-22 fighter jet programs are recent examples of major weapons systems that remain under development notwithstanding significant design flaws and cost overruns.

---

[52] See, for example, Downs (1957); Galbraith (1958); and Pigou (1932).
[53] See Buchanan and Wagner (1977) on "fiscal illusion." See Brunner (1978) and Wallis (1976) on entrepreneurship by public officials.
[54] Aranson and Ordeshook (1977); Buchanan and Tullock (1977); Goff and Tollison (1990); McCormick and Tollison (1981); Olson (1971); and Shepsle (1980).

The F-22 Raptor fighter program remained in production even though the Pentagon point-blank said it didn't want it.[55]

Supply-side, pork-barrel considerations show up in subcontracting patterns for major weapons systems. A former Air Force official noted that "when you see a military aircraft, you are looking at a huge collection of spare parts flying in close formation." Parts contracts are spread around to maximize political support. The degree to which government insiders and symbiotic defense-contractor interests have raised this transaction to an art is exemplified in how being able to relocate a plant to an area represented by members of both the Senate and House Armed Services committees is known as a "double hitter."[56]

In the case of the B-1 bomber, the manufacturer, Rockwell International, spread the work among 5,200 contractors in forty-eight states and 400 congressional districts. A consultant was paid $100,000 to prepare a report detailing how cancellation of the B-1 would affect each district and state. At Rockwell's headquarters, a picture of the B-1 was hung atop a map of the United States with a piece of thread connecting each plane part to the congressional district and state where the part was produced.[57]

Conceptually, public goods' clout is much like the clout acquired by special interests as they promote government growth. Yet, commonly, public goods are used to justify state intervention, so it seems appropriate to isolate their clout as a distinct reason, in addition to special interests, that societies are overgoverned, thereby increasing the potential gains (G) from inside jobs.

Of course, estimating the extent to which public goods may be overprovided is challenging. So is estimating the efficient size of government. As noted earlier, classifying which goods are "public" is problematic and does not hinge on whether they are publicly supplied or supported. Determining the differing values that various citizens derive from a public good is equally difficult. However, studies do show that, at least in developed democracies, the role of government tends to exceed an efficient level. GDP levels and growth rates would be maximized if public spending totaled 15–25 percent of GDP versus what exists in practice generally now – an average of over 50 percent across developed democracies. The studies do not distinguish, however, whether the inefficiency reflects public goods being over-provided, arises from

---

[55] See Fox (1988); Higgs (1990); "A Jet Even the Military Doesn't Want," *Center for American Progress*, July 9, 2009.

[56] "Political Moves in Defense," *Los Angeles Times*, March 6, 1991.   [57] Higgs (1990).

redistributive policies based on equity, or indicates special-interest-group considerations.[58]

Whatever mix of factors driving it, government growth increases the potential gains – the G term in our central equation – that government insiders can derive from co-opting the state. However, factors also exist which can curb government growth. Some of these factors also limit the magnitude of government insiders' profits (P) by reducing one of the other two terms on the right-hand side of our government self-capture equation: the slack in the relationship between citizens and public officials (S) and the extent to which those officials are interested in exploiting this slack (I). The curbs that diminish one of the two latter terms may be externally imposed (as reflected by a lower S term) or involve self-policing (as reflected by a reduced I term), the latter through what political philosophers call the virtue or integrity of public officials.[59] The next two chapters will turn our attention to these factors that either curb government growth or reduce the ability and interest of government insiders to hijack the state.

---

[58] Buchanan and Musgrave (1999); Gwartney, Holcombe, and Lawson (1998); Niskanen (2008); Peden (1991); and Scully (1994).

[59] See, for example, Sandel (2009).

5

What Factors Curb Hijacking by Government Insiders?

$$P = G \times \boldsymbol{S} \times I$$

As many factors increase government size, they increase the potential gains (G) government insiders can secure from hijacking the state. There are also factors that either constrain government growth or diminish the slack (S) in the relationship between citizens and their public officials. The external curbs may be naturally built-in or humanly designed. These factors include the negative consequences associated with government growth; the ability of citizens to vote with their feet; institutional restraints; electoral competition; a quasi-market for political control; and benchmarking across political entities.

NEGATIVE CONSEQUENCES

Government growth has negative consequences, which have a way of catching up even to those who profit from its growth. Scholars such as Francis Fukuyama, Ibn Khaldun, Art Laffer, and Mancur Olson note that, beyond a certain point, government growth diminishes an economy's productivity and thus the tax revenues that a state can collect. Their studies led to plotting the tipping point after which taxes no longer support an economy with services but rather undermine its dynamism with tax burden. Anticipating the Khaldun–Laffer curve, King Chosroes I, who ruled Persia from AD 531 to AD 579, observed that "with justice and moderation the people will produce more, tax revenues will increase, and the state will grow rich and powerful."[1]

---

[1] Fukuyama (2011), p. 220. See also Khaldun (2005) and Olson (1993).

The capacity for government growth to sap a nation's productivity is a naturally occurring, built-in restraint on the inside job. Competition between states enhances this curb on efforts by government insiders to co-opt the state. A private-sector analogy drives home this point. The trade unions in US car and steel production decreased efficiency through the restrictive work rules and costly, defined pension and health benefit obligations that they negotiated for with management, but their efficiency-decreasing effects were limited by competition from Japanese and Korean firms, which did not share these cost burdens.[2] Similarly, when a state excessively burdens its nation's businesses, the global competitiveness of those businesses is hindered and their profits are reduced, thus decreasing the taxes that the state can collect from the enterprises.

Reflecting the inverse relationship that eventually sets in between state size and economic productivity, Singapore incents its political leaders through high base salaries and hefty bonuses tied to national economic performance measures, such as real GDP growth, unemployment, and the real income growth of the poorest 20 percent of its citizens. Singapore's prime minister, Lee Hsien Loong, is the highest paid head of state in the world, having an annual salary of $1.7 million. His salary is three times as high as the next highest, Hong Kong's chief executive, and more than four times as much as the US president. Loong also earns a bonus of six to twelve months of his base if the economic targets are met or greatly exceeded.

While Singapore has been consistently rated as only "Partially Free" politically by Freedom House, it ranks highly on economic freedom measures; for example, it typically runs a close second to Hong Kong among all countries in the *Index of Economic Freedom* measures. Singapore's economic growth rates have remained among the highest in the world over the past several decades. The degree to which the growth stems from how Singapore incents its leaders, however, has not been analyzed, but how the country seeks to align its public officials' personal profit (*P*) with national well-being is a memorable approach.

Beyond the adverse consequences that higher tax rates ultimately can have on an economy's productivity, some other factors naturally limit a state's size in either absolute or relative terms. For one, coordination and control become increasingly difficult as governments grow in size, much the same as with for-profit businesses. Information may be lost or distorted as it is transmitted from lower-level public employees to their

---

[2] Moe (2011).

supervisors to bureau heads and on to senior political executives, and the reverse is equally likely. Communication channels become more complex and difficult to monitor. Decisions require more time to make and implement. Problems of this sort occur in all large organizations – for-profit firms, nonprofits, and governments – and they suggest that the managerial function can provide a natural curb to organizational growth.

Political scientists also have pointed to the potential for over-stretch in that a nation can extend itself beyond its ability to maintain its military and economic commitments.[3] Here challenges in command and control play out geopolitically. The over-stretch may reflect the difficulty of assimilating cultures that are likely to be increasingly more heterogeneous as a nation expands its boundaries or opens its borders. Over-stretch also is felt in the sheer logistical challenges involved with governing an expanding state.

A good way to think about these logistical challenges is by considering an example from the private sector, an analog in the arithmetical relationships fostering first increasing and then decreasing returns to scale. A pipeline's circumference (and hence the amount of material that must be employed to create a unit of pipeline) equals the constant π (approximately 3.14) times twice the radius of the pipeline. In contrast, the volume of goods (such as crude oil) that a pipeline carries depends on the unit area of the pipeline which equals π times the pipeline's squared radius. So, if a pipeline's radius is expanded from 1 to 10 feet, its circumference and approximate construction cost increases by a factor of ten, while its carrying capacity increases by a factor of 100. However, while factors initially favor increasing the size of the pipeline to secure higher returns, they are inherently limited. At some point, as a pipeline is further enlarged, stronger materials may need to be used and proportionately greater amounts spent on pumping crude oil through the pipeline. Analogously, as a nation grows and becomes more far-flung, the logistics involved with managing the state become more challenging.[4] A familiar example is found as the Roman Empire expanded. Rome found it harder to defend against external or internal enemies – more taxing to build and maintain extensive roads, and more disquieting socially to absorb the various cultures that it conquered.

Overall, a state's growth is naturally limited for psychological, sociological, and statistical reasons. Success that leads to growth can be the worst enemy of all to the public interest if it breeds complacency and distracts focus from the ongoing promotion of national well-being.[5] Whether for

---

[3] Kennedy (1987). Hubbard and Kane (2013) provide a critique of the argument.
[4] Huntington (1996).   [5] Pfeffer (2015).

mean-reversion or psychological reasons, success that drives growth may be for nations similar as it is fabled to be for athletic and business leaders who found being featured on the cover of *Sports Illustrated* or *Fortune* turned into a jinx, with their downfall soon following.

Much as Arabic scholar Ibn Khaldun foreshadowed the curve made popular six centuries later by economist Art Laffer, he also anticipated modern-day political theorist Francis Fukuyama's thesis that a nation's success contains within it the seeds of its own decay. Khaldun argues that the initial success of a nation hinges on its social cohesion. Among the factors supporting social cohesion, Khaldun focuses on religious ideology. Different from the evolutionary biology reasons posited by Fukuyama for built-in national decline, Khaldun points to sociological, psychological, and political-economic factors that undermine social cohesion.[6]

Khaldun posits that nations, like individuals, have lifespans and that, toward the end of its lifespan, every state eventually fails because those in power become enamored with sedentary lifestyles, civilization's luxuries, and the perks that come with their positions. To preserve the luxuries and perks, governments raise taxes and violate property rights at the expense of national well-being. According to Khaldun (2005), such "injustice ruins nations," and he describes the cycle nations go through as follows (pp. 230–232):

At the beginning of a dynasty, taxation yields a large revenue from small assessments . . . When the dynasty continues in power . . . qualities of moderation and restraint disappear . . . [due to] the prosperity and luxury in which they are immersed . . . Every individual impost and assessment is increased, in order to obtain a higher tax revenue . . . Eventually, the taxes will weigh heavily on the subjects and overburden them . . . the interest of the subjects in cultural enterprises disappears . . . The result is that total tax revenues go down . . . Business falls off, because all hopes of profit are destroyed, permitting the dissolution of civilization . . . until the dynasty disintegrates.

CITIZEN MOBILITY

Citizen mobility limits government growth. In doing so it limits the magnitude of any capture of the state by government insiders.[7] For example, Florida surpassed New York in 2010 as the third most populous state in

---

[6] Fukuyama (2011, 2014); and Khaldun (2005). Khaldun eloquently expressed the central conundrum associated with effective state building by defining government to be "an institution which prevents injustice other than such as it commits itself."

[7] Hirschman (1970) and Tiebout (1956).

the United States. This change partly reflects citizens changing their residence in light of the different public services and the associated tax costs in the two states. Two states competed, and Florida began to win. Indeed, examples abound in the United States of citizens voting with their feet, as many of them are descendants of people who left harsh conditions in their home countries. My father is a case in point. He fled Yugoslavia in 1955 to escape Tito's dictatorship and to seek greater liberty and better economic opportunity in the United States.

However, citizen mobility only imperfectly limits government growth. There are some natural limits on the potential of voting with one's feet. Job, housing, educational, family, cultural, and language considerations introduce frictions that make migration costly.[8] Visa and citizenship restrictions imposed by countries further restrict citizen mobility when national borders are to be crossed. An extreme example is how challenging it remains to leave North Korea or how difficult most communist nations historically made it for residents to emigrate. Refugees fleeing strife-torn areas in the Mideast are confronting many political barriers at the present time in trying to relocate to safer havens in Europe.

Costlier migration makes it harder for citizens to discipline government insiders by moving to better states with greater benefits for citizens. The restraints against citizen migration work much like greater friction associated with selling stock in a company limits the ability of stockholder-owners to control the behavior of their manager-agents. When citizens can less readily vote with their feet, the slack (S) between them and their public officials will be greater. As slack increases so will government growth and thus the potential gains (G) to public officials from their power. The good news is that while voting with one's feet may be costly, it often is not prohibitively so. This ensures that slack (S) in the relationship between citizens and their officials is less than complete and thus reduces to some degree the potential of an inside job.

It is not just citizens' ability to move away from governments hijacked by insiders that can limit government growth. Also, cross-border fluidity of their assets limits governments' extractive behavior. Simply put, when public officials co-opt the state, citizens and their assets are more likely to take flight. Switzerland's tax-haven status takes advantage of this impulse, as do corporate headquarter inversions. The movement of corporate profits, through transfer pricing arrangements, to more tax-friendly nations such as Ireland, the Netherlands, and Luxembourg, also attests to the phenomenon.[9]

---

[8] DiSalvo (2015).   [9] Hummler (2004).

While citizen mobility often curbs government growth, sometimes instead it fuels the power of government insiders. Specifically, if the citizens who leave are opponents of the government insiders who have co-opted the state, their departure can serve to further entrench the insiders. This has been dubbed the "Curley effect" in recognition of Michael Curley, the four-time mayor of Boston. Curley and his supporters succeeded in chasing out potential opponents using all the tools of government, including property tax hikes and other politically extractive measures, thus insulating themselves in office.[10]

INSTITUTIONAL RESTRAINTS

Institutional restraints limit the slack (S) between citizens and their public officials as well as the potential gains (G) the officials can derive from power. These restraints can work in any institution whether formal (constitutions, laws, property rights) or informal (customs, traditions, behavioral norms, culture).[11]

The Founders of the United States sought to learn from past national failures, mainly in autocracies. They established formal institutions designed to check government growth, prevent the possibility of an inside job, and promote accountability. These institutions included a federal government with three branches and a bicameral legislature with different means of election, term lengths, and bases of representation for the two houses. Other restraints built into the structure of government included freedom of the press and speech, and key rights and responsibilities being denied to the new central government and reserved instead to state governments and citizens.

Operationally, the new federal government ran with key curbs in place. Revenue-raising bills had to originate in the House of Representatives and needed both Senate and presidential approval; two-thirds vote would be required by both houses of Congress to overturn a presidential veto. Congressional tax levies had to be based on state population. The Founders so designed the formal institution to resist government insiders pursuing their own enrichment that taxation based on income even took passing an amendment to the Constitution itself; the 16th Amendment, adopted in 1913, was required to permit income taxes to be levied only

---

[10] Glaeser and Shleifer (2005).
[11] Alesina and Giuliano (2015); Guiso, Sapienza, and Zingales (2015); North (1991); North and Thomas (1973); and North and Weingast (1989).

after invalidating prior legal rulings which had outlawed the imposition of federal taxes on rental, dividend, and interest earnings. Along the same lines, the president's salary could not be increased while the person was in office and any congressional pay raises had to wait until the next election to take effect.

Since the Founders designed a formal institution insulated from government insiders, other laws have added statutory checks on government growth – in the United States as well as in other countries. The Line Item Veto Act of 1996 seeks to limit US federal government growth by enabling the president to nullify specific provisions of a bill without vetoing the entire package. Term limits, such as the 22nd Amendment to the Constitution dealing with presidential tenure, are designed to constrain the time individuals can hold particular political positions – although Putin in Russia and Erdogan in Turkey have shown how the intent of such provisions can be evaded. Also, most US states and several other countries (such as Germany, Austria, Spain, Poland, Switzerland, Italy, and Slovenia) have a formal restraint on growth, a constitutional rule requiring a balanced government budget. Such a rule has been proposed for the US federal government but has yet to be ratified. Balanced budget rules in other countries are not inflexible to the detriment of the public interest, typically allowing for exceptions in times of war, recession, and national emergency. There also tends to be a provision permitting the legislature to suspend the rule by supermajority (e.g., two-thirds) vote.

How effective are such restraints? Economists Torsten Persson and Guido Tabellini analyze the impact of various constitutional features in democracies on the size and performance of government. They compare government spending in two different types of electoral settings, each with different types of restraints on government built in. First, in proportional electoral democracies, legislatures are composed of parties in direct proportion to how citizens voted. On the other hand, in majoritarian electoral democracies, the legislative seats are held on the basis of whichever party wins the majority of a district's popular vote. Compared to proportional electoral rules, Persson and Tabellini find that majoritarian electoral rules reduce overall government spending by almost 5 percent of GDP; welfare spending by 2–3 percent of GDP; and budget deficits by roughly 2 percent of GDP. This trend toward smaller government in majoritarian democracies is rooted in how proportional electoral rules give more political clout to minority interest groups. They thereby increase the slack between citizens and their elected officials, in the process diminishing the accountability of government to the body politic.[12]

For similar reasons, Persson and Tabellini find that within majoritarian democracies, presidential systems reduce the size of government by 5 percent of GDP relative to parliamentary systems. This is due to more checks and balances between the executive and legislative branches in a presidential than a parliamentary system. In a presidential system the chief executive is elected independently from the legislature, whereas in a parliamentary system the prime minister is selected by the legislature's ruling party. The greater checks and balances between the executive and legislative branches diminish the slack (S) between citizens and public officials in presidential versus parliamentary democratic systems. Persson and Tabellini also show, however, that presidential nations perform more poorly economically than do parliamentary ones. The result is driven by Latin-American democracies, nations with presidential systems that are less respectful of property rights.

Beyond formal restraints, informal, cultural factors influence government size and the slack between citizens and their public officials. When touring the country and writing *Democracy in America*, Alexis de Tocqueville noted a unique cultural norm in the young United States. He remarked on the presence of numerous local civic organizations and political associations. Tocqueville believed that such institutions strengthened democracy and limited the possibility of the state being co-opted by government insiders – both because they increased the knowledge of citizens and created curbs against the exercise of centralized political power.[13]

Cultural norms, of course, can cut both ways. Fukuyama notes how the cultural legacy of centuries of ineffective state institutions in Greece and southern Italy is manifest through patronage, nepotism, greater public-sector employment and per capita public outlays, and extensive tax evasion.[14] Culture also appears to play an important explanatory role when it comes to the varying levels of socioeconomic success of Native American tribes. Native Americans are the poorest ethnic group in the United States. Studies show that the socioeconomic success of a given tribe depends only marginally on natural resource and human capital endowments. Rather, the formal constitutional rules chosen by a tribe, such as separation of power between the chief executive and the judicial branch, and how these rules align with underlying cultural norms regarding

[12] Persson and Tabellini (2003).   [13] Tocqueville ([1835–1840] 2003).
[14] Fukuyama (2011, 2014).

political authority and legitimacy are much more influential determinants of a tribe's success.[15]

So, just like some informal cultural norms may curb the growth of government, other norms may be counterproductive, fostering government growth and corruption while, in turn, being amplified by that government growth and corruption. Economists John Garen and Jeff Clark show how at times that government growth may occur even when trust in government is diminishing. If government growth amplifies counterproductive cultural norms such as rent-seeking (either directly or indirectly through increasing the gains from such activity) and the rent-seeking benefits politicians, a vicious cycle sets in involving eroding trust in government, greater rent-seeking, and government growth. A nation can become stuck in a "trust trap," a low-trust/high-rent-seeking/big-government equilibrium.[16] Interestingly, this cycle does not necessarily lead to measures being taken by any party to demand more accountability or to reduce slack between the public and their governing officials.

Greece is mired in such a trap. As Michael Lewis describes, what the Greeks wanted to do "once the lights went out and they were alone in the dark with a pile of borrowed money [from joining the EU], was turn their government into a piñata stuffed with fantastic sums and give as many citizens as possible a whack at it."[17] Lewis cites the national railroad as an example (pp. 44–45):

> The average government job pays almost three times the average private-sector job. The national railroad has annual revenues of 100 million euros against an annual wage bill of 400 million, plus 300 million euros in other expenses. The average state railroad employee earns 65,000 euros per year. Stefanos Manos [former minister of finance] pointed out that it would be cheaper to put all Greece's rail passengers in taxicabs ... "there isn't a single private company in Greece with that kind of average pay."

The public schools and state-owned defense companies are no better (p. 45):

> The Greek public-school system, ... one of the lowest-ranked systems in Europe ... employs four times as many teachers per pupil as the highest-ranked, Finland's. Greeks who send their children to public schools simply assume that they will need to hire private tutors to make sure that they actually will learn

---

[15] Cornell and Kalt (2000). Alesina and Giuliano (2015) address the influence culture and formal institutions have on each other as well as on economic outcomes.

[16] Garen and Clark (2015).   [17] Lewis (2011), p. 44.

something. There are three government-owned defense companies: together they have billions of euros in debts and mounting losses.

Publicly supported pensions add to the problem, notably on account of their early retirement provisions (p. 45):

The retirement age for . . . jobs classified as "arduous" is as early as 55 for men and 50 for women. As this is also the moment when the state begins to shovel out generous pensions, more than 600 Greek professions somehow managed to get themselves classified as arduous: hairdressers, radio announcers, waiters, musicians [etc.].

On top of that, tax cheating is rampant because no one is punished (p. 51):

An estimated two-thirds of Greek doctors reported incomes under 12,000 euros per year – which meant, because incomes below that amount weren't taxable, that even plastic surgeons making millions a year paid no tax at all. The problem wasn't the law – there was a law on the books that made it a jail-able offense to cheat the government out of more than 150,000 euros – but its enforcement.

Can institutional restraints curb public spending, particularly as profligate as Michael Lewis has described? Even as political scientist David Primo offers principles for designing balanced budget rules, he also notes the difficulties involved in design and enforcement. Since budget rules emanate from a political process, special interests are bound to oppose the rules that would restrain public spending from which they benefit. Losing their profit and clout serves as a strong incentive to activate a formidable force of resistance within the political process to such fiscal limits. These special interests operate on both the demand and supply sides of politics, making the force of resistance very great indeed. Moreover, even if a well-designed limit is enacted, it needs to be enforced. It is not uncommon for enforcement to fall to government insiders who were opposed to the restraint and whose resistance may continue through lackluster enforcement.[18]

Here, too, formal institutional restraints may serve the interests of government insiders. Theoretically, a constitutional amendment can provide fiscal discipline, and it can rely on an independent party, such as the Supreme Court in the United States, to ensure enforcement. Constitutional amendments, however, often require supermajority votes, at least in democracies (two-thirds approval by both chambers of Congress in the United States). As with any rules promoting fiscal restraints, demand- or supply-side special interests also are likely to turn

[18] Primo (2007, 2014).

to the political process to advance their minority causes, riddling any proposed amendment with so many loopholes that it becomes toothless. Typically, sufficiently stringent balanced budget rules typically end up relying on self-enforcement, something that is problematic at best or ineffective. Consider the fate, in the United States, of the Gramm Rudman Hollings Act of 1985, the government shutdowns of 1995–1996 and of 2013, federal debt ceilings, the Budget Control Act of 2011, and the No Budget, No Pay Act of 2013. All of these policy actions relied on self-enforcement. Not surprisingly, they were all unsuccessful at restraining the government capture at which their advocates had taken aim.

In addition, attempted fiscal restraints on government growth are not all that they may seem. For example, efforts to balance budgets or otherwise avoid debt as government grows often rely on tax increases and not reduced spending. Tax increases may be more painful than spending cuts for an economy – and for political incumbents – but public officials often still rely on the former to balance public budgets while currying the favor of special interests served by certain public programs. Importantly, if not focused on spending reductions, balanced budget rules may increase the size of the state and its role in society.

Cultural curbs on government growth also present challenges. For example, the occupational guilds and volunteer associations which Tocqueville saw as helpful checks on state power also can promote the interests of their members at the expense of the public interest.[19] Moreover, hopes to alter human nature and thus underlying cultural norms in ways that limit government capture rarely are realized. Contrary to Karl Marx's belief in the positive malleability of human nature, James Madison instead argues, in Essay 51 of *The Federalist Papers*, in favor of formal institutional restraints through constitutions, laws, and elections:[20]

If men were angels, no government would be necessary. If angels were to govern men, neither external nor internal controls on government would be necessary. In framing a government which is to be administered by men over men, the great difficulty lies in this: you must first enable the government to control the governed; and in the next place to oblige it to control itself. A dependence on the people is, no doubt, the primary control on the government; but experience has taught mankind the necessity of auxiliary precautions.

---

[19] Ogilvie (2014).
[20] Marx ([1867] 2009) and Hamilton, Jay, and Madison ([1788] 1982).

ELECTORAL COMPETITION

As Madison imagined, electoral competition is a primary means, at least in democracies, to control government and limit the slack (S) between citizens and their public officials. Much as Adam Smith's Invisible Hand harnesses competition between suppliers in the private sector to promote the interests of consumers, so does competition through the voting booth, between rival prospective suppliers of political representation services, work to advance the public interest.

However effective electoral competition may be, as with other curbs on government growth, there are several reasons why it imperfectly aligns public officials' actions with the public interest.[21] First, citizens typically are presented with all-or-nothing choices between a small number of candidates who, if elected, act on a large number of issues over their tenure and the electoral market meets infrequently – once every six years in the case of the US Senate.

Second, citizens have weak incentives to expend the effort to become and stay well-informed and to exercise their voter-owner rights when the electoral market meets. After all, what difference can one vote make in most democratic elections? The average US congressional district has over 710,000 citizens. Any individual citizen thus has an incentive to hitch a free ride on the policing actions of other voter-owners. This free-rider problem is exacerbated by the fact that political ownership rights are non-transferable. The non-transferability of voter-owner shares limits the gains citizens can realize from promoting superior politicians and policies. By contrast, in the private sector, ownership shares in firms can be bought and sold. The gains associated with promoting better managers and corporate strategies thus are amplified, as are the incentives on the part of owner-shareholders to police the actions of the firm's managers.

The third reason that electoral competition is not entirely effective in reducing slack between citizens and their public officials is that, in most democracies, the provision of representation services takes place under conditions of effective duopoly (e.g., Republicans and Democrats in the United States) or oligopoly. Barriers to entry in these fairly closed systems are significant with respect to the arrival of new parties or the appearance of individual, nonincumbent political candidates. At least in the United States, moreover, the barriers to entry have been growing. The average tenure of US senators has increased from five years in the early 1880s to just

---

[21] See Abrams and Settle (1978); Ferejohn (1977); Fiorina and Noll (1978); Kalt and Zupan (1984, 1990); and Stigler (1971).

over thirteen years in recent congresses. The average tenure of House members has risen from four years in the early twentieth century to nearly ten years today.[22] Heightened congressional tenure has been driven by increases in the proportion of legislators seeking reelection and decreases in the proportion defeated at the polls. While it was common for 30–40 percent of House members not to seek reelection until 1880, the percentage now averages 11 percent. Additionally, only 5 percent of House members seeking reelection since 1940 have been defeated, two-thirds less than the average incumbent defeat rate over 1840–1940.

Various reasons explain why more congressional members are seeking reelection and succeeding.[23] Pre-Civil War, part-time "citizen legislators" were the norm. Life in Washington was less pleasant due to the lack of air conditioning, among other things. Party leaders determined committee assignments and party control changed more frequently, so that seniority conveyed fewer benefits. Careerism rose post-Civil War due to committee assignments and other perks being determined more by seniority than by legislative leaders, the strengthening of the party system, the emergence of more one-party states and districts, and the practice of re-districting further to insulate incumbents from competition. Certain additional advantages emerged post-World War II that helped incumbents increase their tenure prospects, such as garnering publicity and providing facilitation services to their constituents. Communication and transportation improvements also made it easier to remain in touch with constituents. Used as a means in electoral competition, such changes increased the likelihood and attractiveness of a longer congressional career. Another way to look at it is that with time a status quo can take greater root and resist competitors in the electoral arena.

The fourth reason that electoral competition does not entirely reduce slack between citizens and their public officials is that citizens have limited means to curb opportunism by their elected representatives – especially in light of incumbency advantages. Consider how the electorate often relies on agreements or promises made by campaigning officials that, eventually, will depend on self-enforcement, such as when candidates encourage voters to "read their lips." As with fiscal constraints, campaign promises flounder when they rely on self-enforcement.

---

[22] Glassman and Wilhelm (2015).

[23] See, for example, Abram and Cooper (1968); Cain, Ferejohn, and Fiorina (1987); Carson, Engstrom, and Roberts (2006); Fenno (1978); Galloway (1959); Hibbing (1991); Kravitz (1974); Ornstein (1995); and Polsby (1968).

With greater electoral competition, one would expect the slack (S) between citizens and their public officials to be mitigated, thus reducing the profits to public officials from power (P). And it can be to various degrees. However, even highly competitive electoral markets do not ensure that the state's role in society will be optimal, from an efficiency perspective. Nor do they entirely remove the risk of an inside job.

Electorally competitive political markets still promote state growth due to the factors outlined in the previous chapter, such as special interests, public goods' political clout, the common-pool problem, patronage, bureaucratic motives, and transaction costs. Additionally, even if the demand side of politics is perfectly competitive and the political clout of various demand-side interests perfectly mirrors their economic stakes on policies, the supply side may suffer from imperfections. Imperfect competition on the supply side leaves slack in the relationship between citizens and their public officials, and such slack can be exercised by those officials at the expense of the public interest.

A final reason for why electoral competition does not ensure the full accountability of public officials is inherent in voting options. Merely having many candidates from whom to choose does not translate into zero slack between citizens and their public officials ($S = 0$). At certain points in 2015, for example, there were seventeen candidates in the United States for the Republican Party's presidential nomination. One would think that degree of competition would enhance accountability through voting. There did seem to be a range of choice: some had a leg up on others due to their family name, personal wealth, or visibility, but each candidate actually came as a bundle of attributes/stances. Citizens cannot disaggregate a particular aspect from the others a candidate has, choosing Donald Trump without his views on illegal immigrants, or voting for Ben Carson without his stance on gay marriage. Once elected president, the winning candidate acquires further insulation from electoral competition, gaining incumbent advantages that diminish accountability to the public interest. The chief of these is power.

At the extreme, the power that comes with electoral victory can be used to rewrite political rules, including those concerning future elections. In an election in 1933 involving thirteen parties, Hitler and his Nazi party won a plurality of the seats in the Reichstag, the German legislature. Within months of the election, Hitler succeeded in having the Enabling Act adopted, establishing him as a dictator. Imbued with even greater power, Hitler banned all other political parties and disbanded the Reichstag, replacing it with a rubber-stamp parliament composed of Nazis. He used electoral power to gain autocratic power, presumably by legal means. Multiparty elections were not held in (West) Germany again until 1949.

THE QUASI-MARKET FOR POLITICAL CONTROL

Apart and separate from electoral competition, there is another means, in both democracies and autocracies, to control government and limit the slack between citizens and their public officials. It is a quasi-market for political control analogous to the market for corporate control.[24] That is, as actions and policies by public officials diminish an economy's productivity, there is an incentive for government takeover by new, more efficient management. Such a takeover curbs the extent to which government can grow beyond the efficient level, and it also limits the slack between citizens and their public officials.

The good news is that the quasi-market for political control has a disciplinary effect on the behavior of public officials despite their increasing insulation from the electorate. However, there are key impediments limiting the operability of the quasi-market as a control. For one, citizens have little incentive to take over and overhaul political management because the rights by which they own the political state are non-transferable. The gains that they can garner from pursuing efficiencies thus are limited. Not only are the ownership rights of constituents non-transferable, they may be curtailed or nonexistent. Over the course of history, those in political power have limited their citizens' franchise as well as freedoms of speech and assembly. Rulers have also enslaved, incarcerated, or exterminated citizens threatening their power.

The quasi-market for political control also falls short of the private sector in its ability to deliver efficiency-enhancing takeovers because mechanisms to facilitate change of control like golden parachutes are rare in politics. In the private market, managers certainly have incentives to retain power when their firms underperform and they also have means with which to entrench themselves, such as poison pills, supermajority voting requirements, and dual-class shares. In the face of the incentives and means which corporate managers have to cling to power, golden parachutes grease the skids for takeover, thereby promoting efficiency. Even though such buy-out packages may appear unseemly, they are more readily organized in the corporate arena due to the transferability of

---

[24] Manne (1965).

ownership shares. They are also credible to the corporate manager. Their credibility derives from the fact that they are enforced by a third party, the judicial system.

The lack of a similarly reliable third-party enforcement mechanism is what fundamentally limits the extent to which a quasi-market for political control can curtail government growth and prevent inside jobs. The next chapter delves into this particular problem. As we will see, the problem hinges on the currency of politics being power and not primarily money – and how the value of this currency depends on how securely one possesses it. Suffice it for now to say that we rarely see buy-out packages in politics. It is also uncommon for government insiders to cede power through the relatively straightforward process observed in corporate settings. It takes a confluence of legal, constitutional, or cultural curbs to create the clear message to government insiders that they have no other choice.

BENCHMARKING

The effect of policies may not be readily apparent either before or after they are implemented. The accuracy with which a policy's effects are either predicted or perceived is clouded by various factors such as imperfect information, ignorance and other limits to human cognition, the proverbial Law of Unintended Consequences, and assessments being made by the same individuals promoting state intervention. In Orwellian fashion, for example, government insiders may set targets and report numbers so as to justify their regime's success. Manipulating the numbers happens whenever a government program has been hijacked by public officials, in autocracies and democracies alike – although the limits to such hijacking and manipulation tend to be greater in democracies.

The best way to overcome the opacity associated with the effects of a policy is by having benchmarks. As Mark Twain quipped "few things are harder to put up with than the annoyance of a good example." Creating laboratories whereby individual states could experiment with policy innovations and offer illuminating benchmarks was a key argument our nation's Founders made for a limited federal government. At times, indeed, success in individual states has annoyed and even embarrassed the federal government. The Founders' idea has proven sound. According to current-day political scientists, benchmarking is critical to promoting public officials' accountability and diminishing the odds of an inside job.[25] Examples in recent decades support the value of benchmarks as well.

The economic liberalization of China illustrates the beneficial role played by benchmarking. The market economies in Singapore and Japan provided Deng Xiaoping helpful comparisons for how China's productivity could improve through greater reliance on markets and entrepreneurship. From his perspective, and despite the historical political differences between China and its two model economies, it didn't matter: "Whether a cat is black or white, if it catches mice it is a good cat." Deng's international visits in 1978–1979 to these countries generated a flurry of media coverage and created favorable impressions with fellow citizens and Communist Party comrades regarding what could be learned from market-based economies.[26] Deng was relying on tested benchmarks for developing the Chinese economy, and he artfully marshaled support from both the supply and demand sides of his country's political sphere for his liberalizing policies.

India in the early 1990s provides another example of the beneficial role of benchmarking. There had been decades of stifling state intervention at that point. India largely had been closed to the outside world through high tariffs, import licenses, and an inconvertible currency. A labyrinthine bureaucracy, or License Raj, made it difficult to start new businesses. It prevented existing firms from firing workers and closing plants, thus limiting their responsiveness to market changes. Five-year plans, similar to those in the Soviet Union, set output and investment targets by sector and many sectors such as steel, telecommunications, and mining were nationalized.[27] Over 1950–1990, Indian annual GDP growth averaged 3.5 percent, lagging nations with more market-based economies. Over the same time period, annual GDP growth averaged 12 percent in Taiwan, 10 percent in South Korea, 9 percent in Thailand and Indonesia, and 5 percent in Pakistan.

In 1991, India was on the verge of a default. Its foreign exchange reserves were able to finance only three weeks' worth of imports. It took a new Indian government to agree to an International Monetary Fund bailout which required diminished state intervention. Comparisons to other countries would now begin to provide benchmarks for rebuilding the economy. Liberalization allowed India to achieve growth rates in

---

[25] See, for example, Kayser and Peress (2012).   [26] See, for example, Kissinger (2011).

[27] See, for example, Di Lodovico et al. (2001); and Sam Staley, "The Rise and Fall of Indian Socialism: Why India Embraced Economic Reform," Reason.com, June 6, 2006.

line with its more market-based Asian neighbors. Annual GDP growth rate peaked at 9 percent in 2007, the second-highest rate globally, surpassed only by contemporaneously liberalizing China.

Interest in benchmarking the effectiveness of a government or a particular policy has grown over time. The effects of doing so are seen in some of the world's most dynamic economies. The means to benchmark also have expanded due to increased trade and improvements in transportation, communication, and informational technologies such as air travel, Big Data, the Internet, and social media. Benchmarking and its rewards are now easier to achieve. Through comparison, government failures or successes are more readily identified.[28] Whether public officials will be held accountable for them is a different matter.

FROM INCENTIVES TO INTERESTS

We have so far focused on incentives for government insiders to co-opt the state and ways in which those incentives are influenced by changes in both government size and the slack in the relationship between public officials and citizens. Economic theory and considerable empirical evidence argue for incentives having significant influence. Consider, for example, growth in the state's role in society. Its benefit to government insiders through increased possibilities by which to co-opt the state also increases the likelihood that those insiders will hijack the state. Government growth enhances the prospective gains (G) from co-opting the state and thus is an incentive for the inside job. By contrast, with decreases in the slack between citizens and their public officials (S), the cost to government insiders of co-opting the state increases. Decreases in slack are a disincentive reducing the probability of an inside job.

While economists are comfortable with incentives, we find it harder to incorporate and quantify the preferences of individuals for a particular activity – the value or interest (I) they place in the activity. For example, economists are unlikely to ascribe very low beef consumption in India to religious taboos and cultural values. Instead, they have traditionally attributed it to the price of beef consumption being higher in India than most other places around the globe, or to disincentives to consuming beef in India being unusually high. Interests or preference-based explanations are often dismissed by economists with skepticism and left to practitioners

---

[28] Micklethwait and Wooldridge (2014).

from the humanities or other social sciences such as psychology, political science, history, philosophy, and sociology.

To these fields of expertise we now turn as we move from incentives to interests, encountering the possibility of virtue in political behavior. In the government self-capture equation, the presence of interest (I) as a term reflects that possibility as a factor in the inside job. For that reason it is useful to explore preference, or such a taste factor, how it is nurtured, and how it can be relied upon to curb the interest public officials have in profiting from power at the public's expense.

In sum, many external factors, whether naturally present or of human design, can and do limit government growth as well as the slack in the relationship between citizens and their public officials. Now, we move to an internally driven constraint which involves self-policing by public officials. We turn to virtue. In doing so, we will see that, while both external and internally driven factors can and do limit government growth and the likelihood of an inside job, they are not failsafe. And, there is a fundamental reason why.

6

Why Are Government Insiders So Hard to Control?

$$P = G \times S \times \boldsymbol{I}$$

Like the prospective gains from co-opting the state (G), slack in the relationship between public officials and their citizens (S) multiplies the profits to government insiders from inside jobs (P). Mitigating slack requires understanding those factors that give rise to it and then curbing such factors through formal institutional constraints or through supporting naturally occurring restraints, such as the ones noted in the previous chapter. Limiting slack curtails government growth, which also reduces the prospective gains from co-opting the state. So, mechanisms that diminish slack and thus increase the incentive of public officials to promote the public good would seem key guards against inside jobs. However, as we have also seen in the previous chapter, there are limitations with regard to incentives and their ability to constrain the profits public officials derive from power.

Much has been made of how America's Founders focused on checks and balances, relying on incentives to promote the public interest when designing the formal institutions defined by our Constitution. Less clearly laid out is the degree to which the Founders expected, beyond formal restraints and incentives, public officials' interest in exploiting any slack to also play a role in promoting inside jobs. Given any favorable prospective gains (G) and slack (S), inside jobs cannot proceed without public officials who are interested in taking advantage of the situation. That interior, personal factor is represented in the government self-capture equation as interest (I). When public officials are more interested in exploiting any slack in their relationship with citizens, the interest (I) in the equation is closer to its maximum value of unity. As interest increases, government self-capture increases, and the damage imposed on society is greater. A significant curb on interest (I) is virtue.

Virtue has been highlighted for its efficacy in self-policing by public officials not only by political philosophers dating back to Aristotle in the West but across centuries and continents through the history of the world. Virtue was a cultural norm at the time the Founders wrote the Constitution, and to some degree they would have assumed it would influence the magnitude of government self-capture. Challenges with promoting it notwithstanding, virtue can curtail government growth and the possibility of inside jobs. As with incentives designed to mitigate slack and government growth, however, virtue is not able to fully align the behavior of government insiders with the common good. Why this is true in democracies and autocracies alike is this chapter's focus. The obstacle involves the currency of political markets being power and the value of that coinage hinging on who holds power.

In recent centuries, changes in certain factors have promoted a salutary shift from autocracy to democracy. Government *by* the people, however, has been insufficient to ensure government *for* the people. The economic model of politics holds that the primary reason for this problem is the capture of political power by demand-side interests. Yet, there is also the risk of such capture by government insiders operating on the supply side of politics. In contrast to autocracies, democracies tend to have better curbs against co-opting of the state by top leaders, but the potential for hijacking remains, especially below the highest power rungs, where the benefits of electoral competition are greatest. Regardless of autocratic or democratic circumstances, the prospect of an inside job grows with increases in the state's role in society, in the slack in the relationship between public officials and citizens, and in the interest of public officials in exploiting the slack.

PROMOTING VIRTUE

When speaking of virtue, many economists tend to emphasize relying on formal institutions and extrinsic incentives to promote virtuous behavior. Formal institutions, by mitigating slack between public officials and citizens, make non-virtuous behavior more difficult. Electoral competition and term limits, for example, provide incentives for public officials to align their behavior with the common good – a virtuous outcome. Here a public official may behave virtuously but in reaction to external incentives.

However, other social scientists and certain economists such as Deirdre McCloskey advocate promoting cultural norms as a more efficacious means to diminish corruption and better society. Here the idea of virtue becomes an internal factor in a government insider's interest (I) in parti-cipating in an inside job. McCloskey claims that intrinsic motivation and self-policing have greater reach than extrinsically based carrots and sticks: "All that works in the end is ethical change ... It is fruitless to propose 'mechanisms' or [formal] 'institutions,' absent an ethical desire in enough of us to do good."[1]

Daniel Pink, in *Drive*, presents evidence from the field of psychology showing the vital role intrinsic motivation plays in explaining human behavior. To buttress the point, Pink asks how many of us, as parents, would teach our children to be civil through paying them to write thank-you notes versus inculcating them with the right values, including showing gratitude for favors received.[2]

Daron Acemoglu and fellow economist Matthew Jackson model the role which leaders can play in positively shaping social norms.[3] By refusing to be considered for a third term as president, for example, George Washington altered the beliefs of contemporaries who considered the office to be a form of monarchy; he instead established a precedent of limited tenure which succeeding US leaders followed. Washington is a primary figure in the Great Man Theory of history, yet this theory cuts both ways, as Acemoglu and Jackson's model leaves open the possibility that leaders also can influence prevailing social norms in a negative manner.

Political philosophers have long debated the role the state should play in shaping individuals' intrinsic motivations. According to Aristotle, politics is an incubator for virtue. Politics is essential to the good life because participation in the process at the heart of a *polis*, or political community, offers citizens the opportunity to practice moral principles and develop virtuous habits. Successfully relying on the state to promote virtue was more likely in the smaller-scale Athenian democracies with which Aristotle was familiar. In modern nations, where the *polis* is much larger, such a role might further grow the state. Moreover, the larger role of the state, whether in autocracies or democracies, may also reduce the role left to citizens and potentially atrophy their moral "muscles."[4]

Modern-day American political philosopher Michael Sandel similarly argues that a just society cannot be achieved merely by maximizing utility or freedom of choice. Justice involves an interior "right" way to value

---

[1] Deirdre N. McCloskey, "Two Cheers for Corruption," *Wall Street Journal*, February 28–March 1, 2015. See also McCloskey (2010, 2016).
[2] Pink (2011). [3] Acemoglu and Jackson (2015). [4] Zupan (2015c).

things and not just an exterior "right" way to distribute things. From Sandel's perspective, this is best done through strengthening public institutions and promoting a politics of moral engagement.[5]

Aristotle in the fourth century BC and Sandel in the twenty-first century AD both emphasize the *polis* in developing virtue. Doing so, they both credit insufficiently the role non-state institutions play in doing the same. Families, guilds, voluntary associations, and churches give individuals great daily opportunity to learn virtue by doing. Moreover, unlike the coercive means at the core of the laws emanating from a *polis*, non-state institutions rely on noncoercive means when promoting their objectives. In touring America in the early nineteenth century, Alexis de Tocqueville marveled at citizens' involvement with both local voluntary organizations and political associations, crediting it with the effect Aristotle and Sandel credit to the *polis*: "In democratic countries knowledge of how to combine is the mother of all forms of knowledge; on its progress depends that of all the others."[6] Similarly, looking beyond the state as a promoter of virtue, economist Deirdre McCloskey acknowledges the key roles played in developing virtue by "the mother's knee, [and] the pastor's pulpit" while recognizing the influence of "the judge's bench, [and] the schoolmaster's lectern" in promoting ethical change.[7]

Even markets and businesses advance virtue. Both Steven Pinker, in *The Better Angels of Our Nature*, and Matt Ridley, in *The Rational Optimist*, credit markets and business enterprises for improving our species' civility.[8] Over 200 years earlier, Adam Smith intended to spell this out in a third book that was not published due to his death.[9] Free markets, which are based on clearly defined and enforced property rights as well as on the liberty of individuals to pursue their happiness, maximize the opportunity for repeat interaction across time, products, places, and people. The prospect of repeat interaction creates a future and that future, by casting its shadow on the present, promotes integrity.

In his *Lectures on Jurisprudence*, Smith notes how repeat interaction enhances virtue:[10]

When a person makes perhaps 20 contracts in a day, he cannot gain so much by endeavouring to impose upon his neighbours, as the appearance of a cheat would make him lose. Where people seldom deal with one another, we find that they are

---

[5] Sandel (2009).   [6] Tocqueville ([1835–1840] 2003).
[7] Deirdre N. McCloskey, "Two Cheers for Corruption," *Wall Street Journal*, February 28–March 1, 2015.
[8] Pinker (2011) and Ridley (2010).   [9] Zupan (2011).   [10] Ibid.

somewhat disposed to cheat, because they can gain more by a smart trick than they can lose by the injury that it does to their character.

Smith goes on to observe that, when it comes to virtue, politicians are not the most virtuous men in the world because there need to be a[11]

[t]hey are praised for any little advantage that they can take, and pique themselves a good deal on this degree of refinement. The reason for this is that nations treat with one another not above twice or thrice in a century, and they may gain more by one piece of fraud than [lose] by having a bad character. France has had this character with us ever since the reign of Louis XIV, yet it has never in the least hurt either its interest or splendor.

With regard to the non-coercion that is at the heart of market-based exchanges, Tocqueville also points to its beneficial impacts in terms of promoting moderation and understanding between individuals:[12]

Trade is the natural enemy of all violent passions. Trade loves moderation, delights in compromise, and is most careful to avoid anger. It is patient, supple, and insinuating, only resorting to extreme measures in case of absolute necessity. Trade makes men independent of one another and gives them a high idea of their personal importance: it leads them to want to manage their own affairs and teaches them to succeed therein. Hence it makes them inclined to liberty but disinclined to revolution.

From state, from social interactions, from markets, admittedly, it is hard to disentangle virtue's sources. It is harder still to determine the extent to which virtue and other informal, cultural factors affect a nation's formal institutions and are, in turn, influenced by those same institutions.[13] Notwithstanding the empirical challenges, economists Luigi Guiso, Paola Sapienza, and Luigi Zingales conclude that cultural factors such as virtue matter in explaining political outcomes.[14] They reach this conclusion by observing that countries' legal traditions are based on cultural affinities and that when laws conflict with a country's underlying norms, compliance and enforcement are weaker. This comports with Tocqueville's observation that "[t]he best laws cannot make a constitution work in spite of morals; morals can turn the worst laws to advantage."[15]

Social scientists Francis Fukuyama, Lant Pritchett, and Michael Woolcock similarly note the importance of cultural norms such as virtue in "getting to Denmark."[16] To them modern-day Denmark is a worthwhile

[11] Ibid.   [12] Tocqueville (2003).   [13] Alesina and Giuliano (2015).
[14] Guiso, Sapienza, and Zingales (2015).   [15] Tocqueville (2003).
[16] Fukuyama (2011); and Pritchett and Woolcock (2002). See also Duhigg (2016) on the role of norms in determining organizational success. Duhigg argues that norms promoting

destination for nation builders because it is characterized by democratic institutions, low levels of political corruption, inclusivity, peace, and prosperity. Cultural factors appear to play a key role in explaining Denmark. This is because merely replicating Denmark's political institutions, as other nations have tried, does not ensure the same socioeconomic outcome. Analogously, many Latin-American countries have found that just copying the US Constitution does not guarantee achieving the same level of prosperity that prevails in the United States.

Cultural factors as they relate to self-enforcement by government insiders are hard to ignore in seeking to explain why countries such as Denmark, Finland, Norway, and Sweden routinely top the annual Transparency International (TI) index for perceived public-sector integrity. Fukuyama argues that the Protestant Reformation was central to shaping these nations' cultures.[17] The Lutheranism which they adopted through the Reformation encouraged literacy so that all citizens could have direct access to God by reading the Bible. Lutheranism also fostered a work ethic and virtue through stressing that one was directly accountable to God for one's behavior. Responsibility for sins was not mediated by a priest in confession; confession to God was direct.

Of course, it's possible that the adoption of Lutheranism was a fluke, an accident of history which then positively influenced the culture and socioeconomic trajectory of Denmark and its Scandinavian neighbors. It's also conceivable that the spread of Lutheranism in these countries instead might have been due to other, more fundamental, cultural factors, which, in turn, were the source for the noted self-enforcement by public officials. Nevertheless, the observations made by Fukuyama and other social scientists about the role of culture and virtue in "getting to Denmark" are compelling.

Regardless of its antecedents, culture's importance in determining the success of nations and their institutions is quite evident. Its influence affects the magnitude of government self-capture, that is, the extent of inside jobs. Culture directly influences this magnitude by shaping the virtue of public officials; their virtue directly affects the value of interest (I) in the government self-capture equation. Culture also indirectly influences the magnitude of government self-capture by shaping the virtue of a nation's citizens and their collective interest in rent-seeking; it affects the

---

broad-based input from the members of organizational teams lead to superior outcomes over norms favoring more monopolized, autocratic input.

[17] Fukuyama (2011).

size of the state and the potential gains (G) to public officials from co-opting the state.

As with any curb on factors that foster an inside job, culture and the intrinsic virtue of public officials and citizens cannot ensure that we will get to the utopian state of "Denmark." Before examining the evidence, how-ever, let's first further explore why competition fails to ensure efficiency in political markets despite its capacity to promote such an outcome in private markets.

WHY THE INVISIBLE HAND DOESN'T ENSURE EFFICIENCY IN POLITICS

In *The Wealth of Nations*, Adam Smith argued that competition harnesses individuals' self-interested behavior to promote efficiency and social well-being.[18] While economists Gary Becker and Donald Wittman argue that Smith's Invisible Hand Theory also applies to political markets, they neglect an important hindrance limiting the theory's operability in such a setting.[19] The obstacle involves the property rights being indefinite or nonsecure when it comes to political transactions. After all, when it comes to politics, wealth redistributions are the "good" demanded and supplied. Political power gives those who hold it the ability to redefine otherwise secure property rights to the assets in a society. This kind of power, the currency of the realm in politics, allows those who possess it to create wealth redistributions favorable to themselves and others.

The idea of indefinite property rights implies that even with perfect competition on the supply side and demand side of politics, market forces will not result in an optimal outcome. The Invisible Hand has become visible and can subvert the public interest. The Visible Hand holds political power. It cannot readily be harnessed by competitive forces to promote efficiency and social well-being. Instead, the Visible Hand can exercise its power to profit at the public's expense.[20]

The idea of indefinite property rights in politics explains why the qualifier "quasi" defines the concept of a quasi-market for political control introduced in the preceding chapter. This is because the offers to change control which are tendered by outside "raiders" to the incumbent man-agers of underperforming firms are more credible in the corporate setting, where they are reliably enforced by a third party, the judicial system.

---

[18] Smith ([1776] 1937).   [19] Becker (1983) and Wittman (1989).
[20] Acemoglu (2003) and Buchanan (1972).

By contrast, the golden parachutes or other offers to change control which are tendered by outside raiders to public-sector incumbents in an under-performing nation are less definite and credible. There is no similarly reliable third party to ensure that the proffered buy-out terms will be enforced. Because the enforcement of offers in politics depends on who holds power, once government insiders accept a change-in-control offer and relinquish office they also hand over the power to define and enforce the offer. Seen this way, they have no real incentive to relinquish power.

The unique properties of power, which is the currency of the political realm, create complications for efforts to change control and thereby improve efficiency and better serve the public good. This is true for both those raiders seeking to take power and incumbent insiders contemplating relinquishing it. Consider first those seeking to obtain political power. One difficulty they face is the non-transferability of ownership shares across citizens. This limits the prospective gains to raiders from promoting efficiency-enhancing political changes. Another difficulty a prospective raider faces is the effort required to organize an opposing faction in the political sphere. As with all collective endeavors, each prospective raiding member has an incentive to free ride on the organizational work of others. There also tend to be hazards associated with organizing political takeovers – including the prospect of being jailed or killed. Moreover, any takeover offer put on the table runs the risk of being absconded with by those whom one is trying to unseat; as long as they still hold power, public officials have the means to appropriate the offer without relinquishing the power. So, the willingness of incumbent holders of political power to entertain a change-of-control offer may not be credible, and making such an offer may undermine a prospective raider's viability.

Government insiders or political incumbents contemplating the possibility of relinquishing power confront their own challenges. It is difficult to specify in advance all the parameters of a suitable arrangement for public officials and their associates once they are out of office. In addition, political positions provide unique vehicles to promote one's worldviews, whereas the substitute opportunities available to individuals interested in further-ing such ideological objectives are more limited out of office compared to corporate executives motivated by pecuniary goals. Furthermore, the offer may not prove credible: its attractiveness must be discounted due to the fact that one's successor has both an interest in and the means to abrogate the promise. Can government insiders put credence in the value of any promised arrangements in return for ceding power when in doing so they surrender the right to enforce the promises?

It is for the preceding reasons that we rarely see buy-out packages in politics or observe public officials willingly cede power unless institutional factors dictate that it's time. Occasionally, the promise of an alternative government or nongovernment post or of asylum in a different country facilitates exit, especially if this mitigates further harm from one's political successors. Leon Trotsky was the Marxist theorist who was both the founder and leader of the Red Army in the Soviet Union. Once among the top members of the ruling Communist Party, Trotsky lost power due to differences with Joseph Stalin, the leader of the Soviet Union. He spent the last eleven years of his life in four different countries which offered temporary asylum. Stalin, whose control of power was close to absolute, did not make good on any pledges to Trotsky when the latter left the Soviet Union. To him, Trotsky remained a threat to his own hold on power. Trotsky ultimately was assassinated in 1940 in Mexico City at the hands of a Soviet agent.[21]

History shows that the credibility of offers made to incent political incumbents to leave office and cede power is limited, even when there is an assumed divine right of rule or a long-standing monarchic government. For example, Tsar Nicholas II was heir to the great Romanov tsars who had led Russia for three centuries to great heights of culture and power. After abdicating in 1917, when he expected to be exiled with his family, Tsar Nicholas II was held under palace arrest. When Soviet forces began to fear his rescue by counterrevolutionaries in 1918, they executed Nicholas and his family.

For another example of the outcome of a buy-out offer acceptance by a sitting autocrat, in 1791, after attempting unsuccessfully to escape from France in light of growing popular unrest, King Louis XVI agreed to, on the demand of the National Assembly, a new constitution establishing a constitutional monarchy in which he would still have a role. The revolutionary leadership, however, became ever more radicalized in the wake of military defeats in Austria and Prussia. A new National Convention abolished the monarchy in September 1792, declaring France a republic. Louis XVI and his wife, Marie Antoinette, were judged guilty of treason and guillotined in 1793.

---

[21] To facilitate transitions in political power that would improve national well-being, political scientists Bueno de Mesquita and Smith (2011) advocate giving rulers a brief window during which they and their families could leave the country for some safe haven and in return for an offer of perpetual amnesty, guaranteed by international laws established through the United Nations. This incentive for welfare-enhancing political transitions might be further amplified by allowing exiting leaders and their families to retain some significant portion of the rents that they have extracted while in office.

Charles I of England believed the divine right of kings would protect him when, after escaping a besieged city as a disguised servant in 1646, he put himself in the protective custody of the Scottish army. He did not foresee being sold out by this army to the British Parliament dominated by his political opponents. His assertion of sovereign immunity, supported by the House of Lords and all three common-law courts, was ignored by the parliament, which declared an exclusive right to prosecute him. Charles I was judged guilty of treason and beheaded.

These examples illustrate the untoward consequences that can befall rulers who lose power. They also highlight how a quasi-market for political control still may operate, offering buy-outs to those in power as happens in the market for corporate control. Yet, unlike in the corporate setting, self-enforcement of the agreement by those newly in power does not have a credible track record. Nevertheless, monarchies in particular due to their economic cost, at least relative to democracy, have become less common in recent centuries. The opportunity cost of autocracy increases as a society becomes more productive through factors such as specialization, education, and trade.[22] A higher opportunity cost creates greater incentive for "raiders" to change the incumbent governance form. This change, however, tends toward violence given political rulers' vested interest in retaining power – including historic reasons not to rely on nonviolent buy-out options available to corporate raiders.

It is easiest to imagine a quasi-market for political control operating vis-à-vis the highest rungs of government power. However, the concept applies to some degree to all public positions. While lower-level public officials can less directly define and enforce the property rights to society's wealth than higher-level officials, they have the potential to overcome this deficiency through their sheer numbers and influence on top leaders. Their vested interests thus are likely to be politically well-represented, and their indirect exercise of power can be appreciable. For example, the long-standing restriction against printing presses in the Ottoman Empire illustrates the difficulty of altering a political outcome when lower-level

---

[22] Note that this explanation for the shift in governance form to democracy differs from the one posited by Acemoglu and Robinson (2006). Acemoglu and Robinson argue that such shifts are due to the need for elites to make a credible commitment in the face of demands by disenfranchised citizens, demands that are likely to be accentuated by wars or macroeconomic shocks such as depressions or a collapse in the terms of trade. What Acemolgu and Robinson's thesis less readily explains is why shifts to democracy have been occurring over the last two centuries and elites did not make such credible commitments to disenfranchised citizens in the wake of wars and macroeconomic shocks before then.

government insiders have a vested interest in the status quo. Broad use of printing presses was restricted due to the clout of a sizable group of public scribes at the time. The efforts of the Janissaries to expand their influence and perquisites at the expense of the Ottoman Empire's well-being provide another example.

The quasi-market for political control involving lower-level government officials is protected by implied threat to the extent that attempts to alter an existing political equilibrium favoring general state employees are associated with violence. The history of the Janissaries highlights the violence that may accompany efforts to curtail the influence of government insiders below the top rungs of power. After murdering two reform-minded sultans to preserve their influence on the ever-more "Sick Man of Europe," the Janissaries' chokehold was not lessened until 1826 when Sultan Mahmud II abolished the Janissary corps and executed over 6,000 of its members.[23]

THE OSSIFYING AND CORRUPTING INFLUENCE OF POLITICAL POWER

Due to the perks of power, government insiders have an incentive to hang on to power. Due to their positions, government insiders also have the means, or power, to hang on to their perks. Government insiders' perks and power are greater when the supply side of politics is less competitive or accountable.

An examination of regime duration shows that government insiders are more likely to cling to power when the supply side of politics is less accountable to the common good. Lower accountability, or greater slack in the relationship between public officials and citizens, also increases the magnitude of government self-capture. This double whammy of greater co-opting over a longer time period exacerbates the negative impact of inside jobs.

Table 6.1 demonstrates the phenomenon by looking at how regime duration and perceived levels of public-sector corruption vary between autocracies and democracies. Countries are classified as being an autocracy or democracy based on the research of political scientists Barbara Geddes, Joseph Wright, and Erica Frantz.[24] The duration with which an autocratic regime has held power (as of September 7, 2014) represents the total number

---

[23] Acemoglu and Robinson (2012); Fukuyama (2011); and Hubbard and Kane (2013).
[24] Geddes, Wright, and Frantz (2014).

Table 6.1 *Regime duration and perceived levels of public-sector corruption: 2014*

Form of government (number of countries)	Average regime duration measured in days	Average TI score
Autocracies (56)	13,255	33.1
Democracies (118)	1,554	47.8

of days a particular faction has ruled – whether through monarchical, military, party, and/or personal dictatorship.[25] As can be seen from the middle column of Table 6.1, regime duration responds in a predictable manner to the accountability of rulers to their citizens. Regimes retain power nearly nine times longer in autocracies than they do in democracies, presumably due to the lower accountability on the supply side of politics typically found under autocracy compared to democracy.

The third column of Table 6.1 indicates that when rulers are less accountable to a nation's citizens the magnitude of government self-capture also is greater. This magnitude is measured by the index of public-sector corruption compiled for 174 countries in 2014 by Transparency International (TI) on a scale ranging from 0 (highly corrupt) to 100 (very clean).[26] The TI index has been published annually and is the most widely disseminated and highly regarded measure of public-sector corruption across countries.[27] The TI index is based on a composite average of surveys compiled by independent institutions such as the World Bank, Freedom House, Economist Intelligence Unit, Bertelsmann Foundation, IMD Business School, Political Risk Services, Political and Economic Risk Consultancy, and the World Economic Forum. A minimum of three sources must assess a country for it to be included in the TI index.

The TI index reflects the views of observers from around the world, including experts living and working in the evaluated countries. For a variety of reasons, TI argues that its index, which is based on the perceptions of experts, is superior to other potential measures of public-sector corruption. Possible alternative measures include bribes reported, the number of prosecutions brought, and the number of successful court convictions of public-sector malefactors. These alternative measures are likely to indicate how effective the media, prosecutors, and courts are in

[25] Zupan (2015a).   [26] Transparency International (2015).
[27] Svensson (2005). The TI index is highly correlated with alternative cross-country measures of public-sector integrity such as the International Country Risk Guide and the Control of Corruption.

investigating and exposing corruption. They are less likely to reflect prevailing public-sector corruption levels.

As can be seen from the third column of Table 6.1, the perceived cleanliness of a country's public sector is 44 percent higher in democracies than autocracies – the average TI score is 47.8 in the former versus 33.1 in the latter. The lower accountability in autocratic government leads in a predictable fashion to greater government self-capture – at least to the degree government insiders hijacking power is reflected by the TI index. The result comports with the theoretical prediction that greater competition or accountability on the supply side of politics should enhance public-sector integrity and, therefore, lead to less corruption.[28]

Note some of the other implications of the findings in Table 6.1. The performance–reward relationship confronted by suppliers in political markets is the inverse of what we observe in private markets. Firms in private markets that better serve customers are rewarded with more business and greater profits. They also stay in business longer due to their superior service. The exact opposite occurs when we look at suppliers in political markets and compare autocracies with democracies. Specifically, the rulers who pay more attention to their own interests at the expense of the common good both profit more at the public's expense and stay in power longer.[29] They do so because the greater monopoly power on the supply side of politics in autocracies affords rulers greater leeway to pursue their own interests while heightening their incentive to cling to power.

The results of Table 6.1 further indicate that neither self-policing by political leaders nor formal institutional restraints successfully curb power or slack. They cannot perfectly align the actions of political leaders with the public interest. Consider autocracies that give rulers greater slack to pursue their interests and thus better reveal their virtue or lack thereof. A select few autocracies perform exceedingly well when it comes to the perceived integrity of their public sectors. For example, the 2014 TI scores for Singapore, the United Arab Emirates, Qatar, and Botswana are 84, 70, 69, and 63, respectively, and appreciably exceed the democratic average. However, these are rare exceptions to the norm. Only ten of the world's fifty-six autocracies scored higher on the 2014 TI index than the average of 47.8 achieved by democracies. James Madison's assertion that men are not angels is vindicated by Table 6.1 as is his call for imposing formal restraints,

---

[28] Rose-Ackerman (1978) and Shleifer and Vishny (1993).
[29] These results are consistent with those of prior studies. See, for example, Bueno de Mesquita and Smith (2011).

through constitutions, laws, and elections, to promote the accountability of public officials.

While markedly better than most autocracies, democracy does not fully align the behavior of public officials with the public interest, at least as this alignment is measured by the TI index. Although democracies outperform autocracies in terms of public-sector cleanliness, their average score of 47.8 is still below the midpoint of the TI scale. Of the 118 democracies evaluated by TI in 2014, only 2 (Denmark and New Zealand) scored above 90 on the TI public integrity scale; 10 scored at least 80; 23 scored 70 or higher; 33 scored 60 or better; and less than half (50) scored 50 or more and thus exceeded the midpoint of the TI scale. Moreover, over a quarter of all democracies (31) were more corrupt than the average autocracy.

A subtler but important point made by the results of Table 6.1 is that high turnover at the top rungs of power, such as fostered by democratic elections, still can be associated with deeply entrenched co-opting of the state by public officials below the highest levels of power. As previously noted, Italy has had a revolving door for its top government office (prime minister) since World War II. Notwithstanding forty-four changes in the position, Italy scored only 43 on the 2014 TI scale. The average tenure of the Greek prime minister since the end of a military dictatorship in 1974 has been under four years. Yet Greece posted the same lowly TI score of 43 in 2014 for public-sector cleanliness as Italy. Since 1934, Mexico's president has been limited to one six-year term. Notwithstanding the regular presidential turnover, Mexico posted a TI score of 35 in 2014, barely above the average registered by autocracies. These low TI scores where there is high turnover at the top rungs of power suggest that the electoral process proceeds while government insiders on lower rungs of power remain unaffected by the electoral process, and so insulated from the accountability to the public for whom they work.

Co-opting of the state by government insiders, at least as it is measured by TI, is also persistent over time. Consider the nations in Table 6.1 over a ten-year period. The correlation between nations' TI scores in 2014 and 2004 is 0.93.[30] What does this number mean? This is close to the highest possible value for such a correlation coefficient, meaning the degree of

---

[30] While TI began rating the perceived corruption of nations' public sectors in 1995, the initial index comprised only forty-one countries. The list grew to 146 countries by 2004 and 174 countries by 2014. Where a country with a TI measure for 2014 was not rated in 2004, the earliest year for which a rating became available after 2004 was used instead to tabulate the correlation results. In the case of 13 nations rated by TI in 2014 but for which a TI score is not available for 2004, a 2005 score is used instead; in seven cases a 2006 score

co-opting by public insiders in most countries is remarkably consistent over time. That is, a correlation coefficient can take a value as high as 1.0, which occurs when two variables move in perfect lockstep fashion. The lowest possible value for a correlation coefficient is −1.0. It occurs when two variables move in directly opposite ways. The correlation coefficient equals 0 when there is no relationship between two variables.

The correlation coefficient for countries' TI values between 2004 and 2014 is higher for democracies than for autocracies (0.94 versus 0.86), suggesting less change in the level of power co-opted in democracies. While this data initially might be surprising, further reflection suggests an explanation. Autocrats, after all, have greater power to influence the integrity of a nation's public sector – albeit for better or for worse. They also wield power for a significantly longer period of time. By comparison, democratic leaders have both less power and less time to shape the integrity of a nation's public sector. Consequently, although electoral competition is greater and political leadership tenure shorter, overall public-sector integrity is less responsive to a particular leader in democracies than in autocracies.

The influence of democratic political leadership on public-sector integrity can be for good or ill. Democracies such as Denmark, New Zealand, Finland, Sweden, Norway, and Switzerland remained at the top of the TI index between 2004 and 2014 notwithstanding relatively short average tenures (relative to autocrats) for their heads of state. On the other hand, the heads of state of democracies in Haiti, Paraguay, Papua New Guinea, and Kenya had similarly short average tenures, yet these countries remained mired in the bottom fifth of the TI index between 2004 and 2014. This underscores the point that democracy does not ensure government by the people really works for the people, even though democracy does represent an improvement over autocracy (on average) in holding top political leaders accountable and in promoting public-sector integrity.

As testament to democracy's positive overall influence on public-sector integrity, democracies evidenced nearly three times the rate of improvement in TI scores between 2004 and 2014 compared to autocracies. In addition, across all nations, the average TI score increased slightly from 2004 to 2014, suggesting a positive change in some global factors serving to increase public-sector accountability. For example, enhanced trade and ongoing improvements in communication, transportation, benchmarking,

is used. The tenor of the correlation results remains unchanged if only countries having TI scores for both 2004 and 2014 are examined.

and productivity have increased citizen mobility and public knowledge about the impacts of government policies. These developments also make it costlier for government insiders to hijack the state for their benefit.

The upward longitudinal trend in TI scores must be taken with a grain of salt given the short period of time over which the index has been compiled. Transparency International also has altered slightly its methodology over time and progressively increased the number of surveys on which its index is based.[31] At the least, the improvement in TI scores is consistent with a similar upward trend which has been observed over longer time periods in other measures of political and economic freedom across nations. These measures include Economic Freedom of the World, Index of Economic Freedom, Freedom House, and Polity. Over time, they have evidenced a movement toward greater liberty across the globe.[32]

Something not readily apparent from Table 6.1 is that a quasi-market still operates in both autocracies and democracies. Specifically, when one statistically examines regime duration across all nations as well as within just democracies or autocracies, regimes that improve public-sector integrity remain in power longer. Holding other factors constant, that is, changes in a nation's TI score positively influence the length of time a regime remains in power. The impact of public-sector performance on regime tenure is evidenced in both governance forms, but its magnitude and significance are greater for autocracies than democracies. However, the impact is present in both governance forms.[33] While autocracies ossify power more and foster greater public-sector corruption than do democracies, the quasi-market is still at work in both governance forms, limiting

---

[31] Since 2012, TI has relied on a 0–100 scale and draws only on the most recent year's data from each survey comprising its overall index. Prior to 2012, TI employed a 0–10 scale and drew on more than one year's worth of data from the component surveys. From 2012, furthermore, TI has used the raw scores from each of its component surveys. Before 2012, the TI index reflected the rank position of each country in each data source. In comparing nations' 2004 and 2014 TI scores, the 2004 scores are first converted to a 0–100 scale.

[32] See, for example, Zupan (2015a). Freedom House has rated countries' civil liberties and political rights annually since 1972. Economic Freedom of the World ratings of nations' economic freedom began in 1970. The Index of Economic Freedom has rated countries' economic freedom annually since 1995. Polity scores go back to 1800.

[33] Zupan (2015a, 2015b) analyzes the quasi-market in autocracies and democracies. The results for autocracies are consistent with the findings of Holcombe and Boudreaux (2013). Holcombe and Boudreaux examine the influence of economic free-dom measures (such as Economic Freedom of the World scores) on autocratic tenure. They find that while the explanatory power of their overall model is low (as measured by an adjusted R-squared that ranges from .03 to .12 on a 0–1 scale), increases in economic repressiveness reduce an autocrat's tenure.

what autocrats can get away with without being overthrown, and limiting the extent to which democratic leaders can co-opt the state if they wish to remain in office.

PERSPECTIVES TO BE GAINED ACROSS TIME AND PLACE

The foregoing data underscore the need to remain wary of the potential for inside jobs. They also provide room for optimism given that there has been a historical trend away from autocracy and toward democracy. The evidence in Table 6.1 suggests that this trend should be cheered due to the beneficial effects that democracy has, on average, on the accountability of public officials to their citizens and on public-sector integrity. Having now explored the interaction of variables in $P = G \times S \times I$, we can take a closer look at how some empires, states, and cities have declined over the course of time due to subversion from within by government insiders. Chapter 7 will tour salient examples. To balance any optimism warranted by the historic trend toward democracy, Chapters 8 and 9 will examine why government insiders in all forms of government remain a clear and present danger to the well-being of countries around the globe; these chapters do so by focusing on the world's two largest economies, autocratic China and the democratic United States, respectively. The case study on the United States in Chapter 9 illustrates why democracy is not enough to ensure government for the people.

7

Where and When Has the State Been
Co-Opted from Within?

History is replete with stories of the decline of mighty empires, states, and cities. On closer examination, their decline reveals the workings of inside jobs through which they were subverted from within by government insiders. This chapter provides several examples drawn from different centuries and different systems of government. We will start by looking at a few prominent autocracies, because this government form has been prevalent for a longer period of time and has regularly been co-opted by government insiders. The final examples in this chapter involve democratic cities and states in the United States, demonstrating the very real danger of inside jobs in leading democracies, including both at the subnational and the national level.

The examples of decline will illustrate how government insiders first precipitate a decline in a political entity's well-being and, then, exacerbate the decline by clinging to their power and its perks. Paradoxically, the motives, means, and opportunities which public officials have to co-opt the state increase as a state becomes more powerful (absent any counter-vailing institutional restraints). The motives of public officials can be ideological or pecuniary. They may reflect self-interest broadly defined (as argued by Khaldun) or reasons which are narrower or related to evolutionary biology, such as kin selection and reciprocal altruism (as noted by Fukuyama).[1] All of the examples attest to how the interest of public officials (I) in capitalizing on any slack in the relationship with their citizens (S) interacts with the prospective gains from co-opting the state (G) to determine the extent to which government insiders profit at the expense of the public interest (P). As encapsulated by our government self-capture equation, $P = G \times S \times I$.

---

[1] Fukuyama (2011, 2014) and Khaldun (2005).

One heartening trend, despite the co-opting effect of government insiders in autocracies and democracies, is the increase in democratic governments over the last two centuries. As seen in the preceding chapter, democracy improves the accountability of public officials and thereby increases public-sector integrity. So examples of democracy in this chapter also document the democratic trend at work and spell out the quasi-market forces behind it. Just as nation-states and autocratic Leviathans are typically superior to anarchy at promoting national well-being, democracy generally improves on autocracy. However, what is clear from the following examples of democracy is that, even where government is created and elected *by* the people, further governance improvements are needed to better ensure government works *for* the people. Contrary to Fukuyama's thesis in *The End of History*, liberal democracy cannot be the terminus if we seek to promote the common good.[2]

SETTING THE STAGE: THE SYSTEMATIC EVIDENCE

Before turning to the case studies, a review of the evidence on the influence of political-economic institutions on national well-being is in order. Factors in national well-being vary depending on scholarship, but usually include geography, culture, disease, ignorance, religion, natural resources, technology, international relations, vested interests, and institutions.[3] How these factors are influenced by, and contribute to, the decline of empires has long fascinated social scientists.

In *Why Nations Fail: The Origins of Power, Prosperity, and Poverty*, economist Daron Acemoglu and political scientist James Robinson argue that explanations for the decline of nations which are based solely on geography, climate, and natural resources fall short. For example, natural resources are, if anything, a curse: history shows that countries with more readily extractable natural resources are economically less productive and more prone to civil wars than resource-poor countries.[4]

Acemoglu and Robinson argue that national well-being is better explained by political and economic institutions and the interplay between them. The authors point to the extractive potential of these

---

[2] Fukuyama (1992).

[3] See, for example, Caplan (2006); Diamond (1997); Fukuyama (2011, 2014); Gibbon ([1776–1789] 1974); Hubbard and Kane (2013); Kennedy (1987); Khaldun (2005); Marx ([1867] 2009); Olson (1982); Sachs (2006); Toynbee ([1934–1961] 1989); and Weber ([1905] 2002).

[4] For more evidence, see Bueno de Mesquita and Smith (2011); and Warner and Sachs (2001).

institutions, working together, where citizens have insufficient "skin in the game," minimal incentives for innovation, as the force that precipitates national decline.[5] By contrast, non-extractive economic institutions drive prosperity through private property, competitive markets, an unbiased legal system, and the provision of basic public services promoting a level playing field and commerce. These non-extractive economic institutions are closely intertwined with inclusive political institutions. According to Acemoglu and Robinson, inclusive political institutions must be sufficiently centralized so as to enforce law and order, uphold property rights, and encourage commerce through providing basic public services. Beyond that, inclusive political institutions are pluralistic, distributing power broadly and subjecting it to checks and balances.

Acemoglu and Robinson's institution-based argument comports with the research on national well-being. Economist Gerald Scully, for example, examines per capita output growth rates and efficiency measures for 115 market-based nations over the twenty-year period from 1960 to1980. He finds that while measures of political and economic liberty are highly correlated, both positively influence countries' efficiency measures and growth rates. All else equal, open societies grow three times as quickly as, and use resources more efficiently than, states which extensively encroach on citizens' political and economic liberties.[6]

Other studies show that, at least at present levels, increases in state size reduce economic growth. James Gwartney, Randall Holcombe, and Robert Lawson find that real GDP growth in developed nations falls by 1 percentage point for every 10-percentage-point increase in public spending. They also find that secure systems of property rights which limit state encroachment are integral to GDP growth.[7]

William Niskanen estimates that US net after-tax income would be maximized if public spending accounted for 9–12 percent of GDP (exclusive of expenditures for national defense and net interest payments).[8] Gwartney, Holcombe, and Lawson similarly calculate that if public spending was 15 percent of GDP, the economic growth of developed democracies would be maximized. Currently, public spending averages over 50 percent of GDP in such nations, indicating that present-day democracies are not maximizing prosperity.[9]

---

[5] Acemoglu and Robinson (2012).   [6] Scully (1988).
[7] Gwartney, Holcombe, and Lawson (1998).   [8] Niskanen (2008).
[9] Gwartney, Holcombe, and Lawson (1998).

Looking across countries over the twenty-year period from 1975 to 1995, Bernard Heitger finds that secure private property rights and the rule of law significantly and positively influence economic well-being; these factors also foster the accumulation of physical and human capital.[10] Andrei Shleifer and Robert Vishny provide a compendium of studies showing the negative effect of the state's "grabbing hand" on national well-being. One of these studies analyzes European economic growth, as measured by the formation of cities, in the eight centuries before the Industrial Revolution; it concludes that European regions with more limited government evidenced greater economic growth.[11]

Over the past few decades, Economic Freedom of the World (EFW) and Index of Economic Freedom (IEF) have annually rated nations' economic freedom. The ratings are strongly and positively correlated with a variety of indicators, that is, average per capita income levels, per capita income of the poorest 10 percent, life expectancy, citizens' self-reported happiness measures, and the integrity of the political process.[12] Changes over time in countries' IEF scores are positively correlated with real per capita income growth. Over horizons of twenty, ten, or five years, countries with the most improved IEF scores realize higher real per capita GDP growth. For example, the quartile of countries with the most improved IEF scores during the period of 1995–2014 realized average annual real per capita GDP growth of 3.4 percent, compared to 1.5 percent growth for the quartile of countries with the least improved IEF scores.[13]

Studies consistently find a link between economic freedom measures and national well-being, yet the link between political freedom and growth is less regularly verified. Analyzing 100 countries over the period 1960–1990, economist Robert Barro finds that improvements in living standards, as measured by GDP and education, promote political freedom. Accounting for GDP and human capital levels, economic freedom spurs real GDP growth. Political freedom, however, has a more limited positive influence. At best, democracy enhances growth at low levels of political freedom but depresses it beyond moderate levels. Barro argues that this puzzling finding is due to special interests co-opting the state in established democracies at the expense of economic growth. He points to fast-growing countries with limited political freedom, such as Singapore, Saudi Arabia, and China, to

---

[10] Heitger (2004).   [11] DeLong and Shleifer (1993); and Shleifer and Vishny (1998).

[12] See, for example, Gwartney, Lawson, and Hall, Economic Freedom of the World (2013); and Miller, Kim, and Holmes, Index of Economic Freedom (2015).

[13] Miller, Kim, and Holmes (2015).

build a case for the centrality of economic freedom, not political freedom, in economic growth.[14]

Acemoglu and Robinson argue that, while it is possible under extractive institutions, economic growth is unsustainable. After toppling Tsar Nicholas II, the Soviet Union grew robustly because it had some catching up to do with other countries. This growth came from adopting advanced technologies and using central planning to allocate resources toward manufacturing and away from agriculture. The growth was unsustainable, however, due to factors related to low political-economic freedom, that is, weak incentives for innovation in the Soviet command-and-control system. Similarly, Acemoglu and Robinson argue, China's recent growth will be unsustainable without greater political-economic freedom.[15]

Analyzing 175 countries over a fifty-year period from 1960 to 2010, Acemoglu, Robinson, and two coauthors show that democracy increases a nation's per capita GDP by 20 percent over the long run. As a political institution, democracy promotes investment, education, economic reform, public good provision, and social tranquility while not constraining the growth of less-developed countries. However, democracy does more positively influence the growth of highly educated nations, as measured by secondary schooling rates.[16]

Research continues to show that the growth of the state's role in society proceeds at the expense of both economic freedom and national prosperity. Yet, studying the relationship between political freedom and economic growth poses some key analytical challenges which affect conclusions. While the period of time during which economic growth is measured affects data, so are the countries included in studies. Autocracies as a whole are more likely to manipulate reported growth rates in a manner that reflects favorably on their rulers, so their data do not provide credible comparisons among each other or to democracies. Moreover, the repressiveness of certain countries, such as the extreme situations in North Korea and Syria, can hinder as well as skew calculations of their political and economic freedom. In examining the rapid growth of certain autocratic states, appropriate account may or may not have consistently been made for resource endowments, such as oil, that have grown in market value, foreign aid, or changes in (as opposed to levels of) economic and political freedom.

---

[14] Barro (1996).   [15] Acemoglu and Robinson (2012).

[16] Acemoglu et al. (2014). The results contrast with those of Pritchett and Summers (2014), who show that governance changes from autocracy to democracy result in diminished economic growth. Pritchett and Summers, however, do not hold other factors constant and look at just the immediate, versus longer run, impact of transitions to democracy.

More challenging is determining which characteristics comprise measures of economic versus political freedom. For example, is the rule of law an economic freedom (as per Barro) or does it reflect political freedom (as Acemoglu and Robinson assert)? Can we disentangle the independent effects of political and economic freedom measures on economic growth given how highly correlated they are?[17] While the study by Acemoglu, Robinson, and two coauthors finds that democracy increases a nation's per capita GDP, their model does not include a separate measure of economic freedom as an explanatory variable.

Another difficulty in teasing apart economic and political freedoms when assessing their independent influence on national well-being involves the degree of inclusivity in political systems and whether it indirectly promotes economic growth. Economists Friedrich Hayek and Milton Friedman assert it does so through fostering economic inclusivity.[18] Economists Robert Lawson and J.R Clark find similar support for such an indirect relationship by examining nations' political and economic freedom measures over the period from 1970 to 2005. According to their examination, the Hayek–Friedman hypothesis is violated less than 10 percent of the time: it is that rare for countries with high political freedom to not have high economic freedom. Furthermore, Lawson and Clark find that from 1975 to 2005, the percentage of countries violating the Hayek–Friedman hypothesis steadily has declined from 20 to 2.4 percent.[19]

Such challenges in analysis notwithstanding, research generally shows that, as the state's role in society increases, national prosperity is compromised, notably with a correlative decrease in economic freedom as well. Economic freedom and political freedom are shown to be closely intertwined to the point that disentangling their independent influence on economic growth is difficult. The research also suggests that special interests foster government growth and extractive institutions. While the focus of research has tended to be on special interests from the demand side of politics, the following case studies illustrate that supply-side special interests cannot be ignored when explaining government growth and the decline of political freedom, economic freedom, and, existentially, political entities. The demise of many empires, cities, and states can be attributed to public officials pursuing their interests and exploiting slack in the relationship with their citizens so as to capture the prospective gains associated

---

[17] Zupan (2015a). The correlation coefficient is well over 0.5 depending on which particular measures are used.
[18] Friedman (1962) and Hayek (1944).   [19] Lawson and Clark (2010).

with an enlarged government and thereby profit at the public expense (that is, $P = G \times S \times I$).

ANCIENT EGYPT'S NEW KINGDOM

Examples of autocrats subverting the public interest are manifold in history. China's Ming dynasty, renowned for establishing centuries of stability and order after the collapse of Mongol rule, ultimately succumbed to the weight its policies thrust on the population, including taxes. The Mamluk and Ottoman sultanates, which initially achieved great success, were corroded from within by the self-serving policies of government insiders. Mobutu Sese Seko began as a champion against a horrific Belgian colonial power in the Congo, only to increasingly use the power that he captured for profligate enrichment of himself and his family and friends as dictator of the nation he renamed Zaire.

The ossifying and corrupting influence of autocratic power is also seen in other examples which have an archetypal cast of leaders, such as the Roman Empire, China's Han dynasty, the Venetian Republic, and Trujillo's family in the Dominican Republic.[20] After creating a vast empire, Alexander the Great of Macedon squandered much of his nation's wealth through reckless further military forays, lavish spending on vanity projects, and largesse bestowed on favorite government insiders and sycophants. For example, the cost of the funeral pyre Alexander commissioned for his closest companion Hephaestion was equal to the annual tax revenue collected by imperial Athens.[21]

One autocracy where the subversive role played by government insiders is noteworthy but less often popularly noted is ancient Egypt's New Kingdom. During the New Kingdom, which lasted from the sixteenth through the eleventh centuries BC, ancient Egypt achieved its greatest territorial reach and prosperity. Ruling over this regional ascendancy, the Kingdom's pharaohs spanned the 18th through 20th dynasties and included such storied names as Amenhotep IV, Hatshepsut, Nefertiti, Ramses II and III, Tutankhamun, and Thutmose III.[22]

Consistent with Khaldun's theory of the lifecycle of nations, however, the growth of the New Kingdom under the 18th dynasty resulted in

---

[20] See, for example, Acemoglu and Robinson (2012); Acemoglu, Robinson, and Verdier (2004); Fukuyama (2011, 2014); Hubbard and Kane (2013); and Shleifer and Vishny (1998).
[21] Holt (2016).   [22] See, for example, Kuhrt (1995) and Shaw (2003).

a sedentary civilization with a large public sector.[23] The pharaoh, deemed to be of divine lineage, oversaw the tribute to the gods which was facilitated by a sizable priesthood that eventually gained ownership of 30 percent of the Kingdom's lands. The cost of supporting the priests, in addition to the military, was daunting, and it contributed to the shift by Pharaoh Amenhotep IV from worshipping a pantheon of gods to a single sun god, Aten. To further reduce the influence of the established priests, Amenhotep changed his name to Akhenaten and moved the capital from Thebes to Tell-el-Amarna. Successors reversed the changes, however, and Akhenaten was discredited and nearly lost to history.[24] One could say that lower-level government insiders ultimately succeeded in reversing efforts to reduce the degree to which they had captured the political process to pursue their own fortune.

During the 19th dynasty, Ramses II, often called "Ramses the Great," pursued extensive military campaigns and public building programs, expanded government, and increased the Kingdom's costs. The army grew to over 100,000 during his reign. Although displaying personal bravery in battle, Ramses has been criticized for being an inept general due to his waging so many wars and his self-propagandizing; some even consider him unworthy of the title "the Great." History cannot miss his impact: over half of ancient Egypt's temples and palaces extant today are linked to him. He built more colossal statues of himself than any other pharaoh and even converted predecessors' statues and temples to himself, proclaiming his greatness and divine power by having his name prominently and deeply inscribed on them.[25]

Extending the reach of his own power through an expanding state, Ramses II also restored the priesthood's influence and eradicated evidence of Akhenaten's monotheism – and efforts to reduce the size and expense of the priesthood. The capital was moved from Thebes to the new Pi-Ramses (or "Domain of Ramses, Great in Victory"). Its area was dominated by huge temples and a vast personal residence, complete with a zoo. Ramses had himself deified on the 30th anniversary of his ascension to power and fathered over 150 children through various wives and concubines. The tomb he built for his sons in the Valley of the Kings is the largest funerary complex of ancient Egypt.[26]

After Ramses II's death, the New Kingdom lapsed into a decline, which Ramses III of the 20th dynasty sought to attenuate. However, Ramses III's extensive military campaigns drained Egypt's treasury. The fiscal problems

---

[23] Khaldun (2005).   [24] Kuhrt (1995) and Shaw (2003).   [25] Ibid.   [26] Ibid.

even led to history's first recorded labor strike when rations promised to royal tomb-builders failed to be provided. Civil unrest and public corruption intensified. Bickering among Ramses III's heirs over power added to the disorder. As the situation worsened, coupled with below-normal flooding of the Nile, the New Kingdom followed Khaldun's cycle of life and came to an end.[27]

In his poem Ozymandias (Greek for Ramses II), Percy Shelley, in poignantly observing the ultimate result of Ramses the Great's vainglorious propaganda, notes also what could be the epilogue to every storyline in the rise and fall of nations:[28]

> Two vast and trunkless legs of stone
> Stand in the desert. Near them, on the sand,
> Half sunk, a shattered visage lies, whose frown,
> And wrinkled lip, and sneer of cold command,
> Tell that its sculptor well those passions read
> Which yet survive, stamped on these lifeless things,
> The hand that mocked them and the heart that fed
> And on the pedestal these words appear:
> "My name is Ozymandias, king of kings;
> Look on my works, ye Mighty, and despair!"
> Nothing beside remains. Round the decay
> Of that colossal wreck, boundless and bare
> The lone and level sands stretch far away.

THE ANCIEN REGIME

Thirty centuries after the New Kingdom in Egypt, the Valois and Bourbon dynasties ruled France from the fifteenth century until 1789. A patchwork of taxes was collected based on locality and status. Clergy and nobility, members of the First and Second Estates, were largely exempt from taxes as were officers of the crown, judges, and soldiers. Of the clergy, for example, abbots and bishops were considered to be nobility and so required to contribute a grant to the crown only every five years; the grant's size was left up to the abbots and bishops to determine. While the clergy accounted for less than 0.4 percent of the French population in 1780, they owned 10 percent of the land. Meanwhile, peasants were required to pay taxes to the king as well as an annual tithe to the church.[29]

---

[27] Ibid.   [28] Shelley (2013).
[29] Acemoglu and Robinson (2012); Fukuyama (2011); Hibbert (1980); and Schama (1989).

The inequities in collecting taxes were compounded by the practice of selling public offices. This practice provided funds to the crown and cultivated support among the emerging bourgeoisie, but it also created a vested interest on the supply side of politics that would weaken the Bourbon dynasty. Most immediately, however, it diverted entrepreneurial talent toward rent-seeking and away from productive activities, reducing the benefits of innovation. Those who bought public office sought to limit competition to their revenue stream, and they sought more ways to extract rents from their positions (such as tax collections) as a return on their investment in gaining access to the supply-side opportunity.[30]

Bourbon King Louis XIV came to power in 1643 and ruled until 1715. His was a record-setting reign of seventy-two years compared to any major European country. Known as "the Sun King," Louis XIV took key steps to enhance the crown's power. He set a precedent of no longer consulting the Assembly of Notables, a body of nobles and clergy selected by previous kings. He banned private armies and compelled nobles to live in his opulent Versailles palace so that he could more easily monitor them. At levels below the nobility, Louis XIV abolished the local elections through which cities and towns formerly had exercised self-government. His reach extended into the realm of the church, too, at first restricting and then outlawing the practice of Protestantism.[31] The state under Louis XIV expanded its autocratic rule into all facets of political power and governance.

To increase wealth, Louis XIV promoted industry, albeit through state support and under government control. The tax system was rationalized and enhanced to better finance the costly royal court along with the state's large army and its many wars. The number of soldiers grew from 100,000 in 1661 to 400,000 in 1702. The state launched a "capitation" tax in 1695 that affected all citizens, including clergy and nobles who prior had escaped any sizable tax burden. A further tax on income and property, *le dixieme*, was levied in 1710 to support the military. Import tariffs were added to promote domestic industries and raise revenues.[32]

The ever-increasing tax revenues failed to keep pace with spending as the state under Louis XIV expanded. Even with financial restructurings, the crown's indebtedness grew in the eighteenth century. On his deathbed, presumably having learned a hard lesson, Louis XIV advised his heir not to follow his example of excessive military campaigns and encouraged him to

---

[30] Fukuyama (2011). [31] Acemoglu and Robinson (2012) and Fukuyama (2011).
[32] Ibid.

alleviate the tax burden of his subjects. The advice went unheeded. Under the reign of Louis XV spending on the Seven Years' War (1756–1763) added appreciably to the national debt as did his support for the American Revolution and his luxurious lifestyle, the latter following the wanton example set by his two predecessors. In 1749, following the example and not the counsel of Louis XIV, the state under Louis XV added a *vingtieme* (or one-twentieth) levy to the existing tax burden.[33]

Entrenched supply-side interests proved their staying power and bitterly opposed Louis XV's efforts to abolish the practice of selling political offices. Any measures he took had to be rolled back by his successor, Louis XVI. Other reforms sought by the crown to reduce competition for revenues from the same underlying economic pond met similar resistance. For example, efforts to abolish trade guilds and to keep landowners from earning rents through state grants succumbed to resistance from the incumbents in power. With many parties on the supply side of politics fishing the same pond, the state's expenses continued to exceed its tax revenues; slow growth exacerbated the decline.

Ultimately, the Bourbon's profligacy catalyzed a dramatic refusal by the Assembly of Notables to endorse fiscal reforms proposed by Louis XVI in 1789. It was a watershed moment for France, leading to a meeting of the Estates-General, which convened the even more powerful National Assembly which, in turn, proposed a new constitution and led to the French Revolution.[34] From its apex of power, monarchical France collapsed as the damage inflicted by its expanding state took down yet another empire as the quasi-market for political control lurched forward, rejecting the inefficiencies and autocracy of the incumbent regime. At this watershed moment at the end of the eighteenth century AD, autocracies began to give way to an entirely new political system with improved formal and informal institutions to reduce slack between public officials and citizens. It's as if the lyrics from La Marseillaise, the French national anthem, were ushering in a new government not only to replace the Bourbons but also to change the world:[35]

> With luxury and pride surrounded
> The vile insatiate despots dare,
> Their thirst of power and gold unbounded,
> To mete and vend the light and air!
> Like beasts of burden would they load us,
> Like gods would bid their slaves adore.

---

[33] Ibid.   [34] Ibid.   [35] https://en.wikipedia.org/wiki/La_Marseillaise.

AMERICAN CITIES AND STATES

The historical trend away from autocracy and toward democracy has diminished the ability of government insiders to hijack the state for their benefit. However, democracy does not eliminate the ability of public officials to capitalize on slack in the relationship with their citizens (S) to pursue their own interests (I) and to convert the prospective gains from co-opting the state (G) into their profit (P) at the expense of national well-being. The findings cited earlier about the influence of economic and political freedom on national well-being – and its decline – are corroborated by evidence from US states and cities.

Economist Steve Walters shows how US cities have gone boom and bust based on how extractive their political institutions are. For example, during the first two of Michael Curley's four mayoral terms, a period lasting from 1914 to 1923, per capita income growth in Boston lagged all other Northeastern cities. During the 1930s, when Curley served a third term, Boston's population fell by 1.3 percent while New York grew 7.6 percent, Minneapolis 6 percent, Atlanta 11 percent, and Detroit 3.5 percent.[36] Already people were moving elsewhere, voting with their feet to find opportunity which the Curley administration, whose corruption was legendary, could not foster without acting against its own interests.

During Curley's first three mayoral terms, Boston's property tax rate became the highest of any US city. By the time his mayoral reign was over, Boston's property tax rate was five times higher than when he started. Beyond hiking property taxes to pay for his expanding government, Curley encouraged bidders on public projects to add 5–10 percent in "mayoral overhead" that could be doled out to his supporters or used to underwrite his own luxurious lifestyle. Curley built a 21-room mansion, for example, soon after being elected mayor while earning a modest $10,000 annual salary. Dubbed the "Rascal King," Curley was convicted and imprisoned twice for fraud and is considered by historians to be one of the worst big-city mayors in the United States since 1800. His knavery has been memorialized through the so-called Curley effect, that is, the ability of government insiders to entrench and enrich themselves in office by imposing extractive political measures which drive out their political opponents.[37] In a sense, Michael Curley could be a poster child for the inside job in a democratic setting.

Steve Walters also offers a West Coast example of the Curley effect in San Francisco during the period from 1950 to 1975. Manufacturing employment

---

[36] Walters (2014).   [37] Glaeser and Shleifer (2005).

declined by 28 percent from 1947 to 1972. The homicide and total crime rate increased to twice the national average by the early 1970s. And the quality of the city's housing stock moved from being superior to the levels prevailing in other major cities in California such as Oakland, Los Angeles, and San Diego to inferior to the levels in such cities.[38] It is no surprise that people voted with their feet, and the city's population fell by 4 percent in the 1950s and a further 10 percent from 1960 to 1975. While San Francisco lost 35,000 residents just between 1955 and 1965, the city added over 1,500 employees to its payroll during that same time frame, and also increased per capita public spending by 80 percent in real terms. San Francisco financed the spending by more than doubling its effective property tax rate between 1950 and 1970.

In 1978, San Francisco's decline was reversed with the passage of Proposition 13, which was a grassroots initiative led by Howard Jarvis to do three things: cap property taxes at 1 percent of assessed values; roll back assessed values to less-inflated 1975 levels; and limit future annual increases in assessed values to 2 percent until the sale of a property at which point the assessed value would be adjusted to the market price. Opponents opposed its passage with predictions that Proposition 13 would destroy San Francisco, but the exact opposite happened. Population increased by 14 percent between 1980 and 2000, surpassing its 1950 peak. Inflation-adjusted tax revenues decreased for only three years but then grew due to the growing population and investment boom. By 1982, San Francisco was collecting 66 percent more in inflation-adjusted tax revenues, and it was doing so despite the lower property tax rates. From 1978 to 1982, the impact on the city's fiscal well-being was impressive by most measures. Building permit revenues rose 167 percent, sales tax revenues 39 percent, payroll tax revenues 177 percent, hotel tax revenues 204 percent, and business license tax revenues 446 percent. By 1982, Mayor Diane Feinstein was touring the United States touting San Francisco's $160 million surplus.[39]

Beyond cities, as Boston and San Francisco illustrate, states are confronted with the interplay of economic and political freedom and its effect on public well-being. US states with zero income tax are creating jobs at more than twice the rate of high-income-tax states. Between 2003 and 2013, the nine states with no personal income tax saw their nonfarm payroll employment grow by 9.9 percent, compared to 4.3 percent in the nine states with the highest personal income tax rates.[40] Populations shifted too, as citizens voted with their feet in response to the relative

---

[38] Walters (2014).   [39] Ibid.   [40] Laffer et al. (2014).

onerousness of state tax policies. Between 2003 and 2013, states with no personal income tax saw their population increase an average of 3.7 percent due to domestic net in-migration; meanwhile, the nine states with the highest personal income tax lost an average 2.0 percent of their population to net domestic out-migration. Moreover, the differences in migration and job creation patterns between states with zero income tax and high income tax are similar when looking at the last forty years or just the last decade.[41] A different study finds that bank performance is positively related to the economic freedom of the state in which a bank operates. Additionally, political connections (as measured by whether a bank is headquartered in a state where a member of the US Senate or House chairs a congressional banking committee) matter less to banks operating in states with greater economic freedom.[42]

THE RISE AND DECLINE OF THE EMPIRE STATE AND THE FLOWER/FLOUR CITY

The histories of Boston and San Francisco show that even in democracies government insiders profit at the public expense, although, unlike in autocracies, there tend to be stronger mechanisms such as electoral competition to promote their accountability. Now, a final case study focuses on the State of New York and Rochester, one of its largest cities, to show another example of how extractive political institutions undermine the public interest.

In 1790, New York State was not the most populous in the United States. It ranked fifth out of the eighteen states, and it accounted for 8.7 percent of the total US population. Rochester wasn't even on the proverbial map until 1811 when it boasted fifteen citizens. In 1817, it was incorporated as a village on the second try, the initial petition having been turned down due to opposition from neighboring communities.[43] But, Rochester is called the Flower City/Flour City because of its active economy, comprised of seed nurseries and flour mills – the latter on the Genesee River flowing through the town's center.

Water would prove to be a great asset for the city, as Rochester and New York's fortunes changed dramatically through a public investment in

---

[41] States' adoption of right-to-work laws has a similar positive impact on job growth and domestic in-migration.

[42] Gropper, Jahera, and Park (2015).

[43] See, for example, Johnson (1978) and McKelvey (1984).

commerce. Completed in 1825, the Erie Canal linked Albany, which sat on the Hudson River in eastern New York, with Buffalo, which was settled on Lake Erie in the far west of the State. The Erie Canal passed through Rochester along the way, reducing transportation costs by 90 percent. By connecting New York via Albany on the Hudson River with all the Great Lakes, the Erie Canal opened up the Midwest to the rest of the nation and the broader world. New York, which had trailed Philadelphia as America's most populous city until 1810, became "The" city in the United States. New York gained its reputation as "the Empire State" and Rochester became America's first major boom town.[44] The Canal's impact still is felt to this day as nearly 80 percent of upstate New York lives no more than 25 miles away.[45]

Rochester's rise to prominence was historic. By 1830, just five years after the Erie Canal opened, Rochester had become the nation's 19th largest city. It was 13th in 1840, after which the growth of railroads cut into some of its Canal-based competitive advantage. Yet the decline was not sizable, and Rochester remained among the twenty-five most populous US cities through 1940, ranking 22nd in 1930 and 23rd in 1940 with 325,000 residents.

In addition to fostering population growth and prosperity, the Erie Canal facilitated a cultural openness that contributed to the development of political rights, civil liberties, and civic-mindedness. In terms of prosperity, the in-migration carried by the Erie Canal included famed entrepreneurs who came from lowly circumstances and rose to prominence in Rochester in the nineteenth century with names that retain their prominence to this day. John Jacob Bausch and Henry Lomb co-started a major optical company bearing their names, Hiram Sibley was cofounder of Western Union, George Eastman founded Kodak, and Frank Gannett launched the newspaper giant Gannett Corporation.[46]

The entrepreneurial ethic was accompanied by other cultural values along the Erie Canal. Tocqueville spent considerable time in upstate New York and grew to appreciate what he saw there – Americans' penchant for an early breakfast and hard work as well as for volunteerism, equality, and civic engagement. Frederick Douglass and Susan B. Anthony, leading advocates for rights for blacks and women, respectively, called Rochester home. The city also was a hotbed for the Great Awakening spiritual revival that grew out of the industrialization, prosperity, and change induced by the Erie Canal.[47]

---

[44] Bernstein (2005).   [45] www.canals.ny.gov.   [46] Johnson (1978) and McKelvey (1984).
[47] Johnson (1978).

New York State's rise to prominence mirrors Rochester's through 1940. From 8.7 percent in 1790, New York's share of the total US population grew to a peak of 14.9 percent in 1830, notwithstanding several new states joining the union. Even though New York's population share then fell somewhat over the ensuing 100 years, its population remained as high as 10.2 percent of the overall US population in 1940, again, despite the addition of many new states.

For all the success that the Canal brought to Rochester and New York State in the 125 years after its completion, the story changed after World War II. At that time, Rochester's population began to fall in both relative and absolute terms. Although the metropolitan area declined to only 51st nationally in terms of residents by 2014, the city's population fell from 332,200 in 1950 (32nd place) to 210,983 in 2014 (103rd place). Rochester now has fewer residents than Hialeah, Florida; Boise, Idaho; Irving, Texas; and Glendale, Arizona. Other upstate New York cities such as Syracuse and Buffalo underwent a similar decline after World War II. New York State saw its share of the overall US population fall from 9.7 percent in 1950 to 6.2 percent in 2014. New York was surpassed in population by California in the 1960s and more recently by two states with no personal income taxes: Texas in 2000 and Florida in 2014.

The decline of Rochester and New York relative to other cities and states is not readily attributed to the demise of its august firms. Kodak's downward slide, for example, began in the mid-1980s, several decades after the fortunes of Rochester were already slipping. The city even managed to lose relative ground from 1950 to 1980 despite having a robust "Big Three" – that is, Xerox, Kodak, and Bausch and Lomb, along with other sizable area firms such as Canandaigua Wines (now Constellation Brands), Gannett, and Wegmans.

Rather, the timing of Rochester's decline and New York State's decline dovetails with the State becoming more politically extractive, to the benefit of government insiders and at the expense of the public interest. In 1919, New York enacted a personal income tax with an initial top rate at 3 percent on taxable income greater than $50,000 (that is, an income equal to nearly $700,000 in today's dollars). Over the ensuing decades, the top rate was increased while the level of taxable income at which it applied decreased. By 1934, the top rate had risen to 8 percent. In 1959, it was hiked to 10 percent on income greater than $15,000 (that is, an income equal to $125,000 in today's dollars). By 1961, the top rate grew to 14 percent and by 1975 to 15.375 percent, the latter 1975 rate now being applied to income greater than $25,000 (that is, an income equal to $113,000 in today's dollars). New York City entered the fray in 1966 by levying a municipal personal income tax of 2 percent in addition to the State tax. By 1976, the New York City rate had more than doubled to 4.3 percent.

As of 1950, the personal income tax has accounted for half of New York State's total tax revenue. Since the late 1980s, the top personal income tax rate has been reduced; nevertheless, after accounting for all taxes, including those on sales and property, New York's total state and local per capita tax burden on the public has continued to grow. For thirty years starting in the 1980s, the average annual growth in property taxes was 6 percent, double the average inflation rate. As of 2010, the median property tax paid by a New York homeowner ($4,090) was twice the national average ($2,043) and five of the fifteen highest taxing counties in the United States, in terms of median taxes levied per home, were in New York. While not one of the highest taxing counties, the median property tax paid per Rochester home in Monroe County was $4,045 in 2010 and equal to the State average. In 2011, a cap was imposed to limit annual property tax increases to the lower of 2 percent or the rate of inflation.

From the end of World War II, New York has been the nation's leading state in terms of total taxes levied. In 2011, New York's state and local per capita tax burden was $6,622 or 12.6 percent of per capita income – the highest percentage in the United States and nearly 30 percent higher than the average (9.8 percent) for all states. According to the Tax Foundation's 2015 assessment of overall business tax climate, New York ranks dead last due to its per capita income tax being second highest in the nation, sales tax rate 11th highest, and property tax rate fifth highest.[48]

These taxes are feeding multifarious government programs, with the majority spent on those who work on the Empire State's supply side. Public employees account for half of the State's expenditures and 70 percent of local spending. Since World War II, New York has consistently had a relatively large and well-paid state and local workforce. In 1950, for example, while New York accounted for 9.7 percent of the total US population, its shares of total local and state employment and payroll expenses compared to other states were 11.4 percent and 13.8 percent, respectively. Over the past half century, New York's public workforce has grown in absolute terms as well as relative to other states. By 2013, while New York State accounted for 6.2 percent of the US population, it claimed 7.5 percent and 9 percent of total state and local government employment and payroll, respectively.

---

[48] Tax Foundation (2015).

Besides many public employees, New York's political leaders also benefited from government growth. Nelson Rockefeller was the governor of New York from 1959 to 1973 and three-time US Republican presidential candidate. He was a leader on state and national stages. He also exemplifies the ideological benefits power affords. Rockefeller vastly increased the State's role in housing, welfare, education, the arts, the environment, and civil rights – often through public funding. Primary and secondary school aid quadrupled during his tenure. The State University of New York (SUNY) system grew from 29 to 72 campuses, becoming the nation's largest public university system; it now requires over $3 billion in annual state funding. Rockefeller used his clout to convert the University of Buffalo from private to public so that it could serve as a SUNY flagship campus.[49]

In giving a tour of Albany to Holland's Princess Beatrix, Rockefeller was dismayed by the impression made by the city. To remedy this, manifesting perhaps an autocrat's big vision while running a democratically elected government, Rockefeller began a mammoth public works project to house state offices that turned into the Rockefeller Empire State Plaza. The project, which he personally helped design, employed eminent domain to evict 9,000 working-class residents and decimated a shopping district. The colossus took a decade to complete. It included lavish spending on marble and other imported stones, and cost $2 billion ($13 billion in today's dollars).[50] Architectural critics derided the Rockefeller Plaza for epitomizing the International Power Style of the Fifties and mimicking fascist building projects. The site includes one of the world's largest buildings, the tallest skyscraper in upstate New York, and a building modeled after Pharaoh Hatshepsut's Temple in Egypt. There is also a gigantic, egg-shaped theater that many insist looks as if it was deposited by aliens.[51]

In addition to public building projects, many public policies during Rockefeller's tenure fueled his ideological goals and boosted his presidential ambitions, and diminished the well-being of New York's citizens. For example, expanding the SUNY system to nearly every one of the State's sixty-two counties was promoted as a way to make higher education accessible to all residents, but need-based scholarships would have been a cheaper and more effective means to do so. The State already had many private colleges and universities as well as community colleges which could have accommodated more students on need-based scholarships. In addition, the publicly funded SUNY system regressively redistributes income

---

[49] Smith (2014).   [50] Ibid.   [51] Ibid.

by providing reduced tuition ($6,470 per year as of 2016) to all in-state students regardless of financial means. This is because at most campuses the median family income of in-state students benefiting from SUNY's reduced tuition exceeds New York's median family income.

At the city level, nothing better demonstrates government insiders subverting the public interest than the Rochester Unified School District. When it comes to total expenditures and employment at the state and local government level, education is by far the largest category. For the school year from 2012 to 2013, the current expenditure per public elementary and secondary pupil was $20,333 in Rochester versus $19,552 for New York State and $10,705 for the United States overall. When one adds in capital and interest payments, the amount Rochester public schools spent per student during that same period ($23,937) exceeded the annual tuition charged by top area private schools, which cost between $10,000 and $20,000 depending on whether they are religious-based or not.

While spending on education seems laudable, 80 percent of such spending by the Rochester Unified School District is for employee salaries and benefits. The employee benefits are among the highest in the country, thanks to the apt work of the Rochester Teachers Association, a union led for thirty-five years by Adam Urbanski. Urbanski, who is also a vice president of the American Federation of Teachers, has been effective not only at the task of securing increased funding for the Rochester School District in real terms but also doing so despite declining student enrollments.[52] For example, the district's budget grew by more than 15 percent, from $694 million to $802 million, over the period from 2011 to 2016 while during the same time frame K-12 enrollments declined by over 10 percent, from 30,734 to 27,604 students.

The student outcomes associated with such largesse in public school spending have been mediocre at best. Only 51 percent of Rochester's public high school students graduate in four years; this rate is one of the lowest rates in the country.[53] The Rochester Unified school superintendent, Bolgen Vargas, resigned abruptly in October 2015. He had served as the district's permanent head for just over three years and objected to being stripped, by his supervising school board, of the ability to hire and fire the thirty top, nonunionized staff in the district. Historically, these positions

---

[52] Moe (2011).

[53] "Rochester Graduation Rate Up Slightly," *Democrat and Chronicle*, December 16, 2014. The figure is for the cohort entering high school in 2010 and meeting graduation requirements by August 2014.

had been some of the few over which superintendents had control; they had been exempt from what was seen as the restrictive hiring and firing rules stipulated by the collective bargaining agreements negotiated with the Rochester Teachers Association.[54] The Vargas resignation signaled a continued advance against merit-based performance anywhere in the Rochester school system.

Rochester now ranks fifth poorest of the nation's seventy-five largest metropolitan areas. The city's poor educational outcomes have contributed to Rochester's population shrinking by a third since 1960. The population exodus, as citizens have voted with their feet and moved to locations with better returns on educational investment, has diminished the city's tax base, downtown, sustainability, and sense of community while increasing sprawl and commutes. To reverse the trend, Rochester desperately needs better student education outcomes and that means confronting vested special interests entrenched on the supply side of the local political equation.

Until the grip of incumbent government interests is loosened, the relative decline of Rochester and New York State will continue. Ironically, the Erie Canal may now be one of those vested interests, as it requires $55 million annually in public funding, from the State's Thruway Authority, to cover its operating deficit.[55] Whether the investment is recouped through higher (net) taxes collected from the Canal's adjacent homes and businesses has not been examined.

The drag on the economy caused by a large public sector is sizable. Various efforts since 1950 to spur growth have failed to overcome it. Recently, START-UP NY is a program that eliminates state taxes for a decade for new or expanding firms, which operate in fields such as advanced materials and biotech and which partner with a public college or university. The prospect of $1.5 billion in state funding has been dangled, a la "The Hunger Games," in a competition between ten regional councils spanning the state which are composed of community leaders and whose objective it is to promote a compelling strategic plan for their region.[56]

These policies raise questions that challenge New York State's extractive and Visible Hand. By employing tax-free zones which are tied to public

---

[54] "Rochester Schools Chief Bolgen Vargas to Resign," *Democrat and Chronicle*, October 28, 2015.

[55] "State's Erie Canal an Expensive Relic," *Democrat and Chronicle*, August 16, 2015.

[56] "In 'Hunger Game,' State Regions Vie for $1.5B," *Democrat and Chronicle*, October 6, 2015.

colleges and universities in order to generate jobs, New York State raises the question of why such zones are applied only to specific politically selected industries partnering with public institutions. And, by investing public dollars based on regional council proposals, New York State is investing in communities through a political and not a market process, opening further potential for profit at the expense of the public. Yet it is the public which will fund this investment. Taxes will be levied on New Yorkers whose regional council representatives must then vie for their fair share. Okun's leaky bucket concept applies to this New York policy of community investment, just like any other tax and transfer policy, and the administrative costs and disincentive effects eventually will drag down the policy's net impact.[57]

THE SPREAD OF DEMOCRACY AND THE REASONS FOR THE PHENOMENON

These US cities and states highlight an operational problem in democracy, whose officials are elected *by* the people but do not always work *for* the people. This deficiency must be balanced against the fact that democracy has been gaining ground on autocracy for reasons already mentioned. Table 7.1 relies on the Polity ranking of countries on a scale of −10 (autocracy) to +10 (full democracy) over the period 1800–2010.[58] As shown, there has been a steady march toward democracy, albeit with reversals at two points. First, in the 1930s and 1940s the Great Depression gave rise to fascist and communist dictatorships; second, from the 1960s into the 1980s totalitarian states appeared during the Cold War and postcolonial and autocratic states emerged in Africa. Fukuyama notes that while there were no democracies prior to 1776, there were 3 in 1790 (France, Switzerland, and the United States) and 61 by 1990.[59] The percentage of the world's population living under democratic rule has similarly increased over the last two centuries.[60]

As we saw in the preceding chapter, public-sector integrity is lower in autocracies than in democracies. The associated cost grows as a nation

---

[57] Okun (1975).

[58] Marshall (2013). Polity ranks countries with populations over 500,000. Polity2 scores are used to tabulate the data in Table 7.1.

[59] Fukuyama's (1992) own work is based on Doyle (1983) and focuses on countries with over 1 million citizens which have a market economy, representative government, external sovereignty, and juridical rights.

[60] Roser (2015).

Table 7.1 *The rise of democracy: 1800–2010*

Year	Average Polity score (−10 = autocracy, +10 = full democracy)
1800	−7.43
1810	−6.80
1820	−6.74
1830	−5.73
1840	−5.20
1850	−3.95
1860	−3.44
1870	−2.33
1880	−1.09
1890	−0.81
1900	−0.74
1910	0.15
1920	1.80
1930	0.00
1940	−2.37
1950	−0.14
1960	−0.74
1970	−1.77
1980	−1.96
1990	0.58
2000	2.96
2010	3.83

Source: Marshall (2013).

becomes more productive through factors such as specialization, education, and trade. This increasing relative cost explains why quasi-market forces have encouraged a shift toward democracy, albeit often accompanied by violence. As Fukuyama notes, autocracy's costs are both social and economic.[61] The economic costs have been examined in detail already. Fukuyama describes the social costs as stemming from inappropriately recognizing citizens' rights and dignity. Both economic and social costs are likely to be higher when there are fewer restraints on the exercise of power. Such costs also are more likely to be higher when policy decisions are based on the whims, instincts, and information at the disposal of a smaller number of individuals rather than on broader and more open democratic dialogue and the "wisdom of crowds."[62] It is for this reason that Tocqueville observed that democracies even would be more reluctant to

---

[61] Fukuyama (1992).   [62] See, for example, Duhigg (2016) and Surowiecki (2004).

start a war.[63] Finally, as noted by Michael Sandel, autocratic rule gives less opportunity for citizens to engage in political discourse and decision making. So, by contrast, democracies better allow citizens to develop their moral muscle.[64]

Given the greater economic and social costs that autocracy imposes and its adverse impact on public-sector integrity, the trend toward democracy since 1800 is both understandable and heartening. Still, many autocracies continue to operate around the globe and there is no guarantee that the move toward democracy will not suffer reversals, as we saw in the 1930s and then again in the 1960s.

The next chapter turns to the world's largest autocracy (as measured by GDP), China, to explore what the future is likely to hold for the so-called Middle Kingdom absent further political and economic reforms. After that, a closer look at the world's largest democracy (as measured by GDP), the United States, will build on the democratic cases from this chapter and develop further the point that government *by* the people doesn't ensure government *for* the people. Gathering up lessons from all these case studies, we are moving toward an understanding needed to promoting improvements in governance by finding even better ways to keep political entities from being co-opted from within.

---

[63] Tocqueville ([1835–1840] 2003).   [64] Sandel (2009).

8

Government Insiders:
A Day of Reckoning for China?

The potential for autocrats to subvert the public interest is readily understood. The many examples include China under the rule of Mao Zedong from 1949 to 1976. As many as 40 million Chinese died over 1960–1962 directly due to Mao's statist policies, which he was able to enforce by hijacking the full power of the state to advance his ideology. One result was that while life expectancy in China was nearly fifty years before Mao's rise to power, it had fallen to under thirty years by 1960. The cause of such a staggering decline was underscored when, by 1965, in just five years, Chinese life expectancy had risen back to fifty-five years, according to economist Angus Deaton, "once Mao stopped killing people."[1]

Since Deng Xiaoping and his Communist Party began ushering in market reforms in the late 1970s, China has been a different story. The growth reflects the low economic level to which China had sunk under Mao. As we have seen with autocracies, there can be significant benefits to catching up to the rest of the world by liberalizing markets, adopting superior technologies from elsewhere in the world, allocating resources more efficiently (such as shifting labor away from agriculture and toward manufacturing), and investing in human capital through education. China under Deng has followed such policies and has become as big an economic growth phenomenon as Japan after World War II. China surpassed Germany as the world's third-largest economy in 2007 and moved ahead of Japan into second place in 2010. At current growth rates it will pass the United States as the top economy in terms of GDP in 2029. There are now prophesies similar to when Japan became the darling on the world's economic stage that China will own the world because of its superior model for organizing economic activity – a model that other nations

---

[1] Deaton (2013).

would be wise to adopt. Some pundits even claim that economics has more to learn from China than China has to learn from economics.[2]

Although China's development after Mao has been impressive, its economic growth mirrors the economic growth spurts achieved by some other nations over the past century, including Japan in the 1950s through 1980s; the Soviet Union from the 1920s to the 1960s; Germany and Italy during the 1930s; the so-called Asian Tigers (Korea, Hong Kong, Singapore, and Taiwan) between 1970 and 2000; and India since 1991.[3] So, while China's growth rate has been notable, especially since it is the world's most populous country, it parallels what some other countries have experienced over the past century. For example, between 1946 and the first oil shock of 1973–1974, Japan averaged an annual real GDP growth rate of 9 percent. The four Asian Tigers realized annual real GDP growth rates of 7 percent or more between 1970 and 2000. South Korea's real GDP grew 8.2 percent annually between 1980 and 2000. In the wake of economic reforms, India has averaged a 6.8 percent annual real GDP growth rate between 1992 and 2014. Its rate of 7.5 percent for 2015 exceeded China's. Contrary to enthusiasts who would have us believe China presents a superior model for the world to follow, China can look to models around the world and over time for important benchmarks on how to best further enhance economic prosperity and public well-being.

One model for China to avoid is that of the Soviet Union, which was also touted as a global super power when its national income grew by 6 percent per year over the period between 1928 and 1960. This represented one of the most rapid economic growth spurts for any country up until that point in time.[4] Nobel Prize–winning economist Paul Samuelson even predicted, in the 1961 edition of his leading textbook, that the economy of the Soviet Union would overtake that of the United States by 1997. Samuelson and many other learned Westerners were reluctant to question the veracity of the Soviet Union's productivity statistics, despite the knowledge that the Soviet economy remained only half of the size of that of the United States while the reported Soviet growth rate was double that being realized by the United States.[5]

Like these other countries growing rapidly, China faces challenges that are not unique among nations. While certain factors militate toward

---

[2] See, for example, "Why the 'China Model' Isn't Going Away," *The Atlantic*, March 21, 2013.
[3] Pritchett and Summers (2014).   [4] Acemoglu and Robinson (2012).
[5] Levy and Peart (2011).

China's ongoing growth, its economic development will be sustained only through further liberalization. Here the interplay between economic and political spheres will determine the outcome, for, as it does in any political setting, liberalization hinges on whether government insiders are willing to cede some degree of power and risk a diminishment in their perks, ideological and material, for the sake of the common good. In other words, can a nation where the inside job has progressed to the extreme represented by Mao continue to reverse its fortunes? Only if government insiders find ways to forego profit for personal gain (P) through diminishing the prospective gains from co-opting the state (G), reducing slack (S) so as to increase accountability to the public, and self-policing their own interest (I) in profiting at the public's expense ($P = G \times S \times I$).

THE CELESTIAL KINGDOM RISES AGAIN

China, which is also known as the Celestial Kingdom due to its ancient success, does offer an astounding profile in economic growth since the rule of Mao and the beginning of Deng's market-based reforms in the late 1970s. Between 1980 and 2011, China averaged an annual GDP increase of 10.2 percent.[6] Its economy doubled in size every seven years and its growth rate surpassed that of any other major nation, at least in duration, since World War II. A massive shift has occurred from its rural-agricultural base toward cities and industry. China has become both a major market for consumer and capital goods produced by Europe, Japan, and the United States and a major commodity buyer from Latin America, Africa, and the Middle East. In the process, the number of super-wealthy individuals as well as middle-class households has boomed. Millions of Chinese have been pulled out of poverty. Economist Ed Lazear notes that half of the people in the developing world lived on less than $1.25 a day in 1981. By 2011, only 17 percent had such a low standard of living. In China, the percentage of people falling below the $1.25/day threshold fell from 84 to 6 percent from 1981 to 2011.[7]

The average life expectancy in China has continued to increase in the wake of Deng's reforms, reaching 75.4 years in 2014.[8] China's urban population has risen to 700 million as of 2015. That is, it has quadrupled in just

---

[6] Ibid.

[7] Edward P. Lazear, "Want to Reduce Inequality? Consult China, Vietnam, and India," *Wall Street Journal*, March 31, 2015.

[8] CIA World Factbook (2015).

thirty-five years and now represents half of the total population whereas urban dwellers represented 20 percent of the total population in 1980. Over the next thirty-five years, the number of Chinese urban dwellers is expected to grow by 240 million people, increasing the urbanization rate to 75 percent.[9] The Organisation for Economic Co-Operation and Development (OECD) reports that China now has fifteen megacities, which have functional labor markets of over 10 million residents each. By contrast, there were no Chinese cities with more than 10 million residents in 1980 and only two had over 5 million. While the United States has ten cities with at least 1 million residents, China has over 160 as of 2015.[10]

Deng's economic reforms have also improved the wealth of the Chinese people. As recently as 2001, China had only one billionaire and ranked behind many other countries on the *Forbes* annual list of wealthiest individuals, for example, the United States with 269 individuals on the *Forbes* list, Germany with 28, Italy with 17, Canada with 16, and India with four. In 2015, however, China had 213 billionaires and trailed only the United States with its 536 billionaires in terms of superrich individuals.[11] Wealth has not been limited to the wealthiest Chinese. It has been estimated that Chinese middle-class households will account for $2.8 trillion in annual spending by 2020 – nearly half of the overall projected consumer spending of $6.2 trillion.[12] The number of urban households with middle-class annual incomes of $15,000–$33,000 is projected to be 59 percent by 2020, compared to just 8 percent in 2010.[13]

While China's economic growth has been astounding, the reasons for the growth are similar to those behind the rapid development achieved by the many other nations that have enjoyed historic growth spurts over the past century. Let's review the commonalities. First, productivity gains are associated with population shifts from rural to urban settings. Before Stalin began to consolidate his power in the 1920s, most Russians lived in rural settings. Stalin launched a series of five-year plans to promote industrialization. Implemented in a heavy-handed manner, the collectivization of agriculture along the way diminished output in that sector and resulted in famines, but Soviet industrial output grew at a healthy clip. A similar shift toward industry is seen in Japan after World War II, the Asian Tigers between 1970 and 2000, India since 1991, and Italy and Germany during the 1930s.[14] China's

---

[9] OECD (2015).   [10] Ibid.   [11] "The World's Billionaires," *Forbes*, March 2, 2015.
[12] Silverstein et al. (2012).   [13] Atsmon and Magni (2012).
[14] Acemoglu and Robinson (2012). Bloom, Canning, and Fink (2008) argue that urbanization cannot by itself promote economic well-being. While urbanization rates are an

expanded industrial output after Deng's reforms is a factor common to uncommon economic growth in benchmark economies.

Second, productivity improved after Deng's market-based reforms, which began with Chinese output at a nadir created by Mao's ideologically driven policies and totalitarian state. Under Mao, land had been nationalized and the market economy abolished. Industrialization efforts were modeled after Stalin's five-year plans, but they had far less success. Mao's Great Leap Forward in 1958 sought to achieve overly ambitious output targets. Harsh measures were used by government officials driven to meet implausible targets. Meanwhile, agricultural output was devastated by collectivization. The overall failure of these coercive government programs resulted in the execution or starvation of as many as 40 million Chinese people. Unlike in the Soviet case, per capita income fell due to Mao's economic repressiveness.[15]

Although partially discredited by the effects of the Great Leap Forward, Mao reasserted his hold on power through the Cultural Revolution, which lasted from 1966 to 1976. The Cultural Revolution took aim at any remaining capitalist and religious elements in China. Soldiers were dispatched to promote Mao-ism. Suspected opponents and bourgeoisie elements were jailed, killed, or sent to rural work-camps. People purged included largely intellectuals, who were defined as anyone with a secondary school education. The school system was closed. International trade was shunned.[16] Like the Great Leap Forward, the Cultural Revolution set China back at a cost of many lives. By the time Mao died in 1976, China's trade with the United States totaled $336 million, that is, 10 percent of trade between the United States and Taiwan. Yet, Taiwan's population was only 1.6 percent of that of China. Not only did output suffer from the Cultural Revolution. In 1982, less than 1 percent of China's workforce had a college education, 34 percent had only a primary school education, and 28 percent was illiterate or semi-illiterate.[17]

Deng's market-based reforms increased China's growth rate substantially, because the baseline was so low due to the effect of Mao's ideological policies and coercive repressiveness. This result is consistent with what happened in other nations, with the extensive scholarship showing that economic freedom promotes growth. The rapid development achieved by the four Asian Tigers from 1970 to 2000 aptly demonstrates the relationship.[18]

---

indicator of prosperity, changes in urbanization are not casually related to changes in countries' GDP growth rates.

[15] Kissinger (2011) and Zhang (2015).   [16] Kissinger (2011).   [17] Ibid.

[18] Coase and Wang (2012); and Lardy (2014).

One way economic freedom grew under Deng is that economic incentives were introduced. They first appeared as policies in the agricultural sector as collectivization and price controls were reduced. Also, state-owned enterprises (SOEs) were given greater freedom regarding output and pricing decisions. Even local governments, so-called township and village enterprises (TVEs), were permitted to launch ancillary ventures, the profits from which could supplement tax revenues. Of the net revenues generated by ancillary ventures, 70 percent had to be devoted to public purposes, while the remainder was left to be allocated at the discretion of the TVEs and their public overseers. In many other nations around the world such a profit-sharing arrangement quickly would be viewed as an opportunity for abuse by government insiders. However, in China under Deng the policy largely incentivized local officials to promote growth – albeit with the ability to capture some of the profits along the way.[19]

Economic freedom expanded in other ways as well. China under Deng became more open to foreign investment, technology, and trade, most notably through the creation of Special Enterprise Zones along the coast, where firms were granted greater autonomy and investors given added protections. Consumer goods were given priority over heavy industry. In the process, the private sector expanded during Deng's tenure to nearly 50 percent of GDP.[20]

Deng's successor, Jiang Zemin, served from 1989 to 2002, continuing to privatize SOEs and to expand opportunities for foreign investment in China. These actions further expanded the private sector's role in the Chinese economy, so that now the private sector accounts for 70 percent of China's GDP.[21] Zemin was also able to confront inefficiencies which follow where government insiders have operated without accountability to outside forces or scrutiny. He, like Deng, represented a quasi-market force, albeit one operating from within government, when he confronted the problem of industrial SOEs, which were losing money and represented a burden to the state and threatened the banking system due to their nonperforming loans. Zemin initiated a policy to "invigorate large [SOE] enterprises and loosen control over the small."[22] State-owned banks ceased offering "stability and unity loans" to SOEs after the 1997 Asian financial crisis. And, notwithstanding the disincentives associated with disturbing

---

[19] Fukuyama (2014).   [20] Coase and Wang (2012).

[21] Paulson (2015) and "China to Overhaul State Sector," *Wall Street Journal*, September 14, 2015.

[22] Zhang (2015).

the status quo, SOEs were openly criticized for their inefficiency during a "state-out and private-in" process. In 1988 alone, 20 million public employees were let go through the restructuring of SOEs.[23] Reforming an entrenched status quo among government insiders who had escaped Maoist ideological policies was now, again, having a painful impact on the public – no matter how needed the adjustments for eventual and greater well-being.

Economic freedom was even further promoted by tax reforms. Begun in 1994 under Zemin, the tax reforms sought to limit the ability of TVEs to generate profits. Doing so, it limited the opportunities for corruption by local officials and ensured that the central government received a larger share of the tax revenues.[24] In response to a primary complaint of the student protestors in Tiananmen Square in 1989 which involved corruption by government insiders, the tax reforms also encouraged local officials to foster economic development through private-sector means. This came at a cost, however, since the reforms enhanced the potential for inside jobs to occur at the central government level on account of the greater tax revenues flowing to Beijing.[25]

A third reason for the rise of China, like the nations before it, on the world stage was that Deng reversed how Mao's policies shuttered schools and castigated intellectuals. Instead, Deng sought to invest in human capital. In a developed, market-based economy such as the United States, human capital represents 75 percent of the nation's wealth, and education is a central mechanism to cultivate this asset. Accordingly, scientific, technological, and educational undertakings were integral to Deng's reforms. He insisted that "intellectuals are part of the working class" and eligible for Communist Party membership. Sizable investments were made in building up the educational sector. Thousands of students were sent abroad to study because Deng, who had participated as a young teen in a work-study program in France "to learn knowledge and truth from the West in order to save China," was fond of saying in his later life that "we have nothing to fear from Western education."[26]

Whereas enrollments at Chinese universities had fallen to less than 50,000 at the end of Mao's rule, they now total 25 million. Additionally, as of 2014, there were 460,000 Chinese students studying at universities outside of China, over half of whom (275,000) were attending US schools.

---

[23] Ibid. and Coase and Wang (2012).
[24] Ahmad, Keping, and Richardson (2015); and Wang (1998).   [25] Fukuyama (2014).
[26] Stewart (2001).

Postsecondary enrollments in US schools have increased fivefold since 2000. Chinese students account for 31 percent of international enrollments at US universities.[27]

Here, again, policies in China's growth mirror those in the development during periods already defined in Japan, the Soviet Union, and the Asian Tigers.[28] As of 2012, the percentage of citizens between twenty-five and sixty-four years of age with at least an associate's degree among these nations was 53 percent in Russia, 47 percent in Japan, and 42 percent in South Korea, compared to 43 percent in the United States and an average of 32 percent across the thirty-four developed, democratic nations in the OECD. In China, the number is 4 percent, proving policies hostile to growth can take generations to repair.[29] South Korea and China continue to gain ground on other nations when it comes to education. The proportion of China's college-age population which attends college has grown from 1.4 percent in 1978 to nearly 30 percent in 2015.[30] In South Korea, over 98 percent of college-age students now enroll in college.[31]

Fourth and last, like other nations investing in their prodigious growth, China's growth has been accompanied by sizable public investment in infrastructure, such as roads, other forms of transportation, industrial parks, housing, and so on. The infrastructure is designed to keep the economy humming, and investment in the infrastructure is a priority. It is promoted by the party's five-year plans but also, notably, an incentive system with political appointments and promotions being based on the economic growth which party members generate while in office.[32]

Like nations which have undergone historic growth in the century before it, not all of the effects of rapid growth bode well. How those problems have surfaced is more distinct to each circumstance. For example, China's debt in 2015 totaled $28 trillion or 280 percent of GDP (up from 150 percent in 2008). The growing debt has been fueled by local

[27] See, for example, Kissinger (2011); "Record 900,000 International students in U.S.: The Top Countries They Hail From," *csmonitor.com*; and "2015 Chinese College Graduates Employment Report," *People's Republic of China Ministry of Education*, July 20, 2015.
[28] See Goldin and Katz (2008) on the effect of education on economic growth.
[29] "Education at a Glance: OECD Indicators," OECD, September 11, 2013.
[30] UNESCO (2014).
[31] To ensure that South Korean high school students arrive on time to take their college entrance exams and are not distracted, rush hour is rescheduled, airports are closed, and the Seoul stock market opens late. See, for example, "High Performance, High Pressure in South Korea's Educational System," *ICEF Monitor*, January 23, 2014.
[32] Coase and Wang (2012); and Landry (2003).

governments, SOEs (including banks), construction firms, and property developers. Private household debt represents only 40 percent of GDP. Investment accounts for 50 percent of economic output, well above the levels that Japan and South Korea registered during their peak boom years.[33]

This debt and its related considerable investment spending represent a misallocation of capital which appears in the form of excessive office buildings. China had over 60 billion square feet of commercial real estate under development as of 2015, 120 times the total office space in greater New York City.[34] The drive to invest fueled by public policies in China has also led to stranger phenomena, too. Whole new highways and airports exist which have been little used. "Zombie" steel and cement factories remain in business due to loans from state-run banks. "Ghost cities" are fully constructed and waiting with vacant apartment buildings, office towers, and shopping malls. According to China's Academy of Macroeconomic Research, inefficient investment equaled $6.8 trillion between just 2009 and 2013.[35]

Due to the growth and heavy infrastructure investment, China consumes large amounts of commodities. It accounts for 12 percent of the world's oil consumption, 50 percent of coal purchases, 45 percent of steel sales, and up to half of all expenditures on base metals such as copper, nickel, and tin. The heavy reliance on coal to fuel China's growth generates its own adverse consequences. It is estimated that outdoor air pollution contributed to 1.2 million premature deaths in China as of 2010, roughly 40 percent of the global total.[36]

The reliance on public infrastructure investment mirrors the steps taken at high-growth periods in other countries. The fascist governments in the 1930s did so to rebound from the Great Depression. Mussolini is still remembered for promoting investments in infrastructure that made the trains in Italy run on time. Beyond spending profusely on armaments, Hitler's Nazi government invested heavily in Germany's transportation network, including the autobahns.

---

[33] "Coming Down to Earth," *The Economist*, April 18, 2015.
[34] "China Remains a Key Commodities Player Despite Waning Appetites," *Wall Street Journal*, March 31, 2015; and Joe Nocera, "The Man Who Got China Right," *New York Times*, August 25, 2015.
[35] "Why China Will Still Reach Its Target Growth Rate," *Wall Street Journal*, July 31, 2015; and "Zombie Factories Stalk the Sputtering Chinese Economy," *New York Times*, August 28, 2015.
[36] "Air Pollution Linked to 1.2 Million Premature Deaths in China," *New York Times*, April 2, 2013.

To date, China's uncommon growth has shown many commonalities with other nations that have grown dramatically. There have been significant gains in productivity. Economic freedom has been expanded broadly. Education and technological knowledge have been advancing. Infrastructure has been greatly enhanced. Yet, also, investment and debt as well as corruption and reform have generated many difficulties even as overall public well-being improves.

Especially when contrasted with the poverty and misery that prevailed when Mao and his political supporters exercised greater autocratic power to advance their ideological goals, an opportunity exists for China to learn from the post-Deng reform experience. Such learning would allow further gains in national well-being going forward. However, on account of the factors outlined in our government self-capture equation, real risks remain that the public interest will be subverted by those who operate on the supply side of politics in China. The prospective gains to Chinese government insiders from co-opting the state (G) continue to be sizable. There is considerable slack (S) in their relationship with citizens. And they have demonstrated an interest (I) to capitalize on that slack to pursue pecuniary and ideological profit (P) at the public's expense ($P = G \times S \times I$).

ONGOING DRIVERS OF GROWTH

A number of drivers should help sustain China's growth over the coming decades. Even among reasons for its growth thus far there is plenty of room for further catch-up. China's present urbanization rate of 51 percent falls substantially below the OECD average of 80 percent.[37] While incomes are improving, China's income per person is less than 15 percent of that in the United States. There is room for further industrialization that can improve income. Furthermore, public investment in education represents 4 percent of GDP in China and is significantly below the OECD average of 6.3 percent of GDP.[38] Recall the percentage of the Chinese population with a postsecondary degree is only 4 percent of twenty-five- to sixty-four-year-olds compared to an OECD average of 32 percent. There thus appears to be an opportunity for China to benefit from further investment in human capital.

Of course, more investment in education does not directly translate into better economic outcomes. The quality of the schooling and its ability to

---

[37] "China Wants Its People in Cities," *Bloomberg Businessweek*, March 20, 2014.
[38] "China Education," China Education Center Ltd., chinaeducenter.com/en/cedu.php.

enhance students' creativity and skills matter, as do the opportunities a society offers to apply an education productively. In fact, investment in education can be overdone. For example, the unemployment rate for college-educated South Koreans who are between twenty-five and thirty-four years old is 25 percent, among the highest in the OECD. And, nearly 25 percent of the employed graduates in South Korea report being over-qualified for their jobs – three times the OECD average.[39]

Another factor that may sustain China's growth is how Chinese culture values hard work. Diligence has been prized for centuries: Chinese literature and folklore abound with tales about farmers toiling on their crops even during holidays and about peasants working tirelessly on behalf of themselves, their families, and their communities. The Chinese work ethic has attracted the attention of visitors, too. It regularly was noted by nineteenth-century foreign missionaries. Pearl Buck, the daughter of missionaries, had a protagonist in *The Good Earth* who returns to toil in the field right after giving birth.[40] Carl Crow, an American who started the first Western advertising firm in Shanghai in the 1940s, noted in *The Chinese Are Like That*: "If it is true that the devil can only find work for idle hands, then China must be a place of very limited satanic activities."[41] Recent authors of Chinese descent such as Amy Chua and Amy Tan detail the Chinese trait of industriousness.[42]

The Chinese work ethic has a downside. As of 2014, the average Chinese worker logged 2,100 hours on the job compared to 1,770 hours for the average OECD worker.[43] The Chinese state media reports that 600,000 Chinese die annually from overwork or "occupational sudden death" – a term borrowed from the Japanese. Young, worried workaholics can even buy "pressure as big as a mountain" life insurance on Taobao, the Chinese version of eBay. In return for an annual $10 premium, the policy pays $80,000 to those who die from overwork in their twenties.[44]

On a positive note, the Chinese work ethic translates into entrepreneurial energy and activity provided political-economic institutions are conducive to such pursuits. After the state simplified the process for registering new companies and allowed entrepreneurs to use noncash assets as capital, the number of new private business ventures created in China rose to

---

[39] "High Performance, High Pressure in South Korea's Education System," *ICEF Monitor*, January 23, 2014.
[40] Buck (1931).   [41] Crow (1938).   [42] Chua (2011) and Putti et al. (1989).
[43] "Chinese Workers Should Work Less, Spend More, Report Says," *Wall Street Journal*, December 3, 2014.
[44] "The Asian Work Ethic Comes at a Price," *Financial Times*, March 4, 2014.

3.6 million in 2014, that is, a 46 percent increase over the prior year.[45] By contrast, 500,000 new ventures are created annually in the United States and the number has been falling in recent decades.

As reforms are instituted to align political activity with economic growth, China is tapping its cultural legacy of a well-educated, meritocratic bureaucracy dating back to the Qin and Han dynasties (BC 221–AD 220). Fukuyama notes the reestablishment of features of this legacy following Mao's death. In 1978, for example, a merit-based civil service exam was reintroduced. Further reforms in the 1990s and 2000s under Zemin increased competition for civil service posts, enhanced the importance of education as a prerequisite for public office, and instituted disciplinary measures for officials failing to fulfill their responsibilities.[46] Competitive entrance exams were also introduced for university admission. Presently, 1 million Chinese compete annually for 20,000 civil service positions. In terms of selectivity, the 2 percent acceptance rate bests the most elite US colleges (Stanford accepts 5.1 percent of all applicants); the Foreign Service (3 percent of applicants make it through all screens); and the US Navy Seals (of the 1,000 individuals who start training camp each year, 200–250 succeed).[47]

Daniel Bell, head of the Schwarzman Scholars program at Tsinghua University, notes the demanding requirements instituted by China after 1980 (that is, after Mao) for political appointments and promotions and how their rigor increases the higher the level of the post.[48] Town heads must be college educated and have served for two years at a deputy town level. Promotion to county level requires serving in at least two lower-level political capacities. Annually, the Communist Party's Organization Department reviews each higher-level official. The reviews are rigorous and have merit-based components, including 360-degree interviews with subordinates, peers, and supervisors; surveys to gauge the public's satisfaction level; and a vetting of the official's personal conduct.

The ability to serve as a public official is subject to continuous learning and improvement. To make it to the vice-minister level, officials must work their way up through town, county, department, and province assignments – a twenty-year process if one serves the minimum length of time at each level. Along the way, they are rotated through the civil service, SOEs, state-linked organizations such as universities and community groups, and through different regions of China. Supplemental

---

[45] "China's Newly Established Firms Surge 46 Percent in 2014," *Xinhua*, January 22, 2015.
[46] Fukuyama (2014).   [47] Ibid.   [48] Bell (2015).

training is provided by administrative schools and coursework at leading universities around the world, promoting the learning of best administrative practices. Advancement is highly competitive, and it is fair to say that the reforms begun in 1980 have promoted competition on the supply side of the political market. Out of 7 million party members, only 1 out of 140,000 makes it to the province/ministry level. The five to nine members who occupy the top positions of political power and those just below them who comprise the twenty-five-member Standing Committee of the Politburo typically will have been party secretaries or governors of two provinces, have passed a battery of evaluations and exams, and have acquired extensive and diverse administrative experiences.

Fukuyama notes other aspects of post-Mao China distinguishing it from other autocratic regimes. For example, the Constitution limits the president to serving no more than two consecutive five-year terms. In apparent accord with this limit, the last two presidents (Jiang Zemin and Hu Jintao) ceded power after serving for a decade. There are other limits imposed, such as mandatory retirement ages of sixty-eight for top leaders and sixty-five for senior-level officials; these generally have been observed in contrast to Mao's slogan that cadres should "work for the revolution with their last breath and last drop of blood."[49]

For all these external institutional restrictions, however, Fukuyama admits that empirical measures are lacking regarding the meritocracy of China's government compared to Western democracies. It is difficult to determine the extent to which Chinese political appointments are based on merit versus political clout and personal connections, or *guanxi*.[50] Meanwhile, the factors which have driven China's economic growth to date remain in motion, and its ingrained work ethic has been unleashed by the degree of economic freedom already available. As with other nations embarked on growth trajectories, China is in a position to continue to build on the successes it has achieved since 1980.

SEEDS OF DECAY

Despite the preceding drivers for further growth, there are reasons to expect a day of reckoning for China, especially if its reforms fail to promote economic and political freedom and curtail the self-interest of political

[49] "Q and A.: Francis Fukuyama on China's Political Development," *New York Times*, May 1, 2015.
[50] Ibid.

insiders. Economists Lant Pritchett and Larry Summers are agnostic as to the possible reasons for a growth slowdown. Instead, they point to reversion to the average as being economic growth's key feature.[51] Their analysis shows that growth is rarely persistent. Periods of rapid growth in developing nations are often punctuated by sharp drop-offs. They liken it to a baseball hitter with a hot streak who bats fifty points above his average in the last twenty at-bats. In such a case, one would be wise to forecast a return to the overall batting average over the next twenty at-bats rather than to bet on the hot streak continuing. Pritchett and Summers do admit, however, that three aspects of China make a sharp drop-off in growth more likely. These aspects are authoritarian rule, high levels of state intervention in the economy, and corruption.

JAPAN: A BENCHMARK FOR CHINA

Japan, having had tremendous economic growth from the 1950s to the 1980s that then sharply dropped off after 1990, illustrates what may await China without further market and political liberalization. Admittedly, Japan is a democracy, and the relative size of its government, at least in terms of spending, is low compared to other OECD countries as well as China. However, there are notable cultural similarities, such as respect for hard work and for education as well as a meritocratic approach to public bureaucracy. Japan made a similar transition from agriculture to industry, albeit several decades ahead of China. Japan also resembles China both in the extent to which the state has sought to manage the economy and in the lack of competition on the supply side of the political process.

In 1944, Friedrich Hayek presciently forecasted the general failure of command-and-control systems of government in *The Road to Serfdom*.[52] In 1992, Brian Reading similarly and aptly predicted in *Japan: The Coming Collapse* that the Japanese miracle would run aground because:[53]

[i]ts economic system was not capitalist with warts, but communist with beauty spots ... It is a controlled economy, by bureaucratic regulation, designed to eliminate competition for the benefit of powerful producer interests. It is virtually a one-party state, corrupt, paternalistic, and nepotistic, a neo-feudal system operated for the benefit of ... political and industrial dynasties, in which fear and greed dictate how unequal votes are cast in un-secret ballots to select politicians without policies. All are not equal under the law; barons of politics, business, and finance consider themselves to be above it.

---

[51] Pritchett and Summers (2014).   [52] Hayek (1944).   [53] Reading (1992), p. 5.

With the two brief exceptions, Japan's Liberal Democratic Party (LDP) has held power since its founding in 1955. From eight original political factions, four primary ones have produced prime ministers and vie for power within the LDP to this day. The Japanese government is a parliamentary system. The members of the lower house of the bicameral legislature or "Diet" appoint the prime minister. Half of all LDP Diet members are related to one another by blood or marriage. Roughly half are second-generation members who have a better than 50 percent chance of being elected on the first try due to their family's connections and resources.[54]

Securing and retaining public office in Japan is expensive. Between the costs of campaigning, maintaining an office, and giving suitable gifts to constituents and supporters for holidays and celebrations, the estimated annual expenses of being in the Diet are twenty times the after-tax salary associated with the office.[55] The expenses must be offset by other sources. Support for LDP members from demand-side interests is forthcoming because the government actively intervenes in the economy. The Ministry of International Trade and Industry, for example, was the architect of a robust industrial policy through the 1980s by providing protection from import competition, technological intelligence, a source of foreign exchange, assistance with mergers, and help in licensing foreign technology. The Ministry of Finance, long considered the most important bureau, has supervised banks and controlled fiscal, monetary, and foreign exchange policy.[56]

Since the economy's slowdown in the early 1990s, Japan's annual budget deficit has averaged 6 percent of GDP and has added appreciably to the public debt, which now totals 250 percent of GDP.[57] In the 1990s, Japan's public investment splurge focused on wasteful public work projects – such as the much-publicized "bridges to nowhere" – in pursuit of patronage. Since 2000, with Japan's generation of Baby Boomers beginning to retire, public spending on pension obligations and health care has risen. The social welfare spending is politically difficult to curtail given that the elderly are electorally active in Japan, much as they are in the United States.[58] The mushrooming nature of Japan's public debt in the wake of

---

[54] Ibid.   [55] Ibid.   [56] See, for example, Ito (1996); Reading (1992); and Smith (2015).
[57] "Japan's Debt Trap," *bloombergview.com*, September 24, 2014; "Public Finances: A World of Debt," *Financial Times*, January 6, 2015; and "Japan Government Takes On Its Deficit-Ridden Finances," *Wall Street Journal*, June 17, 2015. After accounting for state-owned assets, the net public debt is 140 percent of GDP.
[58] Ibid.

the slowdown in the nation's economic growth has some parallels in present-day China. China's rapidly rising public debt is being driven by excessive public investment. And China faces an aging population with the associated prospect of rising social welfare costs.

Japan has been notorious for "Japan Inc.," the iron triangle alliance between managers, bureaucrats, and politicians. The alliance impedes corporate governance, allowing managers to run their firms more as their private fiefdoms while benefiting lifetime employees and support- ing government insiders.[59] A symbiotic relationship also favors farm interests and government insiders. Farmer-friendly policies, however, harm the Japanese public through the taxes required to underwrite agricultural subsidies as well as through high relative food and housing costs. High food costs result both from land-use policies impeding the development of larger-scale farms and from the protectionist trade policies that shield Japanese farmers from import competition. The tariff rates on rice, butter, and sugar imports are 778, 360, and 328 percent, respectively.[60]

Public policies which protect small farmers also lead to higher housing costs for the population at large. Metropolitan Tokyo, home to 37 million people and the world's most expensive city, still has 20,900 acres of farmland (4,000 in the central city) where one can see weekend farmers raising cabbages and grapes. A mix of policies create this unusual situation, includ- ing farmland being taxed at one-tenth the rate of other land, being not as readily transferable as other property, and being held off the market so as to avoid the hefty taxes levied at the time of sale.[61] Like any entrenched policy which favors the incumbents in power, the vise-grip of farm interests has been hard to undo given their symbiotic links to the LDP and the Ministry of Agriculture. Farmers collectively wield influence through cooperatives, called Japan Agriculture, that employ 240,000 staff around the country and arguably represent Japan's most powerful lobby.[62]

Not surprisingly, housing is expensive and, with space at a premium, claustrophobic. It has a strong impact on society. The average age until first marriage in Japan exceeds that of the United States by 2.5 years for males and three years for females. Moreover, the fertility rate has been falling and Japan's population declining. These trends threaten to exacerbate the nation's public debt problem, for there will be fewer younger workers supporting, through their taxes, the social welfare obligations promised

---

[59] "Abe Topples Japan Inc.," *Wall Street Journal*, June 3, 2015.
[60] "Field Work," *The Economist*, April 13, 2013.   [61] Ibid.   [62] Ibid.

to a growing number of retirees. The impact of these policies thus will have an effect for generations. The policies are the result of government insiders operating symbiotically with special interests on the demand side of Japanese politics to profit at the public's expense.

POLICIES AND GROWTH IN CHINA'S FUTURE

The parallels between the state's role in Japan and in China suggest why China is likely to experience a decline in its growth rate. Government insiders are even more influential in China now than they had become in Japan prior to its economic collapse in the early 1990s. Reliance on public investment to sustain economic activity is much greater in China than it was in Japan either during its peak growth years or in the decade following its economic collapse (a period known as Japan's "Lost Decade"). China's current levels of total and net public debt relative to GDP surpass those in Japan at that time.[63] Ruchir Sharma, head of emerging markets and global macroeconomics at Morgan Stanley, notes: "No emerging nation in recorded history has ever tacked on debt at such a furious pace as China since 2008, and a rapid increase in debt is the single most reliable predictor of economic slowdowns and financial crisis."[64]

Another indicator of ossification in the Chinese economy is that wealth has become increasingly concentrated in the Chinese ruling class. Of the 1,271 richest people in the country in 2015, 203, or more than one in seven, are delegates to the Chinese parliament or its advisory body. The delegates' combined net worth is $500 billion. The eighteen wealthiest delegates have assets which exceed the combined wealth of all 535 members of the US Congress, President Obama and his cabinet, and all nine members of the Supreme Court.[65]

More troubling than even the debt and income distribution, which signals government insiders may be gaining ground after learning to work in a new system, is backsliding in reforms that fueled economic growth in the first place. After two decades of privatization by Deng and Zemin, Hu Jintao ascended to party general secretary in 2002. During Hu's administration, the market became regarded as a problem, so policies were

---

[63] "Coming Down to Earth," *The Economist*, April 18, 2015.
[64] Ruchir Sharma, "A Global Recession May Be Brewing in China," *Wall Street Journal*, September 14, 2015.
[65] "Billionaire Lawmakers Ensure the Rich Are Represented in China's Legislature," *New York Times*, March 3, 2015.

introduced to "perfect the market."[66] The National Development and Reform Commission (NDRC) was broadly empowered to allocate resources, even at the local government level. After the global financial crisis of 2007–2009, the NDRC began focusing on building up "the 10 big industries" deemed to be the capital-intensive backbone of the economy, for example, energy, minerals, banking, transport, telecommunications, electric power, chemicals, and machinery. This led to overcapacity problems in these sectors at the expense of others.

The Chinese solar energy industry was a prime example of public overinvestment through bank loans and local government grants of land and financial subsidies. State-run banks pumped billions of dollars into solar-panel manufacturing, creating hundreds of new factories and making China the world's leading producer. Predictably, prices in the industry plummeted, firms suffered large losses, and many companies, such as market leader Suntech, went bankrupt.[67]

Hu also reversed Zemin's policy of "state-out and private-in" to "private-out and state-in." Officials promoted the growth of SOEs, especially those in energy and steel, at the expense of private firms through discriminatory market access, financing, and taxation. SOEs were encouraged to take over private competitors. At times, the policies used involved coercion, such as the arrest and sentencing of owners of competing private enterprises for "stealing state assets."[68]

Hu, like Deng and Zemin, was faced with the inefficiencies of the SOEs. The State Asset Supervision and Administrative Commission (SASAC) had been established to reform them. However, when SASAC was launched in 2003, the bureaucrats at its helm sought to make SOEs bigger and stronger. Large amounts of stimulus funds and loans were injected into the SOEs by not only local governments but also the four state-owned banks commanding China's financial sector. Li Rongrong, head of SASAC from 2003 to 2010, stated that SOEs are "the oldest son of the People's Republic," and thus are entitled to special privileges, including the ability to exclude private competitors.[69]

The effects of Hu's promotion of SOEs have been profound. While no Chinese SOEs were on the *Fortune* Global 500 list in 1980, by 2014 there were 76. China's largest SOE, Sinopec Group, claimed the number 2 position. China National Petroleum came in at number 4. State Grid

---

[66] Fukuyama (2014); Shambaugh (2016); and Zhang (2015).
[67] "Suntech's Bankruptcy: Beyond Profit," *The Economist*, March 21, 2013.
[68] Zhang (2015).   [69] Ibid.

ranked at number 7.[70] The average Chinese SOE now employs five times as many workers, produces eight times the output, and has fifteen times the assets of the average private firm.[71]

Despite the appreciable state support and their impressive size, SOEs remain highly inefficient. As of 2013, 25 percent of China's SOEs were losing money compared to 8 percent of their private peers. The debt-to-asset ratio for SOEs was 62 percent compared to 53 percent for their private counterparts. The average return on equity for SOEs was 12 percent while for their private peers it was 26 percent.[72] Only fifty-four companies on the *Fortune* Global 500 list in 2014 lost money, and sixteen of them were Chinese.[73] Every one of these was an SOE. Notwithstanding the glaring inefficiencies, Xi Jinping, who succeeded Hu Jintao as party general secretary in 2012, continues to rely on centralized political power for any large-scale economic restructuring.[74]

While the SOEs enjoy protected monopoly or oligopoly positions at home, they not surprisingly struggle outside of China. Still, they operate in close relation to China's rulers and represent a potent vested interest on the supply side of China's political system. Any discipline which China's rulers and bureaucrats exert on them to improve efficiency is attenuated by political interests and objectives behind their sustenance and growth. Economist Harry Broadman notes:[75]

The dirty little secret in China . . . is that the four [principal and state-owned] banks have been technically insolvent for much of the past two decades, with the government bailing them out several times over that period with huge infusions of foreign exchange. It is only a bit of an exaggeration to say that China's state-owned banks pretend to lend money to the SOEs, and the SOEs pretend to pay back the banks.

Fukuyama argues that China's key challenge is the "bad emperor" problem.[76] As an autocratic system, it faces the opportunity and threat that autocrats can more rapidly and decisively shape the public sector's integrity. And China faces the dilemma that the success of authoritarian

---

[70] "The Fortune Global 500," *Fortune.com*, July 22, 2015.
[71] Harry G. Broadman, "Are China's Chickens Finally Coming Home to Roost?," *forbes.com*, July 31, 2015.
[72] "China to Overhaul State Sector," *Wall Street Journal*, September 14, 2015.
[73] "The Fortune Global 500," *Fortune.com*, July 22, 2015.
[74] "China to Overhaul State Sector," *Wall Street Journal*, September 14, 2015; and Shambaugh (2016).
[75] Harry G. Broadman, "Are China's Chickens Finally Coming Home to Roost?," *Forbes.com*, July 31, 2015.
[76] Fukuyama (2014).

systems depends on being able to generate a steady supply of good leaders. On average, autocracies fail to deliver on this score relative to democracies. This is due to the tendency toward government self-capture, whereby government insiders on the supply side of the political process succumb to their interest (I) in using power for personal ideological or pecuniary goals – coupled with the greater slack (S) and prospective gains (G) from co-opting the state in an autocracy. Mao and his policies illustrate China's bad emperor problem. The extent to which government insiders – leaders as well as their comrades below the top power rungs – perceive that their status, ideologies, and wealth hinge on maintaining authoritarian rule is the extent to which China will be unable to overcome its bad emperor problem.

Moreover, as long as the state continues to play such a central role in China's economy, reform efforts to eradicate corruption will at best flail at the symptoms of the problem instead of address the root cause. This is because the power of vested interests will outweigh any effort at real transformation. Whether truly aimed at rooting out malfeasance or just a well-masked effort to consolidate power, Xi's anticorruption campaign nevertheless must confront the drag which any monopolistic state exerts on economic performance. Xi's campaign thus is likely to fail. Cracking down on manifestations of wealth such as overflowing banquet tables, golf, fine liquor and tobacco, and mansions will be a Sisyphean task so long as so much of China's wealth remains aggrandized in autocratic hands.[77]

Beyond the party's influence on the market, its political repressiveness limits other freedoms and restricts the dignity and respect accorded to citizens. This does not bode well for an open dialogue regarding the best use of China's economic resources. Neither does it bode well for fostering the independence of thought and creativity vital to the entrepreneurship central to its growth.[78] Since taking power, Xi has taken steps which suggest less liberalization and reduced economic freedoms by consolidating political power. He has further centralized his own power through taking on a wide range of leadership positions himself while restricting

---

[77] David Shambaugh, "The Coming Chinese Crackup," *Wall Street Journal*, March 7–8, 2015; and "China Cracks Down on Golf, the 'Sport for Millionaires'," *New York Times*, September 10, 2015.

[78] Shambaugh (2016) notes that while the Chinese government has sought to promote innovation from the top–down and, to a lesser degree, from the bottom–up, it continues to severely restrict innovation from the outside in through blocking access to the Internet, foreign search engines, and most international media, as well as through failing to promote an education system based on critical thinking and freedom of thought.

ideological discourse so as to promote the unity and authority of the party. Beyond serving as general secretary and president, Xi leads the Central Military and National Security Commissions and steering committees on overall reform, military reform, and the Internet.[79] From this more powerful position, Xi has championed a more assertive foreign policy leading to disputes with neighboring Vietnam and Japan. He has touted the "Chinese Dream" of a strong nation with a strong military confident of its value system and political structure. He has further asserted China's regional leadership by criticizing the United States' role in Asia and calling on Asian countries to take care of matters on their own, without US involvement.

Despite relaxing China's one-child policy and abolishing the system of "re-education through labor," Xi is more conservative than preceding presidents regarding political and personal liberties. Internet restrictions have increased. Coverage of topics such as human rights and constitutional democracy in educational materials has been forbidden. Dissidents have been regularly arrested and detained.[80] In the wake of a sharp sell-off on Chinese stock markets in mid-2015, the party-run media largely was silent while Wang Xiaolu, a reporter for the top business magazine *Caijing*, was arrested and forced to apologize publicly on state television for writing that authorities planned to scale back their intervention in markets.[81] Chinese police meanwhile took certain prominent financiers into custody and combed through the records of others for evidence of short-selling. The official newspaper of China's state banks, *Financial News*, ran an editorial blaming foreign investment banks such as Goldman Sachs and Morgan Stanley for precipitating the sell-off.[82]

While China may still make its now-lowered annual growth rate target of 6.5 percent over the near term, the accomplishment is likely to involve further capital misallocations toward wasteful local projects and bloated SOEs. Furthermore, given that the party both sets the growth targets and reports the economic data, there is widespread skepticism about the validity of the data by independent analysts.[83] The approach calls to mind the

[79] See, for example, "Rise of the False Reformers," *Bloomberg.com*, September 4, 2014.
[80] Shambaugh (2016).
[81] "China's Response to Stock Plunge Rattles Traders," *New York Times*, September 10, 2015.
[82] "China's Party-Run Media Is Silent on Market Mayhem," *New York Times*, August 25, 2015.
[83] "For All Its Heft, China's Economy Is a Black Box," *Wall Street Journal*, September 25, 2015.

joke circulating in Poland under communism that while "the future is certain, the past is always changing."

Peking University economist Weiying Zhang was a key intellectual behind Deng's reforms. In a political environment growing ever more repressive, Zhang has courageously identified traps that China must avoid to ensure its continued prosperity. These traps echo with lessons learned across centuries with other autocracies where government insiders subverted the public interest. Zhang cautions fellow Chinese citizens and the Chinese government leadership against believing that China's economic success comes from having a unique economic model; that economic liberalization can continue without political reform; that the status quo is good for vested interests; that SOEs are the cornerstone of the Communist Party's ruling power; that power comes from the barrel of a gun; and, most pointedly for the premise of this book, that an unlimited government is stronger than a limited government.[84]

---

[84] Zhang (2015).

9

Government Insiders:
A Day of Reckoning for the United States?

Autocracies with their concentrated powers are more likely to succumb to capture by government insiders, and some like China under Mao have gone to the extreme of that capture. However, democracies are not immune to the disease. Inside jobs occur in democracies despite the safeguards they rely on, particularly at higher levels of political power, to guard against the outcome. The three principal safeguards are electoral competition, rule of law, and accountability.[1]

The vulnerability of these safeguards when it comes to ensuring public-sector integrity is evident in many democracies around the globe. For example, Ecuador has had fourteen different presidents since a military junta relinquished power in 1979, that is, its electoral competition is quite strong and, in theory, the slack between the people and their public officials is low. Yet, Ecuador's judicial system is plagued by delays and inconsistent and seemingly capricious rulings that undermine the rule of law and deter foreign investment. In 2011, for example, an $18 billion judgment against Chevron for pollution contrasted sharply with the government's attestations, a decade prior, to the soundness of the company's environmental remediation.[2] Ecuador achieved a score of only 33 in the 2014 Transparency International (TI) rankings for public-sector integrity, below the average autocratic score of 33.1.

The top post of prime minister in democratic Papua New Guinea (PNG) has changed hands fourteen times since it became independent in 1975 from Australia, so electoral competition is high. Yet, the country scored a lowly 25 on the 2014 TI ratings for public-sector cleanliness. Whether due to cultural reasons or ineffective constitutional and legal safeguards,

---

[1] Fukuyama (2011, 2014).
[2] "Ecuador Court Upholds $8.6 Billion Ruling Against Chevron," *cnn.com*, January 4, 2012.

top PNG officials have not been held accountable for corruption. In 2014, when Prime Minister Peter O'Neill was charged with corruption by an independent task force, he disbanded the task force and fired the attorney general, police commissioner, and deputy police commissioner who were seeking to enforce the charges and arrest O'Neill. Neither PNG laws nor press or protest overcame O'Neill's hold on power.[3]

While blessed with stronger rule of law and political accountability than democracies such as Ecuador and PNG, the United States cannot take its democratic institutions and future prosperity for granted as power becomes more concentrated in the state. As noted before, while members of Congress are subject to electoral competition, they have grown more insulated in office over the last several decades and thus less accountable to the public interest. Beyond the spread of careerism in Congress, the monopoly power of public employees has grown in the United States. Beyond just their sheer numbers, public employees are now a mature and established interest group on the supply side of politics. Individually and as a group, they have become more willing and adept at promoting their agenda with their direct managers as well as with the general electorate. This is the case even when their interests do not align favorably with the public interest.

This chapter focuses on two negative effects of the growth in the state vis-à-vis the monopoly power of public employees in the United States: their unfunded pension and health-care liabilities continue to increase, and deficient K-12 public school outcomes continue to affect new generations of Americans. If unaddressed, the root cause of these effects threatens the republic's viability.

PUBLIC WORKERS' INCREASING MONOPOLY POWER: ITS PERKS AND CONSEQUENCES

As of 2009, there were more members of public-sector unions (7.9 million) than private-sector unions (7.4 million) for the first time in US history. Unionization rates in these two sectors, moreover, have evidenced a classic tale of two cities. As noted earlier, the percentage of nonagricultural workers in the private sector who are union members has plummeted from 38 percent in the early 1950s to less than 7 percent today. By contrast, over

---

[3] "Peter O'Neill Sacks Top PNG Policeman and Shuts Down Corruption Watchdog," *theguardian.com*, June 18, 2014.

the same period, public-sector membership has skyrocketed from 10 percent to 36 percent.

Of the 23.5 million public workers in the United States as of 2015, 18 percent work at the federal level either as civilians or in the military. An estimated 63 percent of federal workers are unionized.[4] That level increased markedly after President John F. Kennedy issued an executive order in 1962 recognizing the right of federal employees to collectively bargain. Kennedy promised to support such a right during the closely contested presidential campaign of 1960 as a way to garner the support of federal employees. Their votes proved critical to his electoral success.[5] Kennedy's executive order represented a breakthrough for federal workers, because the 1935 Wagner Act banned the recognition of unions as formal bargaining units. Although they are still not permitted to strike as per the 1947 Taft–Hartley Act, Kennedy's order enhanced federal workers' political clout. Among other provisions, the order forbade government agencies (unlike private businesses) to campaign against unions and to fire or otherwise take action against union organizers.

As federal employees have grown in number and acquired greater political influence, their compensation, relative to what is earned by comparable state and local government workers or private-sector employees, has increased.[6] The premium was 20–40 percent over 1950–1990 and has grown since then. Based on US Bureau of Economic Analysis data, federal workers now earn an average of 78 percent more in total annual compensation than private-sector workers ($119,934 compared to $67,246) and 43 percent more, on average, than state and local government workers.[7]

The compensation premium earned by federal employees reflects the growth in their numbers and clout over the last century. Their ability to beneficially influence, through lobbying and other means beyond just formal collective bargaining, has allowed members of the federal civil service system to advance their interests. For instance, the 1912 Lloyd–La Follette Act allowed federal employees to join unions without fear of dismissal. As a result, of the half million employees of the Post Office Department in the decades prior to Kennedy's order, 70 percent belonged to unions and were in an exclusive bargaining unit. Well before the 1912

---

[4] "50 Years Ago, Kennedy's Order Empowered Federal Unions," *Washington Post*, January 19, 2012.
[5] Johnson and Libecap (1994).   [6] Ibid.
[7] "Study: Government Workers Make 78 Percent More Than the Private Sector," *Washington Free Beacon*, October 8, 2015.

Lloyd–La Follette Act, moreover, federal unions were active and successful at securing favorable salaries and benefits on behalf of their members.[8]

According to a Harvard Business School report on US competitiveness, out of the federal government's $23.7 trillion in on-balance sheet liabilities as of the 2012 fiscal year, pension and health-care obligations associated with federal workers account for a third of the total. Of the $7.8 trillion in liabilities associated with federal employee benefits, over 80 percent are unfunded.[9] The annual payments made in connection with such promised benefits are primarily underwritten by contributions from various agencies and by the federal government's general fund receipts generated by taxes and borrowing.

The magnitude of the outstanding obligations for federal employee benefits has been growing steadily. In 2010, the government paid $268 billion in pension and health-care benefits to 10 million civil and military retirees or their survivors. This was $100 billion more than had been paid in 2000 after adjusting for inflation. The payments and added commitments made to the 10 million federal retirees or their survivors in 2010 totaled roughly $800 billion and exceeded the $690 billion paid by the federal government to 54 million Social Security beneficiaries.[10]

Few agencies have begun setting aside funds for retiree benefits. One exception is the United States Postal Service (USPS). As of 2007, Congress has required the USPS to switch from a pay-as-you-go system to a system of setting aside funds for retiree health benefits. The requirement was designed to achieve full funding for projected health benefits within a decade from the then-uncovered amount of $45 billion. The plan was to remove the risk to taxpayers that they would end up paying the bill.[11] The problem is that, due to declining mail volume and its effect on revenues coupled with lobbying by unions representing postal workers (over 85 percent of whom belong to unions), the $5.5 billion mandated annual set-aside payment for future health benefits was reduced to

---

[8] Johnson and Libecap (1994). In addition to benefiting public workers, Chen and Johnson (2015) argue that federal employee unionization reflects the influence of US presidents seeking to reduce bureaucratic turnover and thus anchor the ideological composition of like-minded agency workforces. The anchoring ensures that a president's ideological objectives will continue to be promoted even when the party controlling the White House changes.

[9] Kaplan and Walker (2013).

[10] "Federal Retirement Plans Almost as Costly as Social Security," *USA Today*, September 29, 2011.

[11] Michael Schuyler, "Troubles at the Postal Service," *taxfoundation.org*, September 17, 2015.

$1.4 billion in 2009. Since 2011, the USPS has been allowed to default fully on the mandated annual payments for future health benefits. Along the way, USPS has racked up $51.7 billion in losses over 2007–2014 and reached its statutory borrowing limit of $15 billion with the US Treasury. Meanwhile, total unfunded pension and health-care liabilities for USPS retirees have grown by 62 percent since 2007 to over $100 billion in 2014.[12]

The USPS's fiscal viability has not been helped by the contract which was negotiated in 2011 with the 205,000-member American Postal Workers Union. The contract included a 3.5 percent pay raise phased in over three years, an automatic annual cost of living wage hike after 2012, and an expansion of no-layoff protections (for example, lower-cost, part-time employees must be terminated prior to any full-time workers). The negotiated provisions fail to relieve the USPS's fiscal challenges since 80 percent of its expenses involve labor. Postal workers' wages are now 20–25 percent above comparable private-sector levels, and their total compensation is 30–40 percent higher. The incentives for an entrenched workforce are evidenced by the historical annual quit rate, which is less than 1.5 percent and well below the level at private firms.[13]

The numbers and influence of public employees have grown at levels beyond the federal level. The monopoly power of state and local government employees, with its attendant fiscal impact, also has increased in recent decades. Between 1958 and 1984, a majority of states enacted legislation promoting collective bargaining rights for public employees. Whereas only three states permitted collective bargaining by state and local employees in 1959, thirty-three states did as of 1980. Today, only three states entirely proscribe collective bargaining by public employees (North and South Carolina and Virginia).[14]

Several factors have been behind the changes in collective bargaining legislation, according to economist Daniel DiSalvo.[15] First, civil service reforms which typically aim to eliminate patronage and weaken party machines have provided greater job security and prestige to public employees. The demise of patronage has incented politicians to offer greater collective bargaining rights to public workers and expanded government services to increase job opportunities. In return, politicians have been rewarded with the electoral support of public unions. DiSalvo argues that, relative to their Republican counterparts, Democratic politicians have been more willing to support public employees on account of both

---

[12] Ibid.   [13] "The Coming Postal Bailout," *Wall Street Journal*, May 14, 2011.
[14] DiSalvo (2015).   [15] Ibid.

their ideology which favors government playing a greater role in society and private-sector unions, which have been a core part of the support base for Democratic politicians, being on the wane over the last half century.

Second, urban areas acquired greater political power at the state level following Supreme Court decisions in the early 1960s such as *Baker* v. *Carr* (1962) promulgating a "one man, one vote" rule. Prior to the decisions such as *Baker* v. *Carr*, rural voters had been overrepresented in state government since districting had failed to keep pace with the nation's shift from agriculture to industry. The Supreme Court decisions aided both Democrats and public unions: the former because they are more prevalent in urban areas and the latter because Democrats are more sympathetic to unions.

Finally, demographic changes have led to an increase in public jobs, thus favoring public unions. The post–World War II Baby Boom, for example, increased the demand for services such as education, housing, recreation, and police protection. These are services provided by the government mostly at the state and local levels.

As their membership and influence have grown, so have the benefits that public-sector unions at the state and local levels bestow on their members at the expense of the general public. As reported in Chapter 4, cities allowing for collective bargaining spend 9–10 percent more on salaries for police and firefighters and 21–25 percent more on health benefits. Every 10 percent increase in a state's public union membership increases per capita pension liabilities by $1,412, that is, an amount equal to 20 percent of the average state's per capita GDP.[16]

DiSalvo provides further evidence that, after accounting for all forms of compensation, salary and fringe benefits, and the duration for which they hold office, state and local public employees are paid more than their private-sector counterparts. For example, as of 2015, most US public workers can expect a pension when they retire, whereas only 20 percent of private-sector workers receive such a fringe benefit. Private firms have stopped offering pensions, especially given today's ever-more competitive and dynamic global marketplace. Confronted by unexpected factors such as nonunionized firms, technological changes, and/or economic downturns, General Motors, Chrysler, Eastman Kodak, and other iconic firms went bankrupt in part due to hardwired spending on gold-plated pension and health-care packages promised during prosperous times. Now, private-sector pensions, even for unionized workers, are typically defined contributions for which employees

---

[16] Anzia and Moe (2015).

pay the lion's share while they are working. By contrast, public pensions largely are defined benefits where the government not only pays for most (if not all) of the benefit but also guarantees that the promised amount will be paid when the worker retires. Thus, while private-sector workers must worry about how financial market gyrations will affect the value of their retirement accounts, public employees have no similar concern.[17]

Public workers' superior compensation packages reflect their monopoly power in the political arena and the extent to which that power has grown in recent decades through unionization. The monopoly power stems from civil-service–type protections and public positions being more insulated from market forces. After all, the state often is the sole or dominant supplier of the good or service in question.

In addition, public employees get "two bites at the apple" versus the one "bite" available to their private-sector counterparts. That is, not only can they organize themselves to collectively bargain with their managers, as can private-sector employees, they also have the ability to elect and otherwise manage the public officials who are supposed to be managing them on behalf of ordinary voters.[18]

The magnitude of the costs associated with public-sector unionization below the federal level in the United States is staggering. Economists Robert Novy-Marx and Joshua Rauh estimate the unfunded pension liabilities for state and local public employees total $4 trillion.[19] Add to that figure over $1 trillion in unfunded health-care benefits which local and state public workers have been promised and you end up with a fiscal problem of epic proportion. It rivals the one posed by unfunded Social Security obligations, both of which trail the commitments associated with Medicare/Medicaid/ObamaCare.[20] Contrary to the arguments made by Paul Krugman in his *New York Times* op-eds, Detroit's bankruptcy in 2013 is not an anomaly; it is a portent of a looming nationwide problem at the state and local levels.[21] Moreover, the greater the squeeze that pension and health-care obligations put on state and local budgets, the quantity and quality of services they can afford to provide to the taxpayer will decline.

The hard choices needed to solve this problem are not easily made. Rising public-sector unionization has the clout and the numbers; nearly

---

[17] DiSalvo (2015).   [18] Ibid. and Moe (2006).   [19] Novy-Marx and Rauh (2014a, 2014b).
[20] DiSalvo (2015); and Edwards and Gokhale (2006).
[21] See, for example, Paul Krugman, "Detroit, the New Greece," *New York Times*, July 21, 2013.

one in six US employees now work for state and local government, and with their family members and friends comprise a potent voting bloc against ceding gains made over the years. Witness the near political death through recall election that confronted Republican Governor Scott Walker of Wisconsin when he decided to take on public unions after first assuming office in 2010. Alternatively, Democratic Governor Jerry Brown of California successfully promoted a $6 billion tax increase to voters in 2012 arguing that half of the associated revenues would be devoted to public schools. In 2014, Governor Brown signed legislation requiring school districts to increase the funds allocated to teachers' pensions by $3 billion annually within five years. This guaranteed that the proceeds from the 2012 tax increase would primarily reduce the extent to which teachers' pensions were underfunded rather than improve public school performance.[22]

The crush of liability is growing. Assuming realistic rates of return on investments, Illinois' unfunded pension liability is estimated to be $250 billion. This represents over 450 percent of the annual tax revenue collected by the state. Illinois officials have been assuming an average annual return on its investments of 7.75 percent over the next three decades, even though the odds of achieving such an outcome are only 25 percent.[23]

Many state and local governments, aware of the problem whose magnitude the public has yet to grasp, have succumbed to the temptation to take higher risks to avoid disaster. For example, in an effort to make up for the deficit, Illinois has placed 75 percent of its pension portfolio in stocks and other risky assets. Given that the average age of public employees participating in the Illinois retirement system is sixty-two, the typical and prudent approach would involve an allocation of no more than 40 percent of the portfolio to risky assets. Other states similarly have been doubling down and going against basic risk management principles in an effort to reduce their unfunded pension liabilities. The average public plan in the United States places 72 percent of its investments in risky assets. California matches Illinois at 75 percent; New York is at 72 percent; Texas 81 percent; Pennsylvania 82 percent; and New Mexico 85 percent.[24]

---

[22] Steve Malanga, "The Pension Sink is Gulping Billions in Tax Raises," *Wall Street Journal*, January 13, 2015.

[23] "America's Greece," *The Economist*, December 20, 2014.

[24] Andrew G. Biggs, "Public Pensions Need Gamblers Anonymous," *Wall Street Journal*, December 3, 2014.

In September 2015, facing a budget shortfall of $745 million linked to unfunded pensions totaling $20 billion, Chicago's Mayor Rahm Emanuel proposed an array of tax hikes and fees coupled with draconian spending cuts. The spending cuts included shuttering forty-eight fire stations and reducing the number of firefighters and police officers by 40 and 20 percent, respectively. Among the tax increases, Emanuel proposed raising property taxes by $543 million from 2016 to 2018 to help underwrite police and fire pensions. He also proposed raising nearly $50 million through a surcharge on taxi and ride-sharing services and a further $63 million by instituting a monthly garbage collection fee of $9.50 per household.[25]

A few months prior to Emanuel's proposed budget, Moody's Investors Service downgraded the credit rating for bonds issued by Chicago to junk status. The downgrade stemmed from the city's pension shortfall and came on the heels of an announcement by Chicago's Public Schools System that it would borrow $1 billion to cover a $600 million payment for outstanding pension obligations. Due to the downgrade, Chicago's borrowing costs increased to nearly 8 percent on taxable bonds – twice the rate paid by a typical home buyer for a thirty-year mortgage loan.[26]

Other localities such as Dallas are approaching Chicago's status while some have progressed beyond that point. Following Detroit in 2013, three California cities (San Bernardino, Stockton, and Vallejo) and Puerto Rico either have declared bankruptcy or gone into default. In Detroit's bankruptcy case, unfunded pension ($3.5 billion) and health-care ($5.7 billion) obligations accounted for half of the city's debt. Puerto Rico's outstanding debt of $72 billion is far larger than the $20 billion that precipitated Detroit's bankruptcy, and it exceeds 100 percent of the territory's GDP. The territory's fiscal challenges have been exacerbated by a flight of human capital to the mainland United States and an anemic economy linked to high taxes and generous welfare benefits. What is common among all these localities are unfunded obligations for public workers. As of 2015, Puerto Rico's public pension system is only 7 percent funded, $34 billion in the red, and expected to run dry by as soon as 2018.[27]

Without significant changes in what is promised to public workers, the fiscal squeeze on US cities and states will grow more acute – especially for those that are unable to attract or develop firms to enhance their tax base.

---

[25] "Chicago Mayor Pushes Massive Tax Hike over Crippling Cuts," *reuters.com*, September 22, 2015.

[26] "Pensions and Politics Fuel Crisis in Illinois," *New York Times*, May 25, 2015.

[27] "America's Greece," *Wall Street Journal*, July 3, 2015.

The services that they can provide to their citizens will shrink. Pennsylvania and its municipalities epitomize the problem. Philadelphia's public pension plan requires $600 million in funding per year, one-sixth of the city's budget. At least 53 percent of the city's outstanding pension obligations remain unfunded. Pennsylvania's other cities and towns paid $867 million in 2015 for their pension plans and averaged 24 cents in spending on pensions for every dollar paid in salaries to their employees. As recently as 2005, this rate was only 9 cents on the dollar. The contributions made by taxpayers to Pennsylvania's unified school pension plan have increased even more sharply. In 2010, funding for pensions was 4 cents per dollar in salaries paid to employees. By 2014, the rate had grown to 16 cents per dollar and is projected to rise to 30 cents per dollar by 2019.[28]

SACRIFICING THE NEXT GENERATION

A critical sector of the US economy increasingly co-opted by government insiders is K-12 education. The supply side of the sector has become more monopolized due to growing unionization as well as a consolidation of school districts. Consequently, it has become less accountable to the public interest to the detriment of the development of the country's most important asset, its human capital. The negative impact reaches into the national ability to provide opportunity, the degree to which the urban areas remain viable and even vibrant, and the productivity of society's scarce resources.

The growth of union power in public K-12 education mirrors what occurred for state and local government workers in general over the past fifty years. Prior to 1955, only one state authorized collective bargaining by teachers; by 1980, forty-three states had adopted such laws. Similarly, in 1955 no state imposed a duty to engage in collective bargaining with teachers; by 1980, thirty states had done so. Except in the remaining twenty-five "right-to-work" states (located primarily in the South and the upper Midwest), teachers also acquired the ability, by majority vote, to designate a specific union as their representative and to legally require all fellow employees to contribute to the union's support through "agency fees."[29]

A watershed strike in 1961 by the newly certified affiliate of the American Federation of Teachers (AFT) in New York City led to the first

---

[28] "Crushing Pension Obligations Are Pushing Stressed Governments," *Philadelphia Inquirer*, July 19, 2015.
[29] Moe (2011).

major collective bargaining contract for public teachers in the United States. While illegal, the successful work stoppage demonstrated to public teachers nationwide the benefits of forceful collective action. The strike led to substantial improvements in pay, benefits, and working conditions and it established a checkoff for union dues (the checkoff allows the government to automatically withhold a portion of public employees' salaries to cover union dues and agency fees).[30]

Prior to the New York City's teachers' strike, only a small number of teachers were members of unions advocating on behalf of their interests. The National Education Association (NEA), established in 1857, promoted professionalism, progressive education, and administrative interests but was largely opposed to teachers unions during its first century of existence. During the decades after the watershed strike, however, union membership and collective bargaining agreements in the United States increased dramatically. By 1993, 80 percent of public K-12 teachers belonged to such interest groups. The percentage of teachers covered by collective bargaining agreements soared from 0 percent in 1960 to 65 percent by 1978, leveling off there since. Along the way, the NEA shifted to a pro-union stance when faced, in the 1960s, with growing competition from the AFT. Now, the NEA represents an estimated 86 percent of all unionized teachers.[31]

Beyond unionization, the monopoly power on the supply side of K-12 public education has grown through school district consolidation. Between 1950 and 1980, the number of districts declined by 81 percent, from 83,642, to 15,987. This trend has been driven by an increase in urbanization in which process several trends are occurring, for example, increased pressure to take advantage of economies of scale; heightened importance of state aid aiming to reduce any cross-district differences in quality; and teachers unions seeking to lower their organizational costs and increase their political influence.[32]

As public school districts have consolidated, the potential diminishes for citizens to hold officials accountable by voting with their feet if they are unhappy with the services provided. By looking across US school districts, economist Caroline Hoxby shows that the lower competition brought about by district consolidation has its effect in lower student academic achievement and increased per-pupil spending.[33]

Hoxby also shows that unionization results in greater per-pupil spending and poorer student outcomes, the latter being measured by high school

[30] Ibid.   [31] Ibid.   [32] Kenny and Schmidt (1994).   [33] Hoxby (2000).

dropout rates. Over the period 1972–1982, per-pupil spending grew by 12.3 percent more in unionized school districts than in nonunionized districts, holding all other factors constant. Three-quarters of the added spending in unionized districts was devoted to either higher teacher salaries or hiring more teachers. Unlike for nonunionized schools, however, the added spending in unionized districts was unproductive. High school dropout rates for unionized schools were 2.3 percentage points worse than for nonunionized schools, holding constant demographic factors such as median household income, population in poverty, racial/ethnic composition, total K-12 enrollment, private K-12 enrollment, average adult education level, median monthly rent, and percentage of the population aged 16–19.[34] The negative effect of per-pupil spending on student outcomes in unionized districts stands in marked contrast to the positive effect of additional spending on student outcomes in nonunionized districts. A similar positive influence of additional spending on student performance has been documented by studies examining student cohorts educated prior to 1960 and the onset of unionization of K-12 public teachers in the United States.[35] Whereas additional spending in nonunionized districts appears to be applied toward enhancing student outcomes, such spending in unionized districts is consumed by government insiders. In unionized districts, government insiders are profiting by a greater amount at the public's expense (P) both because there is greater slack (S) in their relationship with citizens and because the prospective gains (G) for co-opting the political process are larger ($P = G \times S \times I$).

Political scientist Terry Moe corroborates Hoxby's findings by examining a large sample of California school districts. He finds that, after controlling for demographic factors and school/district characteristics, the restrictiveness of the district's collective bargaining contract has a large negative impact on student achievement; it also exceeds the effect of any other organizational aspect of schools and districts. The negative effect is most pronounced for schools with a high percentage of minority students. This suggests that unionization by public school teachers extracts an especially heavy toll on how much minority children learn and hence the opportunities available to them later in life.[36]

In his book *Special Interest*, Moe details how teachers unions have become a potent vested interest.[37] They exercise influence from the

---

[34] Hoxby (1996).
[35] See, for example, Card and Krueger (1992a, 1992b); Johnson and Stafford (1973); and Welch (1966).
[36] Moe (2009).   [37] Moe (2011).

bottom-up, through collective bargaining that benefits them at the expense of our educational system's effectiveness and children. They also shape schools from the top-down, through electing favorable school boards and legislators (largely Democrats) and blocking or weakening attempted reforms running counter to their interests.

According to Moe, the ability of teachers unions to promote their interests is unrivaled by any other special-interest group. The 4 million members across the two leading unions, the AFT and NEA, are the nation's top contributing interest group to federal elections, influencing outcomes of ballot measures and school board elections which directly impact school district management. In examining Los Angeles County school board elections in 1997 and 1999, Moe finds that only 7 percent of registered voters cast ballots. By contrast, 46 percent of teachers living in the district turned out to vote, thus magnifying their political impact.[38]

On top of their direct voting impact, teachers unions collect nearly $3 billion in dues annually. These dues allow teachers unions both to field an army of grassroots activists spanning the nation's various political districts and to spend over $60 million per year at the local level in support of measures and elections favorable to their members. Over 85 percent of the local funding goes to Democrats, as does 95 percent of the $5–$6 million which teachers unions spend annually at the federal level.

Teachers unions' political clout has ossified antistudent policies, such as teacher tenure, seniority preferences, and lock-step pay. The more that teacher employment and compensation are based on tenure, seniority, and degree status, the less strongly they are linked to student outcomes. Moreover, studies find little evidence that the contractual provisions regularly supported by unions – requiring state teaching licenses, tenure, basing pay on years of service and graduate degrees earned, and so on – increase teacher effectiveness in the classroom.[39]

According to the NEA, the average base salary of public school teachers as of 2012–2013 is $56,103. This figure can be misleading. The NEA does not tabulate the salaries for teachers covered by collective bargaining agreements (presumably higher due to the influence of union power) versus for those that are not. The NEA salary statistic does not incorporate factors such as fringe benefits, job security, and vacation time (typically three months per year).[40] Nor does it account for the opportunity teachers have to earn more through taking on extra duties (tutoring or after-school assignments) or by cashing out unused vacation time, sick/personal days,

[38] Moe (2006, 2011).   [39] Moe (2011).   [40] DiSalvo (2015) and Moe (2011).

and medical coverage. The salary statistic also does not reflect the cost of administrative personnel.

In the Los Angeles Unified School District (LAUSD), 45 percent of payroll expenses go toward employees who do not interact with students in the classroom ($2.1 billion per year out of $4.7 billion) and the pay of administrators and centralized staff exceeds that of teachers. As of 2014, LAUSD teachers, who are covered by a collective bargaining agreement, earned a median of $75,504 after taking into account base salary, other duties, and cashed in vacation/sick leave/personal days. The teachers earned an average of $21,000 in estimated pension and health-care benefits beyond their regular pay, or a total annual compensation package of over $95,000.[41]

LAUSD teachers work 182 days a year (two days without students) and have twenty-two paid holidays. By comparison, a full-time worker in the private sector has two weeks of paid vacation, six paid holidays, and works 249 days annually. In addition, LAUSD teachers receive ten sick days per year and their workweek is 35 hours long when school is in session, compared to 40 hours for private-sector professionals. On average, urban public school teachers are absent 5–6 percent of all school days, almost three times as high as the absentee rate for the average professional or managerial worker in the United States.[42]

At the time of a successful union strike in 2012, the average Chicago public school teacher earned a reported $76,000 in salary and $15,000 in annualized benefits, compared to Chicago's median household income (not counting annualized benefits) being $47,000.[43] Through the strike, teachers secured a 17.6 percent pay increase spread over four years, the elimination of provisions allocating pay based on merit, and reduced weighting of student test scores in teacher evaluation formulas.[44]

Whereas 28.5 percent of Chicago Unified School District's 11th graders met or exceeded Illinois testing standards, only 0.1 percent of teachers were let go for performance reasons from 2005 to 2008.[45] In Chicago, as in other districts covered by collective bargaining agreements, teachers receive tenure after only a few years of probationary service and then are nearly impossible to fire.

---

[41] "LAUSD Educators Typically Earned $75,504 Last Year," *Los Angeles Daily News*, March 21, 2015.

[42] Moe (2011).

[43] "Rahmbo at the School Barricades," *Wall Street Journal*, September 15–16, 2012. The salary figure was reported by the city while the union calculated the average to be $71,000.

[44] DiSalvo (2015).   [45] "Why We Must Fire Bad Teachers," *Newsweek*, March 5, 2010.

Indeed, merit has been increasingly eliminated from the compensation formula. In Illinois, a tenured teacher could not be dismissed for poor performance prior to 1985. Even after legislative reforms to promote greater accountability in 1985, however, it has remained extremely difficult to fire a tenured teacher. Of 95,000 tenured Illinois public school teachers, an average of only seven per year had their recommended dismissals approved by a state hearing officer in the eighteen years after the legislative reforms. Of the seven, on average only two were for performance reasons while the others were based on misconduct charges. The average cost per dismissal case was at least $219,000 – an amount large enough to make administrators think twice about attempting to fire a bad teacher.[46]

In the LAUSD, only 2 percent of the hired teachers are denied tenure after their two-year probationary period. Upon receiving tenure, an average of only eleven of the district's 43,000 tenured teachers faced termination charges each year from 1995 to 2005. Most of these charges were for reasons other than performance issues. During the same time, the high school graduation rate for LAUSD was barely above 50 percent. A union representative stated: "If I'm representing them [poorly performing teachers], it's impossible to get them out . . . Unless they commit a lewd act."[47] It cost LAUSD $3.5 million in legal fees and took nearly a decade to try to dismiss seven teachers. Four ended up being dismissed, although two of them negotiated significant payout packages as part of their exit.[48]

In California, 0.002 percent of public teachers are dismissed for poor performance per year. In comparison, 1 percent of all public workers and 8 percent of private workers in the United States are let go each year for performance-based reasons. As noted by the movie *Waiting for Superman*, while one out of every fifty-seven doctors and one out of every ninety-seven lawyers lose their licenses, nationally, only one out of 1,000 teachers end up being dismissed on account of poor performance.[49]

The difficulty of firing poorly performing teachers who have tenure and are union members includes high costs to society, as portrayed by a *New Yorker* article by Steven Brill. Of the teachers hired in New York City, 97 percent are granted tenure after their third year of teaching. Moreover, until the advent of reforms introduced by Mayor Bloomberg in 2002, 99 percent of New York City's tenured teachers received satisfactory ratings.[50] Brill's article focused on the 700 teachers assigned in 2009 to one of New York City's so-called Rubber Rooms. Deemed to be unsuited for teaching, they still collected full pay and benefits, including summers

---

[46] Moe (2011).   [47] Ibid.   [48] DiSalvo (2015).   [49] Ibid.   [50] Brill (2009).

off and the usual vacation days. Meanwhile, they spent their days solving crossword puzzles, sleeping, reading books, chatting with each other, and occasionally fighting over a folding chair. They did so while waiting two to five years for their cases to be heard by an arbitrator.[51] The annual cost to the school district was $65 million in salary and benefits for the bad teachers alone. On top of that, the district had to hire substitute teachers, rent the Rubber Rooms to warehouse the bad teachers, and even pay $500,000 per year for security guards to keep the bad teachers safe – largely from each other while they were warehoused. Still, warehousing was better than trying to fire the educational lemons and thus challenge the teachers union, collective bargaining contracts, and state tenure laws.

Job security is indeed valuable to public school teachers as confirmed by the results of a survey undertaken by Terry Moe. Of the K-12 public teachers surveyed, 47 percent stated that they would be unwilling to give up tenure even in return for a 50 percent increase in their base salary.[52] While valuable to their members, tenure and other key collective bargaining provisions promoted by teachers unions are detrimental to student outcomes. Whether measured by high school graduation rates or student performance on standardized tests, the United States has lost ground relative to other nations over the past half century. This especially is true for unionized public school districts in major cities, such as Rochester, New York, which was showcased in Chapter 7. As of 2010, the percentage of students entering high school who graduated on time was 43 percent in Rochester; the comparable percentages for other major cities with heavily unionized public schools were 45 in Cleveland, 50 in Detroit, 51 in Syracuse, 53 in Buffalo, 59 in Philadelphia, 60 in Los Angeles, 61 in Baltimore, and 64 in Milwaukee. In 2015, only 4 percent of eighth graders in the Detroit public school system were proficient in math and only 7 percent in reading.[53]

Up through the first half of the twentieth century, the United States had arguably the leading K-12 educational system in the world. However, according to the most recent cross-country Programme for International Student Assessment (PISA) study, US students start off ahead of those in other OECD countries in the early grades, lose educational ground in the middle school years, and trail most of the pack by high school. In terms of middle school educational attainment, US students rank below average among OECD countries in mathematics, close to average in reading and

---

[51] Op cit.   [52] Moe (2011).
[53] "Detroit's Public School Plague," *Wall Street Journal*, January 22, 2016.

science, and barely above average in problem-solving. These results are despite the facts that the United States spends more per pupil than almost all other OECD nations and, in real terms, twice as much per pupil as it did in 1970 and three times as much as in 1960.[54] As of 2012, the Slovak Republic spent only 54 percent as much per K-12 pupil as the United States but achieved comparable student outcomes. Shanghai-China, Singapore, Hong Kong-China, and Macao-China – all non-OECD members but PISA participants – appreciably outperform the United States in reading, science, and mathematics educational outcomes while spending much less per pupil.

In the concluding chapter of *Special Interest*, Moe summarizes the critical juncture facing American education (pp. 342–343):

[Our nation's] leaders fully agree that improving . . . public schools is . . . critical to the economic and social well-being of the country, and . . . are willing to invest heavily to bring that improvement about. But we also see an education system . . . protected from change . . . by a special interest group that has a deep stake in the status quo and has used its formidable power . . . to prevent real reform . . . making it impossible for governments to correct for the system's pathologies and create organizations . . . built for top-flight performance.

Due to the vested interest of teachers unions, Moe argues that we have a (p. 343):

system that can't even get bad teachers out of the classroom. Is that good for children? Obviously not . . . and this just scratches the surface. Seniority rules for teacher transfers, excessing, and layoffs ensure that . . . teaching resources get allocated in ways that have nothing to do with productivity or quality. The single salary schedule ensures that good teachers get paid exactly the same as bad teachers and that the criteria on which they are paid – seniority, formal credentials – have nothing to do with how much children . . . learn. We have accountability systems that don't . . . hold anyone accountable.

A growing amount of data and studies concur that promoting teacher accountability and rewarding superior teaching performance promises to improve appreciably students' long-term opportunities and outcomes. Using school district and tax records for more than 1 million children, economists Raj Chetty, John Friedman, and Jonah Rockoff find that students assigned to high value-added teachers – as measured by the teachers' impacts on students' test scores – are more likely to go to college, attend a higher-quality college, earn higher salaries, and invest in a 401(k) retirement savings plan; they are also less likely to have children as teenagers.

---

[54] Moe (2011) and OECD (2012).

Replacing a poorly performing K-12 teacher, whose value added ranks in the bottom 5 percent, with an average one is estimated to increase the present value of students' lifetime earnings by $250,000 per average-size classroom. These results suggest that substantial socioeconomic gains can be realized in the United States by a K-12 system empowered to dismiss poorly performing teachers and to reward highly performing ones.[55]

On a larger scale, it has been estimated that replacing the bottom 5–10 percent of public K-12 teachers with average teachers would be sufficient to move the United States from below average to near the top of the cross-country PISA measures of student outcomes. The performance-based accountability system such a change suggests would also increase cumulative future GDP by $102 trillion over the lifetime of the generation born in 2010.[56] By comparison, the US GDP was estimated to be nearly $18 trillion as of 2015. According to another study, relying on high-impact instead of just average teachers for four to five consecutive years would suffice to eliminate entirely the educational gap that presently exists between low-income students on free or reduced-price lunch programs and average students not on such programs.[57]

Studies of the potential gains from promoting teacher accountability focus on the benefits to students from improved teacher quality. However, there are other sizable gains, albeit more difficult to quantify, with respect to diminishing inequality, revitalizing cities, and promoting sustainability. For example, poorly performing urban schools foster suburban flight.[58] It is true that many cities have been investing in enhancing their infrastructural core. Those investments have had very real positive impact attracting more young professionals to live in cities, but this trend is unlikely to continue if the public school system does not improve by the time young professionals begin raising families.[59]

Publicly funded but privately run charter schools have gained market share since their inception two decades ago. Their growth indicates the

---

[55] Chetty, Friedman, and Rockoff (2014).   [56] Hanushek (2009) and Moe (2011).

[57] Rivkin, Hanushek, and Kain (2005).

[58] "America's Immigrants Are Moving to the Suburbs," *National Journal*, December 11, 2014.

[59] Other factors cited for the recent gentrification trend include declining crime rates; the negative effect of the 2007–2009 economic downturn on the wealth of young professionals and thus on their ability to make a down payment on a suburban home; a growing number of two-earner couples seeking to decrease the cost, in terms of time and other resources, of commuting; and superior Internet connectivity in urban areas leading to expanded job opportunities and living amenities. See, for example, Greenstein (2015); and Paul Krugman, "Inequality and The City," *New York Times*, November 30, 2015.

public's disaffection with the public school system. As of 2015, 2.9 million public school students, or 5.8 percent of the total, were enrolled in one of the nation's more than 6,700 charter schools. Enrollment was up from 300,000 students in 2000, 0.7 percent of the total at that time. Charter schools hold the highest market share in urban areas, which have been traditionally characterized as having the worst-performing public schools. For example, in the wake of a massive overhaul of the school system following Hurricane Katrina, 61 percent of students in New Orleans attend a publicly funded charter school; likewise, 53 percent in Detroit; 38 percent in Washington, DC; 32 percent in Kansas City; 16 percent in both LAUSD and Baltimore; and 15 percent in Boston.[60] Furthermore, the wait lists to enroll in charter schools are long: 13,000 additional Boston families were seeking to switch to charter schools as of 2015.[61]

Although not without challenges or hiccups, charter schools are gaining market share due to their perceived potential to improve student outcomes. School networks which offer multiple charter schools such as the Knowledge Is Power Program (KIPP), Aspire, and Success Academy are not unionized. As a result, they are able to be more directly organized to advance learning over the special interests promoted by teachers unions. The track record these school networks are building attests to the potential of charter schools for improving student outcomes. Among other things, these charter school networks control their budgets, are able to determine which teachers are hired and fired, and decide classroom instruction time without having to negotiate with competing interests.[62]

When students enter KIPP, the measures of their academic performance fall well below district averages. That gap is eliminated by KIPP's educational process. The charter Success Academy Harlem West provides a stark contrast to student outcomes in public schools. Success Academy Harlem West operates out of the same building as the public Wadleigh School, and it operates on less funding than the $20,331 per pupil which New York City spends through schools such as Wadleigh. Despite having virtually identical student demographics and using the same cafeteria, gym, and outdoor courtyard (for recesses), the student outcomes are vastly different. As of 2014, of the Wadleigh students in grades six through eight, not a single one met state standards in math or English. By comparison, 96 percent of the

---

[60] See, for example, "Detroit's Public School Plague," *Wall Street Journal*, January 22, 2016.

[61] See, for example, Moe (2011); and "Charter Battle Heats Up," *Wall Street Journal*, October 12, 2015.

[62] Moe (2015).

students in the same grades who enrolled in the Success Academy were proficient in math and 75 percent in English. Compare this performance to all students in grades six through eight in New York City (not charter) schools, where proficiency in math hovers at 35 percent and in English at 30 percent.[63]

The gains made by charter schools have been hard-won. They receive less funding than their traditional public counterparts; in most states, they receive no capital support for facilities. They also are opposed by teachers unions and political allies of those unions, that is, they face the entrenched status quo with its comfortable alliances among government insiders. In New York City, for example, Mayor Bill de Blasio's administration has sought to block the spread of charter schools such as those operated by Success Academy, despite their track record of generating superior results and pleased parents. But parents' expectations are no match for the clout of teachers unions and their political allies. Indeed, many states limit how many charter schools can operate across the state or in individual districts.[64] Several states, including Alaska, Hawaii, and Maryland, require charter schools to be unionized. And United Teachers of Los Angeles is building support to add the twenty-six schools and more than 600 teachers in the city's largest charter system, Alliance College-Ready Public Schools, to its union rolls[65] – in other words, to co-opt them by government coercion into a broken system that serves the interest of government insiders at the expense of the public interest.

In their book *Liberating Learning*, Moe and John Chubb argue that technology promises to relax the chokehold exercised by teachers unions over K-12 public education.[66] Much as Hurricane Katrina swept away entrenched educational interests in New Orleans and permitted the rapid growth of charter schools, online learning may have a similar tsunami-like power to disrupt the K-12 status quo for the better. Since the book's publication in 2009, however, the power of online technology to improve student outcomes markedly has yet to be manifest. Meanwhile, teachers unions have protected their turf, as strikingly illustrated by the outcome of the $100 million gift made in 2011 by Facebook founder Mark Zuckerberg to transform Newark's public school system. Zuckerberg's vision was more teacher accountability, pay-for-performance, and charter schools. The gift

---

[63] "A Tale of Two Schools, One Building," *Wall Street Journal*, October 6, 2015.
[64] Ibid. and Moe (2011).
[65] "Unions Eye Charter Schools," *Wall Street Journal*, November 17, 2015.
[66] Moe and Chubb (2009).

was inspired by a cross-party partnership between then Democratic Mayor Cory Booker of Newark and Republican Governor Chris Christie of New Jersey, and attracted matching funds from other individuals such as financier Bill Ackmann. Nevertheless, the lion's share of these ample funds ended up increasing the salaries of existing, unionized K-12 teachers. Little progress was made in linking teacher pay to productivity, enhancing the ability of administrators to fire poorly performing teachers, and expanding charter options.[67]

The Newark outcome mirrors the limited effect other individuals and organizations have had in improving student outcomes in other states and cities through philanthropy. Philanthropic leaders such as the Walton family, the Bill and Melinda Gates Foundation, and the Broad Foundation have proved no match to the ability of teachers unions to block or dilute these reform efforts. It will take more powerful internal or external forces to overcome their co-opting role.

The deleterious influence of the United Auto Workers (UAW) on the efficiency of the Big Three auto manufacturers in the United States was eventually undone by global competition. Two of the companies (Chrysler and General Motors) ended up declaring bankruptcy so as to restructure their balance sheets, breaking the stranglehold of unions and their allies on the viability of those corporations. Similarly, it took moving into the existential extreme for the "Sick Man of Europe" to break the detrimental hold on its treasury and trajectory which the Janissaries and public scribes had on the once preeminent Ottoman Empire. Ultimately, it may take further losses in the relative standing of the United States on the world stage to acknowledge the impact of a poorly performing K-12 educational sector to precipitate changes that have so far been foiled by entrenched interests operating on the supply side of politics.

UNFINISHED WORK

Unlike in autocracies, examples of how democracy *by* the people is not sufficient to ensure outcomes *for* the people can be more complicated, perhaps because they are surrounded with the activities and rhetoric of democracy even as the slack in the relationship between the public and its officials grows. The pending crisis from growing unfunded pension and health-care liabilities for public workers eludes public outcry perhaps mostly because the problem is complicated and often mischaracterized.

---

[67] Russakoff (2015).

Declining K-12 student outcomes are couched in battles over spending far more often than how funds are spent. These are but two illustrations of the greater issue for the United States. Democracy, notwithstanding virtues that include promoting citizens' civil liberties and political rights, does not ensure economic well-being. A key reason for this is the ability of government insiders to subvert the public interest – albeit not as readily as in autocracies from the most visible top rungs of power. In China, the inside job has moved to a totalitarian extreme from which some reformers seek to retreat to some degree. In the United States, the inside job has progressed not due to autocracy but, thanks to the activities of entrenched interests, mostly on lower rungs of the supply side of politics. The following, concluding chapter turns to steps that can be taken to prevent such outcomes – and move the forces behind the inside job into retreat.

10

How Can We Form a More Perfect Union?

James Madison in *The Federalist Papers* noted that "the great difficulty is this: you must first enable the government to control the governed; and in the next place oblige it to control itself."[1] As democracy replaces autocracy around the globe, this difficulty remains freshly challenging for democratic nations. Whatever changes contemporary democracies might employ to limit the possibility of inside jobs also have broader import to whatever degree China and other autocracies seek to promote the public interest and prosperity to uplift their own nations.

The economic model of politics illuminates the worthy effort to limit power in democracies, especially when enhanced by insights from the study of history, political science, and sociology. Using this lens in this book to survey the arc of governing systems in autocracies and democracies over the broad course of time, a lesser-known factor in government capture emerges when politics is seen for the marketplace it can be. The supply side of the political market emerges as a central factor, a Visible Hand if you will, in determining the fate of nations. This key factor has until now been treated, at least by most economists, largely as a black box.

Prying open the black box has proven revelatory. It highlights the influence of political-economic institutions on national well-being and it indicates the pivotal role government insiders play in determining the extent to which democracies *and* autocracies operate for the people. The more the role of the supply side of the political market is understood, the more we are able to identify some steps that might be taken to better ensure government for the people. These steps are the topic of this concluding chapter.

---

[1] Hamilton, Jay, and Madison ([1788] 1982).

RESTRAINING PUBLIC TRUSTS

The state often is the sole supplier of a good or service. And, in its role as supplier, interests other than its market – or constituents – influence how that good or service is provided. Consider the double impact of public employees, who have some ability to manage their managers through their unions and through their influence on the electoral process (at least in democracies). Consequently, policies permitting collective bargaining by public employees enhance monopoly power on the supply side of politics. They merit scrutiny.

US public workers could not collectively bargain until the late 1950s. Historically, even labor champions like AFL-CIO president George Meany and Franklin Delano Roosevelt opposed such rights for public employees. Contrary to President Kennedy and others who strengthened the public employee unions, Meany and Roosevelt resisted them due to their concerns about the quality and quantity of public services, fiscal responsibility, and protecting democracy. Roosevelt argued:[2]

The process of collective bargaining ... cannot be translated into the public service ... The very nature and purposes of Government make it impossible for representative officials to represent fully or to bind the employer in mutual discussions with Government employee organizations. The employer is the whole people, who speak by means of laws enacted by their representatives in Congress. Accordingly, administrative officials and employees alike are governed ... by laws which establish policies, procedures, or rules in personnel matters.

Courts similarly ruled against collective bargaining by public workers. In 1943, a New York Supreme Court judge held:[3]

To tolerate ... civil service employees ... as a labor ... union is not only incompatible with the spirit of democracy, but inconsistent with every principle on which our government is founded. Nothing is more dangerous to public welfare than to admit that hired servants of the State can dictate ... the hours, wages, and conditions under which they will carry on essential services vital to the welfare, safety, and security of the citizen. To admit as true that government employees have power to halt or check the functions of government unless their demands are satisfied is to transfer to them all legislative, executive, and judicial power. Nothing could be more ridiculous.

Since services such as police and fire protection are supplied by the state on a near-monopoly basis, the possibility for the public to be held hostage was clear to those who opposed these unions. Abraham Raskin, a long-time

---

[2] DiSalvo (2010, 2015).   [3] Ibid.

New York Times writer on labor matters, argued in 1968 that "The com-munity cannot [be] defenseless at the hands of organized workers to whom it has entrusted responsibility for essential services."[4]

But as we have seen, the right of US public workers to collectively bargain has increased markedly over the last half century. As economist Daniel DiSalvo has documented, the change has adversely impacted the quality and quantity of public services, the fiscal soundness of state and municipal budgets, interparty polarization, and citizens' trust in government.[5] The United States can take some solace by falling below other countries where the power of public unions is far greater along with the measurable damage to the public interest. The percentage of the public workforce which is unionized is over 70 percent in Canada, 56 percent in Britain, 60 percent in Germany, and well over 50 percent across the rest of continental Europe versus 36 percent in the United States.[6] The conse-quences to the economy of Greece, where 29 percent of the workforce is employed by the public sector and approximately 60 percent of public employees are unionized, have previously been noted.

The details are astounding. Britain's Labour Party gets 80 percent of its financial backing from public unions. The last time the party held power, from 1997 to 2010, public spending increased from 40 to 50 percent of GDP and 1 million workers were added to the public-sector payroll. In Brazil, civil servants can retire on full pay after thirty-five years on the job (30 for women) and teachers can retire after thirty years (25 for women). Brazil spends as much on public employee pensions (12 percent of GDP) as does Britain, despite having a much younger population. In Poland, police officers and soldiers can retire after just fifteen years on the job.[7] Yet, efforts to roll back drains on state coffers meet with strong, if not violent, rejection. When former French president Nicolas Sarkozy sought to increase the retirement age of public employees by two years, millions of them turned out to protest. Large numbers also have taken to the streets of Italy, Greece, Portugal, Spain, Ireland, Poland, Brazil, and Britain to oppose proposed austerity measures targeting the public sector since the recession of 2007–2009.[8]

There are arguments in favor of public unions. DiSalvo reviews them, for example, ensuring labor peace; enabling industrial democracy; providing

---

[4] Ibid.   [5] Ibid.
[6] "(Government) Workers of the World Unite!" *The Economist*, January 6, 2011.
[7] Ibid. and "The Battle Ahead," *The Economist*, January 6, 2011.
[8] "(Government) Workers of the World Unite!" *The Economist*, January 6, 2011.

political representation; reducing power inequalities between employers and workers; improving workers' compensation; protecting collective bargaining rights; and promoting investment in public goods. DiSalvo concludes that only two of the many claims advance the public interest: ensuring labor peace and promoting investment in public goods such as defense and secure property rights that simultaneously benefit multiple citizens. The others focus on how public unions advance their members' interests but not the public interest.[9] DiSalvo also argues the benefits from the few claims are too minor to support having public employee unions. That is, benefits from greater labor peace are minimal, and the increased spending on public goods largely has been channeled in ways that do not benefit the public (for example, increased pensions and other fringe benefits often are provided at the expense of reduced services). DiSalvo (2015) concludes that the result is a government (p. 217):

That spends more but does less ... hardly the sort of broad public provision that liberals champion. And it's a less attractive version of the "big government," which conservatives already oppose.

Certain US states and municipalities have begun dealing with the symptoms of public union power. They are meeting with varying degrees of success. These efforts have included wage freezes, employee furloughs, modest reductions in pension benefits, increased retirement ages, switching from defined benefit to defined contribution plans, expanding the number of years from which an employee's final peak salary is calculated for pension purposes, and caps on property taxes. While not without some benefits, efforts to deal with the symptoms of public union power fail to address the root cause. The public interest will require focus on the root cause, especially as the fiscal challenges to state and local governments mount while the quantity and quality of services delivered to citizens diminish. Dealing with the root cause will require citizens to rethink how much latitude they are willing to give public employees to organize and exercise monopoly power to the determinant of public well-being.

The ability of public trusts to coalesce and sustain themselves either directly or through facilitating practices merits scrutiny. President Grover Cleveland's motto was "a public office is a public trust." While "trust" referred to public officials' fiduciary responsibility, the growth of public union power has altered, in a diametrically opposite way, the manner in which Cleveland's motto can be interpreted. If anything, we now have to fear

---

[9] DiSalvo (2015).

the power of public trusts, or combinations in restraints of trade. In the analogy to worries about the marketplace that their private-sector counterparts generated over a century ago, there is a hint of a solution. For the same reason that antitrust statutes were enacted to limit the monopoly power that firms in the private sector can exercise to the detriment of consumers, so too can legal limits be placed on the monopoly power that public workers exert, at the expense of citizens, through collective bargaining and lobbying. Furthermore, practices facilitating public union formation, such as public workers being required to pay "agency fees" for collective bargaining whether they belong to unions or not, can be outlawed.

Some states have done just that, seeking to limit public unions' ability to bargain over pensions and health care. Wisconsin Governor Scott Walker successfully promoted such a legal change in 2011 to restrict public unions from negotiating over fringe benefits. Other legal proceedings have sought to keep union membership dues from being used for lobbying (versus collective bargaining) or to eliminate public-sector agency shops. Ten teachers, for example, sued the California Teachers Union in 2015 for requiring them to pay advocacy fees, $650 of the $1,000 in annual dues. The fees, used to underwrite lobbying, are collected by school districts automatically from teacher paychecks. The US Supreme Court deadlocked, 4–4, in its March 2016 decision on the suit, following the death of Justice Antonin Scalia in February 2016. The suit, which challenged laws allowing the automatic collection of agency fees in twenty-three states, may be reheard once a new, ninth Supreme Court Justice is confirmed.[10] Indiana, Michigan, and Wisconsin have moved even further by adopting right-to-work laws covering public- and private-sector unions. Right-to-work laws, now governing twenty-five US states, prohibit closed shops through which an established union requires workers to become members and pay dues as a condition of employment.

Public unions have contributed to the demise of autocracies also, offering a similar lesson in how government insiders consolidate power and exploit opportunity at the expense of public well-being, indeed ultimately at the expense of their own interests as they bring down their host nation. The ability of Janissaries and scribes to block progress, for example, undermined the Ottoman Empire. The decline of ancient Egypt's New Kingdom can be attributed at least partly to a sizable,

[10] Steve Malanga, "The Legal Case Unions Fear They Cannot Win," *Wall Street Journal*, November 14–15, 2015; and "Victory for Unions as Supreme Court, Scalia Gone, Ties 4–4," *New York Times*, March 29, 2016.

publicly supported priesthood. In communist workers' states, in which the collectivized proletariat theoretically owns the means of production, a well-known quip among the (ostensibly ruling) working class is "they pretend to pay us and we pretend to work." As the "they" and the "we" of the quip intimates, the extent to which workers own the means of production and can exercise their rights collectively under communism is questionable – even though the state-reported union membership numbers are sizable. Part of the reason for Trotsky's fall from power was due to his arguing that the workers' democracy established in the Soviet Union had been betrayed. According to Trotsky, the Soviet Union had turned into a "degenerated workers' state" in which bureaucrats really owned and oversaw the means of production.

How workers' states operate in practice highlights a caveat regarding whether restraining public trusts serves the public interest in the case of autocracies. The caveat stems from the potential for public unions to constrain the pernicious effects of autocrats. Solidarity, the Polish trade union led by Lech Walesa, demonstrates this point. At its peak, Solidarity had 10 million members and was responsible for Poland's semi-free elections in 1989 and the end of communist dictatorship.[11] Unfortunately, no similar constraining effects by public unions on Communist Party dictatorship can be found in present-day China – much as public-sector unions failed to check the Communist Party's autocratic rule of the Soviet Union.

Given the lack of beneficial impacts on national well-being by public unions coupled with their clout and growth in many democracies, such as the United States, checking and rolling back their influence would advance the public interest. Too often, such public trusts operate to the detriment of national well-being. They increase the slack between public employees and citizens (S) and the potential gains (G) from inside jobs. Along the way, public unions also raise the likelihood of attracting individuals who are interested (I) in profiting from their positions (P) at the public's expense ($P = G \times S \times I$).

PROMOTING COMPETITION IN THE SUPPLY OF GOVERNMENT GOODS AND SERVICES

Peering into the black box, we can also see how the public interest can be enhanced by promoting competition in the supply of government goods

---

[11] Ogilvie (2014) analyzes guilds and provides arguments for why unions (public or private) can promote or subvert the public interest in autocracies.

and services. As a nation, we are averse to a single firm providing all of our military goods or computer hardware, as evidenced by the formal procedures designed to foster competitive bids from prospective private-sector suppliers. So too should we be wary of the state being the sole or predominant supplier of K-12 education, medical care for veterans, and postal delivery. Options such as vouchers, charter schools, competitive outsourcing, and franchise bidding are all possible parts of the solution. They all diminish reliance on a sole public provider and thereby the likelihood of inside jobs.[12]

Take the case of the United States Postal Service (USPS), which has a government-enforced monopoly on mail delivery. It lost $5.5 billion in 2014 on revenue of $67.8 billion. Since 1971, when the USPS became more like a private company, it consistently has lost money. Its reform in 1971 sought to make the USPS self-financing, albeit preserving its monopoly, a variety of subsidies, and tax-exempt status. It has been unable to do so. Now, the USPS is exploring fairly dramatic cost-cutting such as suspending Saturday delivery; shuttering smaller and inefficient post offices; and creating "cluster boxes" whereby entire neighborhoods would be served through a common delivery location.

Under market pressures, the USPS operations struggle. Meanwhile, what often goes unnoticed is that the USPS contracts out for activities like rural mail delivery, scanning and encoding letters that are not easily readable, and ferrying express mail (Fed Ex and UPS help with the latter). Ten percent of rural routes are operated by private carriers, who collect and deliver mail, sell stamps, and handle express mail. An internal USPS analysis found that such outsourcing cuts costs by up to 50 percent while improving service quality.[13] The evidence suggests that broader reliance on competitive outsourcing can advance the public interest. Initiatives to do so will need to confront established and theoretical arguments in favor of the state being the sole supplier, such as economies of scale and scope.

Rethinking the conventional wisdom of ever-larger public school districts and municipal service territories also is in order. The trend toward monopolization often has been justified by moral and economic reasons: for example, desegregation, equalizing per-pupil spending, and achieving economies of scale and scope. Yet, monopolization has diminished competition on the supply side of government services and thus has had some

---

[12] See, for example, Demsetz (1968); Friedman (1962); Hoxby (2011); Moe (2011); Shleifer and Vishny (1998); Williamson (1976); and Zupan (1989).

[13] Merewitz and Zupan (1993).

adverse consequences for the public interest. Decisions cannot be driven solely by arguments focused on economies of scale or scope. Political-economy considerations – that is, the deleterious potential for government insiders or other special interests to co-opt the state – also must be incorporated into the policymaking calculus. Policies merit scrutiny if they increase the slack between public officials and citizens (S), the prospective gains from inside jobs (G), or the interest of public officials (I) in profiting at the public's expense.

In promoting competition on the supply side of politics, however, care must be taken not to amplify any common-pool problems. As political scientist Christopher Berry shows, the proliferation in the United States of political jurisdictions focused on providing a single service such as sanitation, education, and health care has exacerbated a common-pool problem. This is because the jurisdictions have the ability to fish for revenues from the same tax base. Overall taxes and the size of local government have grown. The influence of special interests has increased. And the accountability of local officials to citizens has diminished.[14]

LIMITING OPPORTUNITIES TO HOLD PUBLIC POSITIONS FOR LIFE

America's Founders realized that competition for public positions through elections is a primary means to control government. Over time, Americans and the citizens of many other countries also have come to appreciate the value of term limits as a means to curb the potential for political power to ossify in place. In too many nations, however, the possibility of being president (or holding other public positions) for life cultivates opportunity for the inside job because ways to limit political power are weak or null: term limits are lacking, and/or the ballot box lacks sufficient legitimacy or competitiveness.

The negative repercussions when public officials are encrusted in their positions are most evident in autocratic rule. We saw this earlier through the adverse socioeconomic consequences associated with Mao's dictatorship in China, the Kim family's multi-generational vise-hold grip on power in North Korea, the reigns of Bourbon Kings Louis XIV through Louis XV in France, Venezuela under the Chavez-Maduro regime, and Trujillo's kleptocracy in the Dominican Republic. Robert Mugabe's iron-fisted control of Zimbabwe since 1980 provides but another compelling piece of

[14] Berry (2009).

evidence. While his country's social well-being indicators have regressed to their 1960 levels, Mugabe's cronies organized a 91st birthday bash in 2015 for the president for life. Held at a posh golf course at Victoria Falls, the guest list included 20,000 of Mugabe's closest friends. The menu featured elephant, buffalo, antelope, impala, and lion donated by a local farmer. In addition to the $1 million raised by the cronies for the feast, every teacher in Zimbabwe was forced to contribute up to $10.[15]

The negative effects of political power calcifying are not limited to autocracies. We saw this through cases such as Mayor Michael Curley of Boston; Boss Tweed of Tammany Hall; Robert Moses, the domineering force in New York's public works programs in the middle of the last century; and Governor Nelson Rockefeller's role in making the state of New York the high-tax leader in the United States in the process of advancing his political agenda and presidential ambitions. A recent example demonstrates that history at least rhymes if not repeats itself regarding both the corrupting effects of political power calcification in the United States and how it spans political parties. In 2015, New York State's second and third most powerful politicians were arrested on corruption charges: Sheldon Silver, a Democrat, and Dean Skelos, a Republican. Skelos, the Senate majority leader, had served in that body since 1985 and was accused of using his power to advance construction companies that, in turn, funneled jobs and payments to his son. Silver, who served in the state assembly for nearly forty years and as state Speaker for over two decades, became known for his imperious management of the assembly and for his ability to enrich himself and his loyalists through the power that he accumulated.[16] These examples underscore how the danger of political power ossification remains present in democracies as well as autocracies.

Commonly, term limits are considered a logical curb on the longevity of political power, but they are not without their weaknesses. For instance, term limits applied to legislators can impede their ability to acquire expertise and govern effectively, including exercising oversight over the executive branch.[17] Government insiders also are creative at finding ways to evade the intent of term limits – as evidenced in Russia by Vladimir Putin and in Turkey by Recep Erdogan who have managed to rule two countries with term limits on their political chief executive positions. After serving as

---

[15] "Robert Mugabe Eats a Zoo for 'Obscene' 91st Birthday Party," www.independent.co.uk, March 2, 2015.

[16] "Silver & Skelos, New York's Corruption-Trial Double Feature," *New York Post*, November 16, 2015.

[17] See, for example, Cain and Kousser (2004); and Querebin (2016).

prime minister from 2003 to 2014, Erdogan was constitutionally precluded from serving a fourth term as Turkey's political head. He ran instead for the largely ceremonial post of president, was elected, and then began to redefine and consolidate power from that alternative office.[18]

Below the top political rungs, certain policies that insulate public positions merit closer scrutiny in order to limit government insiders from ossifying in office. Some of these policies were instituted for well-intentioned reasons, such as eliminating patronage and party machines through civil service reforms, including competitive exams, qualifications, and regular schedules for advancement and pay raises.[19] Others, such as tenure for US K-12 public school teachers after only two to three years of probationary service, have been justified as a means to prevent discriminatory treatment and to attract talent to the teaching profession. Regardless of intent, however, by strengthening public employees' grip on their positions, the policies diminish the accountability of those employees to the public interest.

Research indicates teachers unions and their efforts to benefit members have nevertheless failed to attract talent to the profession.[20] Moreover, tenure fails to positively impact teacher effectiveness and student outcomes as do other provisions for which teachers unions have collectively bargained, such as requiring a state teaching license to teach and guaranteeing an automatic pay bump for earning a master's degree.[21] By decreasing the emphasis on teaching quality, the ossifying tenure and dismissal systems which are employed by K-12 public systems disproportionately disadvantage the prospects of minority and low-income students.[22] (Furthermore, it is similarly difficult to rationalize tenure on the basis of promoting scholarship and protecting academic freedom, as go the arguments offered in its defense at the university level.) As noted in Chapter 9, it is nearly impossible to fire incompetent K-12 public teachers in the United States. Attempts to weed out poor performers require protracted, expensive, and uphill battles against entrenched unions and collective bargaining rules. Because of the high costs associated with attempted dismissals, poor performers typically end up receiving satisfactory ratings and, if need be, are warehoused or reassigned to new positions and/or schools. Here, a dismissal process, which was intended to protect teachers from arbitrary termination, has been under union influence turned into de facto job

---

[18] "Erdogan Continues to Consolidate Power," *Al-Monitor*, December 26, 2014.
[19] Johnson and Libecap (1994).   [20] Hoxby and Leigh (2004).   [21] Moe (2011).
[22] Chetty, Friedman, and Rockoff (2014).

security – even for public employees whose poor performance is at the expense of the public well-being.

Public job security is not unique to the United States. A law in Greece prevents public workers from being fired solely on the basis of poor performance. Instead, Greeks talk about parking incompetent workers "in the fridge" with pretend jobs. In France, they are positioned "in the cupboard" while Brazilians quip that public employees show up on day one, drape their jackets over the backs of their new chairs, and disappear after that.[23]

The job security of public employees in autocratic settings, if anything, may exceed that of their counterparts in democracies. According to the World Bank, public workers account for a larger share of total employment in the still largely autocratic Arab world than in any other region around the globe. Professor Hala al-Said, at Cairo University, argues that many of these workers "do no work at all" because it is so difficult to lose one's job, even for incompetence.[24] Absenteeism is common due to lack of accountability, while promotions are often based on connections and seniority rather than on merit.[25] In China, while civil servants are expected to undergo an annual review and may be dismissed for poor performance, very few are removed and thus effectively enjoy life tenure. The Ministry of Personnel reports that only 0.06 percent of China's civil servants are dismissed due to poor performance in any given year.[26]

Whether in autocracies or democracies and whether at the highest rungs of power or at lower levels of state employment, institutions such as term limits that curb the ability of public officials to hold onto office merit consideration. By diminishing the slack between public officials and citizens (S), such institutions also curtail the potential gains associated with inside jobs (G) and the likelihood of attracting individuals who are interested (I) in profiting at the public's expense to public service.

GOVERNANCE FORMS PROMOTING GREATER ACCOUNTABILITY

In economics, promoting the public interest is taken to mean maximizing a society's total net economic benefits given an initial resource distribution, and by this benchmark, however idealized it may be, various systems of

---

[23] "(Government) Workers of the World Unite!" *The Economist*, January 6, 2011.
[24] "Aiwa (Yes) Minister," *The Economist*, November 14, 2015.   [25] Ibid.
[26] Burns (2007).

government measure up in different ways. While we have seen that democracy, on average, does better than autocracy in diminishing public-sector corruption, there are exceptions. Realpolitik can involve a more limited and less-appealing set of options, for one example, and the "best" form of government thus has to be calibrated against what else is available. Autocracy, in other words, may better serve the public interest if the only other option is civil war or a nonfunctioning, corrupt democracy.

While autocracy has declined over the past two centuries, this does not imply that it lacks favorable features. Indeed, it may be the preferred form of government relative to other available options. Consider hereditary monarchy. Most would agree that it is superior to anarchy. In addition, it has some virtues. For example, as with family-run firms, hereditary monarchs are likely to make decisions from a longer-run perspective if they care about promoting their genes (for evolutionary biology reasons) or the general interests of their families.

In addition, by specifying a clear succession plan, hereditary monarchies reduce the prospect of a disruptive civil war. This was a critical failing of the Ottoman Empire when it relied on an open, or survival of the fittest, succession model. Until a less-disruptive approach to succession was established in the seventeenth century, the passage of power hinged on either a sultan's favorite concubine at the time of his death or each male offspring of the sultan and his proximity to Constantinople.[27] Consequently, many aspiring sultans-to-be ended up either being placed in golden cages or murdered by their brothers. Such untoward demises resulted from being the offspring of less-favored concubines or governing more faraway provinces, thus being at a disadvantage of getting to the capital "the fastest with the most-est" upon learning of their father's death.

The trend away from autocracies, including hereditary monarchy, since the 1800s, is the result of a quasi-market for political control, upheavals which often were triggered by the relative cost of autocracy. The relative cost of an autocracy increases as a nation becomes more productive through specialization, education, and trade – and on account of the inside jobs that are more likely to occur in such a form of government. A higher opportunity cost incents change toward a governance form with better checks and balances on the supply side of politics. Relative to autocracy, democracy on average improves public-sector integrity and limits the

---

[27] Bueno de Mesquita and Smith (2011) and Fukuyama (2011). In the seventeenth century, an agnatic approach to succession was adopted whereby power passed to a ruler's younger brother upon the death of a sultan.

extent to which a nation's rulers can hang on to political power – at least before its supply side begins to capture political power to the detriment of the people *by* whom it is elected and *for* whom it presumably works.

Beyond promoting democracy over autocracy, opportunities remain for increasing public-sector integrity through limiting government growth and enhancing checks and balances on the supply side of politics in democracies. This is because democracy, government *by* the people, does not ensure government *for* the people. The research of Persson and Tabellini, noted in Chapter 5, suggest some potential constitutional improvements in democracies. For example, Persson and Tabellini find that majoritarian electoral rules outperform proportional ones. Proportional electoral rules enhance the holdout or monopoly power of minority interest groups. This greater power, which operates both through the demand and supply sides of politics, increases government spending and public budget deficits relative to democracies with majoritarian voting.[28]

Persson and Tabellini also find that presidential systems reduce the size of government by 5 percent of GDP, or at least as much as majoritarian elections. Relative to parliamentary countries, which have fewer checks and balances between the executive and legislative branches, presidential systems promote greater overall accountability of the supply side of politics in democracies, at least as accountability is reflected by fiscal performance.[29]

The Persson and Tabellini findings have implications for subnational democracies. For instance, it might seem that cities run by a professionally trained manager who is not popularly elected but appointed by a city council might be more efficient than ones in which a popularly elected mayor hires and fires key officials outside of the merit system. A popularly elected executive (mayor), however, can provide a check on the legislature (city council), in keeping with Persson and Tabellini's comparison of presidential versus parliamentary forms of government. The net impact of these opposing forces appears to be a wash. At least in US cities, there is no difference in the relative efficiency of city manager and mayor-council forms of government when it comes to the costs of providing various services such as police, fire protection, and waste collection.[30]

Whether comparing autocracies to democracies or different governance forms within democracies, such as parliamentary and presidential systems, the extent to which public officials profit at the public's expense (*P*) is determined by the three factors in our government self-capture equation.

[28] Persson and Tabellini (2003).   [29] Ibid.   [30] Hayes and Chang (1990).

Specifically, governance forms will more effectively promote national well-being when they diminish the slack between public officials and citizens (S), the prospective gains from inside jobs (G), and the interest of public officials in co-opting the state for their benefit (I).

IMPROVING GOVERNMENT TRANSPARENCY AND MONITORING BY CITIZENS

Many different methods are available for improving government transparency that enables citizens to monitor their public officials more effectively – thus reducing slack between citizens and their public officials, the prospective gains from inside jobs, and the likelihood of attracting individuals interested in profiting from public positions at the expense of national well-being. Advances in communication, transportation, information, and productivity increase citizen mobility, reduce the cost of collective action, and enhance benchmarking with respect to public policies. These effects all make it costlier for government insiders to subvert the public interest. Anything that can be done, therefore, to improve government transparency and monitoring by citizens should be championed. A free press helps along these lines as do measures such as Transparency International, Freedom House, Economic Freedom of the World, and the Index of Economic Freedom that independently assess public-sector integrity and political and economic freedom across countries. Technological innovations that increase "reporting" by a broader public and disseminate information more rapidly and extensively also foster government transparency while boosting the policing by citizens of their public officials.[31] To mitigate the damage that autocrats can do to their nations, political scientists Bruce Bueno de Mesquita and Alastair Smith recommend using foreign aid to provide mobile phones for the poor and establishing broad-based wireless access to the Internet.[32] In other words, a relatively small increment of aid can trigger significant improvements in the quasi-market operating in the political sphere.

Autocrats, still governing a third of the world's countries, are increasingly at risk of ouster by popular revolt. The proportion of autocrats ousted by revolt tripled from 4 percent during the Cold War to 12 percent since the Cold War's end in 1989. The proportion increased further to 25 percent

---

[31] The goal of American Transparency's project, Open the Books, is to put all public spending (federal, state, and local) information online through a mobile app. See Tom Coburn, "Tracking Government Waste – There's an App for That," *Wall Street Journal*, October 6, 2015.

[32] Bueno de Mesquita and Smith (2011).

over 2010–2012.[33] Political scientists note that technologies such as email, Twitter, YouTube, and Facebook increase the potential for autocrats to be removed by popular revolt. Social media lower the costs of collective action by broadly and quickly publicizing regime abuses that can serve as triggering events. Social media also provided models for taking to the streets in its vivid images during the Arab Spring and the color revolutions which unseated autocrats in Georgia, Kyrgyzstan, and Ukraine in the prior decade. It became the conduit for ousting unpopular rulers.[34]

Of course, a Facebook friend is not the same as a real friend. Social media have advantages in terms of speed and breadth of coverage but they lack depth. In a *New Yorker* essay, Malcolm Gladwell notes that social media foster weak-tie connections, compared to the strong-tie connections that are vital to strategic and disciplined activity:[35]

Social media [enthusiasts] would ... have us believe that [Martin Luther] King's task in Birmingham would have been made infinitely easier had he been able to communicate with his followers through Facebook, and ... [Tweeted] from a Birmingham jail. But networks are messy: think of the ceaseless pattern of correction and revision ... and debate, that characterizes Wikipedia ... [If King] had tried to do a wiki-boycott in Montgomery, he would have been steamrolled by the white power structure. And of what use would a digital ... tool be in a town where 98 percent of the community could be reached every Sunday morning in church? The things that King needed ... discipline and strategy ... were things that online social media cannot provide.

Although Gladwell's point is well taken, both weak- and strong-tie connections can increase the accountability of public officials. When the connections are enhanced through advances in communication, information, transportation, and productivity, government transparency and monitoring by citizens improve.[36]

CONSTITUTIONAL CURBS ON PUBLIC SPENDING AND DEBT

When it comes to political collective action, taxpayers are the most poorly organized interest group and suffer the consequences. They are not motivated

---

[33] Kendall-Taylor and Frantz (2014).

[34] Ibid. The manner in which autocrats get ousted affects a nation's political trajectory. While autocratic exits lead to democracy only 20 percent of the time, the odds of such a transition increase markedly when the exit is due to popular revolt. Ouster through popular revolt led to democracy 45 percent of the time between 1946 and 2012 versus only 10 percent of the time when autocrats were overthrown by coups.

[35] Gladwell (2010), pp. 46–49.   [36] Micklethwait and Wooldridge (2014).

like other interest groups to organize more actively due to how widely diffused their benefits are from any reduced public spending. Future taxpayers are even more poorly represented in politics because they are not even present to represent their interests in the present-day political arena.[37] The less-organized, motivated, and present the taxpayers, the greater the ability of government insiders and special interests from the demand side of politics to co-opt power for their benefit and at the expense of the public interest.

Even with better techniques for monitoring, well-organized taxpayers face the challenge that deficit spending makes the present-day cost of public policies opaque. Moreover, compared to future taxpayers, government insiders focus on near-term payoffs which they can secure while still in power. Due to these considerations, constitutionally mandated speed bumps limiting public officials' ability to overspend, or otherwise to slough off obligations to future generations merit consideration. Prospective speed bumps include budget rules limiting government growth and deficits. Examples are a balanced budget rule and a "debt brake" rule such as the one approved in 2001 by 85 percent of Swiss voters.

As noted by political scientist David Primo, effective budget rules must overcome significant design and enforcement difficulties. Since budget rules emanate from a political process, special interests are incented to oppose fiscal limits. Moreover, even if a well-designed limit is enacted, it needs to be enforced.[38]

In a democracy with multiple government branches such as the United States, the Supreme Court could enforce a balanced budget rule, and making it a constitutional amendment would offer an added safeguard. However, amendment passage requires, among other things, two-thirds approval by both the House and the Senate. In 1995, vested interests successfully fought approval of a balanced budget amendment while ensuring that any proposed cap was loaded with loopholes.

The Swiss debt brake rule caps any increases in federal government spending to average tax revenue increases over a multiyear period. To enforce the limit, any reliance on debt has to be approved by both chambers of parliament. Furthermore, any spending that would increase taxes requires a double-majority referendum, meaning a majority of voters in a majority of Switzerland's cantons must approve. This is unlikely given that Swiss voters have historically much more regularly approved tax cuts

---

[37] See, for example, Kotlikoff and Burns (2012).   [38] Primo (2007, 2014).

than tax increases.[39] Prior to the debt brake rule being enacted in 2003, Swiss federal spending increased 4.3 percent per year. Since then, spending has increased by 2.6 percent annually.[40] While the average debt-to-GDP ratio for euro-zone nations rose from 70 percent in 2005 to 92 percent in 2014, Switzerland's ratio declined from 53 percent to 35 percent over the same period.

The success of the Swiss debt brake rule suggests that constitutional speed bumps that protect a nation's taxpayers are likely to advance the public interest. Such speed bumps diminish the slack between public officials and their citizens (S), the prospective gains from inside jobs (G), and the likelihood that individuals interested (I) in profiting from power at the public's expense will be attracted to public office.

IN CLOSING

While we have covered considerable ground in terms of time, place, and across governance forms in an effort to show how the potency of the economic model of politics can be enhanced through a better understanding of the supply side of politics, many related issues remain to be explored. For example, what is the impact of general government insiders, apart from leaders, on national well-being and can this effect be disentangled from the role played by leaders? Can we develop better measures of government insider interests and how they maintain their hold on the apparatus of the state? While political scientists have made some headway in gauging the duration of autocratic regimes, more work remains to be done on the extent and means through which government insiders hang on to power in democracies as well as autocracies, especially when looking below the easier-to-measure level occupied by top leaders. For instance, can the successive US presidencies of Ronald Reagan and George H. W. Bush be considered to be one continuous political regime? How about the successive hold over the position of prime minister of the United Kingdom by Margaret Thatcher and John Major?

To what extent can the symbiotic capture of power by government insiders and special-interest groups from the demand side of politics be curtailed by mechanisms such as term limits, constitutionally mandated speed bumps that protect general taxpayers, and promoting competition in

---

[39] Daniel Mitchell, "How the Swiss 'Debt Brake' Tamed Government," *Wall Street Journal*, April 25, 2012.
[40] Ibid.

the supply of government goods and services? To what extent is symbiotic capture facilitated by policies such as the landmark US Supreme Court decision in 2010 in the *Citizens United* case that overturned a long-standing ban on unions and corporate spending to advance the electoral prospects of candidates for political office?[41]

What explains the global trend toward greater political and economic freedom over the past two centuries as well as over the last several decades? What about the drivers of increased public-sector integrity in both democracies and autocracies? Are there certain curbs on government insiders that are gaining traction and from which we further can take heart, or is the trend a temporary aberration? A century ago, the prevalence of autocracies was greater and the average tenure of political leaders was longer than today. One can conjecture that the curbs imposed by benchmarking as well as citizen mobility and monitoring have been acquiring greater bite on account of improved communication technology and lower transportation and information costs. In addition, the opportunity cost associated with extractive behavior by government insiders has arguably grown over the past century due to increases in per capita real productivity and the relative importance of human capital to national well-being. The quasi-market which operates in politics, albeit often with violent strings attached, appears to have responded to this increase in autocracy's opportunity cost and the diminished slack between citizens and their rulers. However, systematic empirical verification of the influence of such factors remains to be done.

Speculating even more broadly, to what extent do inside jobs pose a greater problem in the political arena versus other settings such as non-profit institutions and for-profit firms? While there are more mechanisms fostering accountability in such alternative settings, the alignment remains imperfect between an organization's principals/owners and the managers who are hired as their agents to run the organization.[42] The imperfect alignment is attested to by the inside jobs that have occurred at various points in organizations such as Kodak, the Catholic Church, Satyam, United Way, FIFA, Adelphi University, the International Olympic Committee, and Tyco. In these settings beyond the political arena it is often termed the principal–agent problem.[43] Whether the damage is less extensive there than in the political arena is a testable hypothesis.

Suffice it to say, there appears to be a lot in what has heretofore been treated, at least by most economists, as a black box with regard to the

---

[41] Mayer (2016).   [42] See, for example, Jensen and Murphy (1990).
[43] Jensen and Meckling (1976).

supply side of politics. This book's overriding purpose has been to suggest that prying open the black box enhances our understanding of national well-being. Admittedly, it has done so with a minimum of figures (one), equations (one), and tables (two), while drawing on insights from other fields in the social sciences and humanities such as history, political science, sociology, and psychology so as to better illuminate the potency of the economic model of politics.

In conclusion, this chapter's proposed steps leave room for optimism regarding better mitigating the potential for an inside job. Like Dorothy and her red slippers in the film *The Wizard of Oz*, we, the people, have it within our ever-increasing power to form a more perfect union. While the historical and global trend toward democracy is to be cheered, we must remain mindful that government *by* the people also must operate *for* the people. Democracy, simply put, is not sufficient. This book has been written to help, at least in some small measure, to rededicate us to the noble cause of ensuring government for the people.

Bibliography

Abram, Michael and Joseph Cooper (1968). "The Rise of Seniority in the House of Representatives." *Polity* 1 (1): 52–85.

Abramowitz, Moses (1986). "Catching Up, Forging Ahead, and Falling Behind." *Journal of Economic History* 46 (2): 389–406.

Abrams, Burton A. and Russell F. Settle (1978). "The Economic Theory of Regulation and Public Financing of Presidential Elections." *Journal of Political Economy* 86 (2): 245–257.

Acemoglu, Daron (2003). "Why Not a Political Coase Theorem? Social Conflict, Commitment, and Politics." *Journal of Comparative Economics* 31 (4): 620–652.

Acemoglu, Daron and James A. Robinson (2006). *Economic Origins of Dictatorship and Democracy*. New York: Cambridge University Press.

(2006). "Economic Backwardness in Political Perspective." *American Political Science Review* 100 (1): 115–131.

(2012). *Why Nations Fail: The Origins of Power, Prosperity, and Poverty*. New York: Crown Publishers.

(2013). "Economics versus Politics: Pitfalls of Policy Advice." *Journal of Economic Perspectives* 27 (2): 173–192.

(2015). "The Rise and Decline of General Laws of Capitalism." *Journal of Economic Perspectives* 29 (1): 3–28.

Acemoglu, Daron, James A. Robinson, and Thierry Verdier (2004). "Kleptocracy and Divide-and-Rule: A Model of Personal Rule." *Journal of the European Economic Association* 2 (2–3): 162–192.

Acemoglu, Daron and Matthew Jackson (2015). "History, Expectations, and Leadership in the Evolution of Social Norms." *Review of Economic Studies* 82 (1): 1–34.

Acemoglu, Daron, Suresh Naidu, Pascual Restrepo, and James A. Robinson (2014). "Democracy Does Cause Growth." Unpublished manuscript, Department of Economics, MIT.

Acemoglu, Daron, Tristan Reed, and James A. Robinson (2014). "Chiefs: Economic Development and Elite Control of Civil Society in Sierra Leone." *Journal of Political Economy* 122 (2): 319–368.

Ackerman, Kenneth D. (2011). *Boss Tweed: The Corrupt Pol Who Conceived the Soul of Modern New York*. Falls Church, VA: Viral History Press.

Aghion, Philippe, Alberto Alesina, and Francesco Trebbi (2008). "Democracy, Technology, and Growth." In *Institutions and Economic Performance*, 511–543. Edited by Elhanan Helpman. Cambridge, MA: Harvard University Press.

Aghion, Philippe, Yann Algan, Pierre Cahuc, and Andrei Shleifer (2010). "Regulation and Distrust." *Quarterly Journal of Economics* 125 (3): 1015–1049.

Ahman, Ehtisham, Li Keping, and Thomas J. Richardson (2002). "Recentralization in China," IMF Working Paper, Number 2/168.

Alchian, Armen A. and Harold Demsetz (1972). "Production, Information Costs, and Economic Organization." *American Economic Review* 62 (5): 777–795.

Alesina, Alberto and Paola Giuliano (2015). "Culture and Institutions." *Journal of Economic Literature* 53 (4): 898–944.

Anzia, Sarah F. and Terry M. Moe (2015). "Public Sector Unions and the Costs of Government." *Journal of Politics* 77 (1): 114–127.

Aranson, Peter H. and Peter C. Ordeshook (1977). "A Prolegomenon to a Theory of the Failure of Representative Democracy." In *American Re-evolution Papers and Proceedings*, 23–46. Edited by Richard D. Auster and Barbara Sears. Tucson, AZ: University of Arizona Press.

Atsmon, Yuval and Max Magni (2012). "Meet the Chinese Consumer of 2020." *The McKinsey Quarterly* 50 (1): 1–10.

Barro, Robert J. (1996). "Democracy and Growth." *Journal of Economic Growth* 1 (1): 1–27.

Becker, Gary S. (1983). "Competition Among Pressure Groups for Political Influence." *Quarterly Journal of Economics* 98 (3): 371–398.

Bell, Daniel A. (2015). *The China Model: Political Meritocracy and the Limits of Democracy*. Princeton, NJ: Princeton University Press.

Bensel, Richard F. (1990). *Yankee Leviathan: The Origins of Central State Authority in America, 1859–1877*. New York: Cambridge University Press.

Bernstein, Peter L. (2005). *Wedding of the Waters: The Erie Canal and the Making of a Great Nation*. New York: W. W. Norton & Company.

Berry, Christopher R. (2009). *Imperfect Union: Representation and Taxation in Multi-level Governments*. New York: Cambridge University Press.

Bloom, David E., David Canning, and Gunther Fink (2008). "Urbanization and the Wealth of Nations." *Science* 319: 772–775.

Borcherding, Thomas E. (1977). Editor. *Budgets and Bureaucrats: The Sources of Government Growth*. Durham, NC: Duke University Press.

Borcherding, Thomas E., Werner W. Pommerehne, and Friedrich Schneider (1982). "Comparing the Efficiency of Private and Public Production: The Evidence from Five Countries." *Zeitschrift fur Nationalokonomie* 42 (2): 127–156.

Brill, Steven (August 31, 2009). "The Rubber Room: The Battle over New York's Worst Teachers." *The New Yorker*: 30–36.

Browder, Bill (2015). *Red Notice: A True Story of High Finance, Murder, and One Man's Fight for Justice*. New York: Simon & Schuster.

Browning, Edgar K. (1975). "Why the Social Insurance Budget Is Too Large in a Democracy." *Economic Inquiry* 13 (3): 373–388.

(2008). *Stealing From Each Other: How the Welfare State Robs Americans of Money and Spirit*. Westport, CN: Praeger.

Brunner, Karl (1978). "Reflections on the Political Economy of Government: The Persistent Growth of Government." *Swiss Journal of Economics and Statistics* 114 (3): 649–680.

Buchanan, James M. (1972). "Before Public Choice." In *Explorations in the Theory of Anarchy*, 27–37. Edited by Gordon Tullock. Blacksburg, VA: Center for the Study of Public Choice, Virginia Polytechnic Institute.

Buchanan, James M. and Gordon Tullock (1977). "The Expanding Public Sector: Wagner Squared." *Public Choice* 31 (1): 147–150.

Buchanan, James M. and Richard E. Wagner (1977). *Democracy in Deficit: The Political Legacy of Lord Keynes*. Indianapolis, IN: The Liberty Fund.

Buchanan, James M. and Richard A. Musgrave (1999). *Public Finance and Public Choice*. Cambridge, MA: MIT Press.

Bueno de Mesquita, and Alastair Smith (2011). *The Dictator's Handbook*. New York: Public Affairs.

Buck, Pearl S. (1931). *The Good Earth*. New York: P. F. Collier & Son.

Burgess, Robin, Remi Jedwab, Edward Miguel, Ameet Morjaria, and Gerard Padro Miquel (2015). "The Value of Democracy: Evidence from Road Building in Kenya." *American Economic Review* 105 (6): 1817–1851.

Burns, John P. (2007). "Civil Service Reform in China." *OECD Journal on Budgeting* 7 (1): 57–81.

Cain, Bruce E. and Thad Kousser (2004). *Adapting to Term Limits: Recent Experiences and New Directions*. San Francisco, CA: Public Policy Institute of California.

Cain, Bruce, John Ferejohn, and Morris Fiorina (1987). *The Personal Vote: Constituency Service and Electoral Independence*. Cambridge, MA: Harvard University Press.

Camerer, Colin (1983). *Behavioral Game Theory: Experiments in Strategic Interactions*. Princeton, NJ: Princeton University Press.

Cameron, Averil (1993). *The Later Roman Empire*. Cambridge, MA: Harvard University Press.

Caplan, Bryan (2006). *The Myth of the Rational Voter*. Princeton, NJ: Princeton University Press.

Card, David, and Alan Krueger (1992a). "Does School Quality Matter? Returns to Education and the Characteristics of Public Schools in the United States." *Journal of Political Economy* 100 (1): 1–40.

(1992b). "School Quality and Black-White Relative Earnings: A Direct Assessment." *Quarterly Journal of Economics* 107 (1): 151–200.

Carlin, John (2009). *Invictus*. New York: Penguin Press.

Carlyle, Thomas (1841). *On Heroes, Hero-Worship, and the Heroic in History*. London: James Fraser.

Caro, Robert A. (1974). *The Power Broker: Robert Moses and the Fall of New York*. New York: Alfred A. Knopf, Inc.

(2012). *The Passage of Power*. New York: Alfred A. Knopf, Inc.

Carson, Jamie L., Erik J. Engstrom, and Jason M. Roberts (2006). "Redistricting, Candidate Entry, and the Politics of Nineteenth-Century U.S. House Elections." *American Journal of Political Science* 50 (2): 283–293.

Chayes, Sarah (2015). *Thieves of State: Why Corruption Threatens Global Security*. New York: W. W. Norton & Company.

Chen, Jowei, and Tim Johnson (2015). "Federal Employee Unionization and Presidential Control of the Bureaucracy: Estimating and Explaining Ideological Change in Executive Agencies." *Journal of Theoretical Politics* 27 (1): 151–171.

Chetty, Raj, John N. Friedman, and Jonah E. Rockoff (2014). "Measuring the Impacts of Teachers II: Teacher Value-Added and Student Outcomes in Adulthood." *American Economic Review* 104 (9): 2633–2679.

Chua, Amy (2011). *Battle Hymn of the Tiger Mother*. New York: Penguin Press.

Chubb, John E., and Terry M. Moe (1990). *Politics, Markets, and American Schools*. Washington, DC: Brookings Institution.

Coase, Ronald H. (1937). "The Nature of the Firm." *Economica* 4 (16): 386–405.

 (1960). "The Problem of Social Cost." *Journal of Law and Economics* 3 (1): 1–44.

 (1964). "The Regulated Industries: Discussion." *American Economic Review* 54 (2): 194–197.

Coase, Ronald H., and Ning Wang (2012). *How China Became Capitalist*. New York: Palgrave MacMillan.

Cornell, Stephen, and Joseph P. Kalt (2000). "Where's the Glue? Institutional and Cultural Foundations of American Indian Economic Development." *Journal of Socio-Economics* 29 (3): 443–470.

Corruption Perceptions Index (Annual). Berlin, Germany: Transparency International.

Cost, Jay (2015). *A Republic No More: Big Government and the Rise of American Corruption*. New York: Encounter Books.

Cowen, Tyler, and Daniel Sutter (1997). "Politics and the Pursuit of Fame." *Public Choice* 93 (1–2): 19–35.

Cowen, Tyler, Amihai Glazer, and Henry McMillan (1994). "Rent Seeking Can Promote the Provision of Public Goods." *Economics and Politics* 6 (2): 131–145.

Crew, Michael A., and Paul R. Kleindorfer (1993). Editors. *Regulation and the Nature of Postal and Delivery Services*. Boston, MA: Kluwer.

Crow, Carl (1938). *The Chinese Are Like That*. New York: Harper and Brothers.

Dalberg-Acton, John E. E. (1907). "Letter to Bishop Mandell Creighton, April 5, 1887." In *Historical Essays and Studies*, 504. Edited by John N. Figgis and Reginald V. Laurence. London: Macmillan.

Deaton, Angus (2013). *The Great Escape: Health, Wealth, and the Origins of Inequality*. Princeton, NJ: Princeton University Press.

DeCelles, Katherine, D. Scott DeRue, Joshua D. Margolis, and Tara L. Ceranic (2012). "Does Power Corrupt or Enable?: When and Why Power Facilitates Self-Interested Behavior." *Journal of Applied Psychology* 97 (3): 681–689.

DeLong, Bradford J., and Andrei Shleifer (1993). "Princes and Merchants: European City Growth Before the Industrial Revolution." *Journal of Law and Economics* 36 (2): 671–702.

Demsetz, Harold E. (1968). "Why Regulate Public Utilities?" *Journal of Law and Economics* 11 (1): 55–65.

Diamond, Jared (1997). *Guns, Germs and Steel*. New York: W. W. Norton.

Diermeier, Daniel, Michael P. Keane, and Antonio M. Merlo (2005). "A Political Economy Model of Congressional Careers." *American Economic Review* 95 (1): 347–373.

Di Lodovico, Amadeo M., William W. Lewis, Vincent Palmade, and Shirish Sankhe (2001). "India: From Emerging to Surging." *The McKinsey Quarterly* 4 (Special Edition): 28–50.

DiIulio, John J., Jr. (2014). *Bring Back the Bureaucrats*. West Coshohocken, PA: Templeton Press.

DiSalvo, Daniel (2010). "The Trouble with Public Sector Unions." *National Affairs* 5: 3–19.

   (2015). *Government Against Itself: Public Union Power and Its Consequences*. Oxford, UK: Oxford University Press.

Dobbie, Will, and Roland G. Fryer, Jr. (2015). "The Medium-Term Impacts of High-Achieving Charter Schools." *Journal of Political Economy* 123 (5): 985–1037.

Downs, Anthony (1957). *An Economic Theory of Democracy*. New York: Harper.

Doyle, Michael W. (1983). "Kant, Liberal Legacies, and Foreign Affairs." *Philosophy and Public Affairs* 12 (4): 205–235.

Duhigg, Charles (2012). *The Power of Habit: Why We Do What We Do in Life and Business*. New York: Random House.

   (2016). *Smarter Faster Better*. New York: Random House.

Edwards, Chris, and Jagadeesh Gokhale (2006). "Unfunded State and Local Health Costs: $1.4 Trillion." *Tax and Budget Bulletin 40*. Washington, DC: Cato Institute.

Eliot, T. S. (1943). "Little Gidding." *Four Quartets*. New York: Harcourt, Inc.

Ellison, Sarah (January 2015). "Which Blair Project." *Vanity Fair*, 54–68.

Farr, W. Ken, Richard A. Lord, and J. Larry Wolfenbarger (1998). "Economic Freedom, Political Freedom, and Economic Well-Being: A Causality Analysis." *Cato Journal* 18 (2): 247–262.

Fenno, Richard (1978). *Homestyle: House Members and Their Districts*. Boston, MA: Little, Brown.

Ferguson, Niall (2006). *The War of the World: Twentieth Century Conflict and the Descent of the West*. New York: Penguin Books.

Fiorina, Morris P., and Roger G. Noll (1978). "Voters, Bureaucrats and Legislators: A Rational Choice Perspective on the Growth of Bureaucracy." *Journal of Public Economics* 9 (2): 239–254.

Fisman, Raymond, Florian Schulz, and Vikrant Vig (2014). "The Private Returns to Public Office." *Journal of Political Economy* 122 (4): 806–862.

Fox, J. Ronald (1988). *The Defense Management Challenge*. Boston: Harvard Business School Press.

Freedom House (Annual). *Freedom in the World: Annual Survey of Political Rights and Civil Liberties*. Boston: Freedom House.

Freeman, Richard B. (1986). "Unionism Comes to the Public Sector." In *When Public Sector Workers Unionize*, 365–398. Edited by Richard B. Freeman and Casey Ichniovski. Chicago: University of Chicago Press.

Friedman, Milton (1962). *Capitalism and Freedom*. Chicago: University of Chicago Press.

Friedman, Milton, and Rose D. Friedman (1984). *Tyranny of the Status Quo*. New York: Houghton Mifflin Harcourt.

Fukuyama, Francis (1992). *The End of History and the Last Man*. New York: Free Press.

   (2011). *The Origins of Political Order: From Prehuman Times to the French Revolution*. New York: Farrar, Straus and Giroux.

(2014). *Political Order and Political Decay: From the Industrial Revolution to the Globalization of Democracy.* New York: Farrar, Straus and Giroux.

Galbraith, John Kenneth (1958). *The Affluent Society.* Boston: Houghton Mifflin.

Galloway, George B. (1959). "Development of the Committee System in the House." *The American Historical Review* 65 (1): 17–30.

Gandhi, Jennifer, and Adam Przeworski (2007). "Authoritarian Institutions and the Survival of Autocrats." *Comparative Political Studies* 40 (11): 1279–1301.

Garen, John, and Jeff R. Clark (2015). "Trust and the Growth of Government." Unpublished manuscript, Gatton College of Business and Economics, University of Kentucky.

Geddes, Barbara, Joseph Wright, and Erica Frantz (2014). "Autocratic Breakdown and Regime Transitions: A New Data Set." *Perspectives on Politics* 12 (2): 313–331.

Gibbon, Edward ([1776–1789] 1974). *The History of the Decline and Fall of the Roman Empire.* Edited by John Bagnell Bury. New York: AMS Press.

Gladwell, Malcolm (October 2010). "Small Change." *The New Yorker*, 42–49.

Glaeser, Edward L., and Andrei Shleifer (2005). "The Economics of Shaping the Electorate." *Journal of Law, Economics, and Organization* 21 (1):1–19.

Glaeser, Edward L., Joseph Gyourko, and Raven E. Saks (2005). "Why Have Housing Prices Gone Up?" *American Economic Review* 95 (2): 329–333.

Glassman, Matthew E., and Amber H. Wilhelm (2015). *Congressional Career: Service Tenure and Patterns of Member Service, 1789–2015.* CRS Report for Congress 7-5700. Washington, DC: Congressional Research Service.

Goff, Brian L., and Robert D. Tollison (1990). "Is National Defense A Pure Public Good?" *Defence Economics* 1: 141–147.

Goldin, Claudia, and Lawrence F. Katz (2008). *The Race Between Education and Technology.* Cambridge, MA: Harvard University Press.

Goodwin, A.J.H. (1957). "The Medieval Empire of Ghana." *South African Archaeological Bulletin* (12): 108–112.

Greenstein, Shane (2015). *How the Internet Became Commercial: Innovation, Privatization, and the Birth of a New Network.* Princeton, NJ: Princeton University Press.

Grief, Avner (1994). "Cultural Beliefs and the Organization of Society: A Historical and Theoretical Reflection on Collectivist and Individualist Societies." *Journal of Political Economy* 102 (5): 912–950.

Gropper, Daniel M., John Jahera, and Jung-Chul Park (2015). "Political Power, Economic Freedom, and Congress: Effects on Bank Performance." *Journal of Banking and Finance* 60:76–92.

Guiso, Luigi, Paola Sapienza, and Luigi Zingales (2015). "Corporate Culture, Societal Culture, and Institutions." *American Economic Review* 105 (5): 336–339.

Gwartney, James D., Randall G. Holcombe, and Robert A. Lawson (1998). "The Scope of Government and the Wealth of Nations." *Cato Journal* 18: 163–190.

Gwartney, James D., Robert A. Lawson, and Joshua Hall (Annual). *Economic Freedom of the World.* Vancouver, BC: Fraser Institute.

Hamilton, Alexander, John Jay, and James Madison ([1788] 1982). *The Federalist Papers.* Toronto: Bantam Books.

Hansmann, Henry B. (1986). "The Role of Nonprofit Enterprise." In *The Economics of Nonprofit Institutions: Studies in Structure and Policy*, 161–184. Edited by Susan Rose-Ackerman. New York: Oxford University Press.

Hanushek, Eric A. (2009). "Teacher Deselection." In *Creating a New Teaching Profession*, 165–180. Edited by Dan Goldhaber and Jane Hannaway. Washington, DC: Urban Institute Press.

Harrell, Stevan (1985). "Why Do the Chinese Work So Hard?" *Modern China* 11 (2): 203–226.

Hayek, Friedrich A. (1944). *The Road to Serfdom*. Chicago, IL: University of Chicago Press.

Hayes, Kathy, and Semoon Chang (1990). "The Relative Efficiency of City Manager and Mayor-Council Forms of Government." *Southern Economic Journal* 51 (1): 167–177.

Heitger, Bernhard (2004). "Property Rights and the Wealth of Nations: A Cross-Country Study." *Cato Journal* 23 (3): 381–402.

Hibbert, Christopher (1980). *The French Revolution*. New York: Penguin Press.

Hibbing, John R. (1991). "The Modern Congressional Career." *The American Political Science Review* 85: 404–425.

Higgs, Robert (1990). Editor. *Arms, Politics, and the Economy*. New York: Holmes and Meier.

Hirschman, Albert O. (1970). *Exit, Voice, and Loyalty: Responses to Decline in Firms, Organizations, and States*. Cambridge, MA: Harvard University Press.

Hodler, Roland, and Paul A. Raschky (2014). "Regional Favoritism." *Quarterly Journal of Economics* 129 (2): 995–1033.

Holcombe, Randall G. (2012). "Make Economics Policy Relevant: Depose the Omniscient Benevolent Dictator." *The Independent Review* 17 (2): 165–176.

(2015). "Political Capitalism." *Cato Journal* 35 (1): 41–66.

Holcombe, Randall G., and Christopher J. Boudreaux (2013). "Institutional Quality and the Tenure of Autocrats." *Public Choice* 156 (3): 409–421.

Holderlin, Friedrich (2008). *Hyperion*. Translated by Ross Benjamin. Brooklyn, NY: Archipelago Books.

Hollyer, James R., and Leonard Wantchekon (2015). "Corruption and Ideology in Autocracies." *Journal of Law, Economics, and Organization* 31 (3): 499–533.

Holt, Frank L. (2016). *The Treasures of Alexander the Great: How One Man's Wealth Shaped the World*. New York: Oxford University Press.

Hoxby, Caroline M. (1996). "How Teachers Unions Affect Education Production." *Quarterly Journal of Economics*. 111 (3): 671–718.

(2000). "Does Competition Among Public Schools Benefit Students and Taxpayers?" *American Economic Review* 90 (5): 1209–1238.

Hoxby, Caroline M. (2011). Editor. *The Economics of School Choice*. Chicago: University of Chicago Press.

Hoxby, Caroline M., and Andrew Leigh (2004). "Pulled Away or Pushed Out: Explaining the Decline of Teacher Aptitude in the U.S." *American Economic Review* 94 (2): 236–240.

Hubbard, Glenn, and Tim Kane (2013). *Balance: The Economics of Great Powers From Ancient Rome to Modern America*. New York: Simon & Schuster.

Hummler, Konrad. (2004). "Globalization: Phase 2," *Wegelin Investment Commentary No. 232*.

(2009). "States Under Stress." *Wegelin Commentary No. 264*. Wegelin & Company.

Huntington, Samuel P. (1996). *The Clash of Civilizations and the Remaking of World Order*. New York: Touchstone.

Hurwicz, Leonid (2008). "But Who Will Guard the Guardians?" *American Economic Review* 98 (3): 577–585.

Isaacson, Walter, and Evan Thomas (1986). *The Wise Men: Six Friends and the World They Made*. New York: Simon & Schuster.

Ito, Takatoshi (1996). "Japan and the Asian Economies: A Miracle in Transition." *Brookings Papers on Economic Activity* 27 (2): 205–272.

Jensen, Michael C., and William H. Meckling (1976). "Theory of the Firm: Managerial Behavior, Agency Costs and Ownership Structure." *Journal of Financial Economics* 3 (4): 305–360.

Jensen, Michael C., and Kevin J. Murphy (1990). "Performance Pay and Top-Management Incentives." *Journal of Political Economy* 98 (2): 225–264.

Johnson, George E., and Frank P. Stafford (1973). "Social Returns to Quantity and Quality of Schooling." *Journal of Human Resources* 8 (2): 139–155.

Johnson, Paul E. (1978). *A Shopkeeper's Millennium*. New York: Hill & Wang.

Johnson, Ronald N., and Gary D. Libecap (1994). *The Federal Civil Service and the Problem of Bureaucracy: The Economics and Politics of Institutional Change*. Chicago: University of Chicago Press.

Kahneman, Daniel (2011). *Thinking, Fast and Slow*. New York: Farrar, Straus, and Giroux.

Kalt, Joseph P., and Mark A. Zupan (1984). "Capture and Ideology in the Economic Theory of Politics." *American Economic Review* 74 (3): 279–300.

(1990). "The Apparent Ideological Behavior of Legislators: Testing for Principal-Agent Slack in Political Institutions." *Journal of Law and Economics* 33 (1): 103–131.

Kaplan, Robert S., and David M. Walker (2013). "Government Debt and Competitiveness." Harvard Business School U.S. Competitiveness Project. Cambridge, MA: Harvard Business School.

Kau, James B., and Paul H. Rubin (1979). "Self-Interest, Ideology, and Logrolling in Congressional Voting." *Journal of Law and Economics* 22 (2): 365–384.

Kauffmann, Daniel, Aart Kray, and Massimo Mastruzzi (2003). "Governance Matters III: Governance Indicators for 1996–2002." World Bank Policy Research Working Paper No. 3106, Washington D.C.

Kayser, Mark A., and Michael Peress (2012). "Benchmarking Across Borders: Electoral Accountability and the Necessity of Comparison." *American Political Science Review* 106 (3): 661–682.

Keech, William, and Michael Munger (2015). "The Anatomy of Government Failure." *Public Choice* 164: 1–42.

Kendall-Taylor, Andrea, and Erica Frantz (2014). "How Autocracies Fall." *Washington Quarterly* 37 (1): 35–47.

(2015). "Mimicking Democracy to Prolong Autocracies." *Washington Quarterly* 37 (4): 71–84.

Kennedy, Paul (1987). *The Rise and Fall of the Great Powers*. New York: Random House.

Kenny, Lawrence W., and Amy B. Schmidt (1994). "The Decline in the Number of School Districts in the U.S.: 1950–1980." *Public Choice* 79 (1–2): 1–18.

216 Bibliography

Khaldun, Ibn (2005). *The Muqaddimah: An Introduction to History*. Translated by Franz Rosenthal. Princeton, NJ: Princeton University Press.

Kinross, Patrick (2001). *Ataturk: The Rebirth of a Nation*. London: Phoenix.

Kissinger, Henry (2011). *On China*. New York: Penguin Press.

(2014). *World Order*. New York: Penguin Press.

Klein, Benjamin, Robert G. Crawford, and Armen A. Alchian (1978). "Vertical Integration, Appropriable Rents, and the Competitive Contracting Process." *Journal of Law and Economics* 21 (2): 297–326.

Knack, Stephen, and Philip Keefer (1997). "Does Social Capital Have an Economic Payoff? A Cross-Country Analysis." *Quarterly Journal of Economics* 112 (4): 1251–1288.

Kolko, Gabriel (1963). *The Triumph of Conservatism: A Reinterpretation of American History, 1900–1916*. New York: Free Press.

Kotlikoff, Laurence J., and Scott Burns (2012). *The Clash of Generations: Saving Ourselves, Our Kids, and Our Economy*. Cambridge, MA: MIT Press.

Kravitz, Walker (1974). "Evolution of the Senate's Committee System." *Annals of the American Academy of Political Science* 411: 27–38.

Krueger, Anne (1974). "The Political Economy of the Rent-Seeking Society." *American Economic Review* 64 (3): 291–303.

Kuhrt, Amelie (1995). *The Ancient Near-East c. 3000–330 BC*. London: Routledge.

Kumar, Krishna B., and John G. Matsusaka (2009). "From Families to Formal Contracts: An Approach to Development." *Journal of Development Economics* 90 (1): 106–119.

Kuziemko, Illyana, Michael I. Norton, Emmanuel Saez, and Stefanie Stantcheva (2015). "How Elastic Are Preferences for Redistribution? Evidence from Randomized Survey Experiments." *American Economic Review* 105 (4): 1478–1508.

Laffer, Arthur B., Stephen Moore, Rex A. Sinquefield, and Travis H. Brown (2014). *Inquiry Into the Nature and Causes of the Wealth of States: How Taxes, Energy, and Worker Freedom Change Everything*. Hoboken, NJ: John Wiley and Sons.

Landry, Pierre F. (2003). "The Political Management of Mayors in Post-Deng China." *The Copenhagen Journal of Asian Studies* 17: 31–58.

Landsberg, Henry A. (1958). *Hawthorne Revisited*. Ithaca, NY: Cornell University.

Lardy, Nicholas (2014). *Markets Over Mao: The Rise of Private Business in China*. Washington, DC: Peterson Institute for International Economics.

Lasswell, Harold D. (1936). *Politics: Who Gets What, When, and How*. New York: Whittlesey House.

Lawson, Robert A., and J. R. Clark (2010). "Examining the Hayek-Friedman Hypothesis on Economic and Political Freedom." *Journal of Economic Behavior and Organization* 74 (3): 230–239.

Lemos, Margaret H., and Max Minzner (2014). "For Profit Public Enforcement." *Harvard Law Review* 127 (3): 853–913.

Levitt, Steven D. (1996). "How Do Senators Vote? Disentangling the Role of Voter Preferences, Party Affiliation, and Senator Ideology." *American Economic Review* 86 (3): 425–441.

Levy, David M., and Sandra J. Peart (2011). "Soviet Growth and American Textbooks: An Endogenous Past." *Journal of Economic Behavior and Organization*. 78 (1–2): 110–125.

Lewis, Bernard (1995). *The Middle East: A Brief History of the Last 2,000 Years.* New York: Touchstone.

Lewis, Michael (2011). *Boomerang.* New York: W.W. Norton & Company.

(2014). *Flash Boys: A Wall Street Revolt.* New York: W.W. Norton & Company.

Lott, John R., Jr. (1987). "Why is Education Publicly Provided? A Critical Survey." *Cato Journal* 7 (2): 475–501.

MacMillan, Margaret (2014). *The War That Ended the Peace: The Road to 1914.* New York: Random House.

Manne, Henry G. (1965). "Mergers and the Market for Corporate Control." *Journal of Political Economy* 73 (2): 110–120.

Marshall, Monty G. (2013). "Polity IV Project: Political Regime Characteristics and Transitions, 1800–2013." North Vienna, VA: Center for Systematic Peace.

Marx, Karl ([1867] 2009). *Das Capital: Critique of Political Economy.* Washington, DC: Regnery Publishing.

Mayer, Jane (2016). *Dark Money: The Hidden History of the Billionaires Behind the Rise of the Radical Right.* New York: Doubleday.

McChesney, Fred S. (1997). *Money for Nothing: Politicians, Rent Extraction, and Political Extortion.* Cambridge, MA: Harvard University Press.

McCloskey, Deirdre N. (2010). *Bourgeois Dignity: Why Economics Can't Explain the Modern World.* Chicago: University of Chicago Press.

(2016). *Bourgeois Equality: How Betterment Became Ethical, 1600 to 1848, and Then Suspect.* Chicago: University of Chicago Press.

McCormick, Robert E., and Robert D. Tollison (1981). *Politicians, Legislation, and the Economy: An Inquiry Into the Interest Group Theory of Government.* Boston: Martinus Nijhoff Publishing.

McDonald, Patrick J. (2009). *The Invisible Hand of Peace: Capitalism, The War Machine, and International Relations.* New York: Cambridge University Press.

McKean, Roland N. (1965). "The Unseen Hand in Government." *American Economic Review* 55 (3): 496–506.

McKelvey (1984). *Rochester: A Brief History.* New York: Edwin Mellen Press.

Meltzer, Allan H., and Scott F. Richard (1981). "A Rational Theory of the Size of Government." *Journal of Political Economy* 89 (5): 914–927.

(2014). "A Rational Theory of the Growth of Government and the Distribution of Income." The Wharton School Research Paper No. 67.

Merewitz, Leonard, and Mark Zupan (1993). "Franchise Bidding, Contracting Out, and Worksharing in the Production of Postal Services: Can They Collect, Sort, and Deliver?" In *Regulation and the Nature of Postal and Delivery Services,* 69–89. Edited by Michael A. Crew and Paul R. Kleindorfer. Boston: Kluwer Academic Publishers.

Micklethwait, John, and Adrian Wooldridge (2014). *The Fourth Revolution: The Global Race to Reinvent the State.* New York: Penguin Press.

Milgram, Stanley (1974). *Obedience to Authority: An Experimental View.* New York: HarperCollins.

Miller, Terry, Anthony B. Kim, and Kim R. Holmes (Annual). *Index of Economic Freedom.* Washington, DC: Heritage Foundation and Dow Jones & Company, Inc.

Moe, Terry M. (2006). "Political Control and the Power of the Agent." *Journal of Law, Economics, and Organization* 22 (1): 1–29.

(2009). "Collective Bargaining and the Performance of Public Schools." *American Journal of Political Science* 53 (1): 156–174.

Moe, Terry M. (2011). *Special Interest: Teachers Unions and America's Public Schools.* Washington, DC: Brookings Institution.

(2015). "Vested Interests and Political Institutions." *Political Science Quarterly* 30 (2): 277–318.

Moe, Terry M., and John E. Chubb (2009). *Liberating Learning: Technology, Politics, and the Future of American Education.* San Francisco: Jossey-Bass.

Morck, Randall, and Bernard Yeung (2014). "Corporate Governance in China." *Journal of Applied Corporate Finance* 26 (3): 20–41.

Mueller, Dennis C. (1979). *Public Choice.* Cambridge, UK: Cambridge University Press.

Nietzsche, Friedrich (1909). *Thoughts Out of Season.* Edinburgh, UK: Edinburgh Press.

Niskanen, William A., Jr. (1971). *Bureaucracy and Representative Government.* Chicago: Aldine-Atherton.

(2008). *Reflections of a Political Economist: Selected Articles on Government Policies and Political Processes.* Washington, DC: Cato Institute.

North, Douglass C. (1968). "Sources of Productivity Change in Ocean Shipping, 1600–1850." *Journal of Political Economy* 76 (5): 953–970.

(1991). "Institutions." *Journal of Economic Perspectives* 5 (1): 97–112.

North, Douglass C., and Robert P. Thomas (1973). *The Rise of the Western World: A New Economic History.* New York: Cambridge University Press.

North, Douglass C., and Barry R. Weingast (1989). "Constitutions and Commitment: Evolution of Institutions Governing Public Choice in 17th Century England." *Journal of Economic History* 49 (4): 803–832.

Novy-Marx, Robert, and Joshua D. Rauh (2014a). "Revenue Demands of Public Employee Pension Promises." *American Economic Journal: Economic Policy* 6 (1): 193–229.

(2014b). "Linking Benefits to Investment Performance in U.S. Public Pension Systems." *Journal of Public Economics* 116: 47–61.

Nye, Joseph S., Jr., Philip D. Zelikow, and David C. King (1997). *Why People Don't Trust Government.* Cambridge, MA: Harvard University Press.

OECD (2012). *PISA 2012 Results.* Paris: OECD Publishing.

(2015). "Urban Policy Review: China 2015." Paris: OECD Publishing.

Ogilvie, Sheilagh (2014). "The Economics of Guilds." *Journal of Economic Perspectives* 28 (4): 169–192.

Okun, Arthur M. (1975). *Equality and Efficiency: The Big Tradeoff.* Washington, DC: Brookings Institution.

Olson, Mancur (1971). *The Logic of Collective Action: Public Goods and the Theory of Groups.* New York: Shocken.

(1982). *The Rise and Decline of Nations: Economic Growth, Stagflation, and Social Rigidities.* New Haven, CT: Yale University Press.

(1993). "Dictatorship, Democracy, and Development." *American Political Science Review* 87 (3): 567–576.

(2000). *Power and Prosperity: Outgrowing Communist and Capitalist Dictatorships.* New York: Basic Books.

Ornstein, Norman (1955). Editor. *Congress in Change.* New York: Praeger Publishers.

Paulson, Henry M., Jr. (2015). *Dealing With China: An Insider Unmasks the New Economic Superpower.* New York: Hachette Book Group.

Peden, Edgar A. (1991). "Productivity in the United States and its Relationship to Government Activity: An Analysis of 57 Years, 1929–1986." *Public Choice* 69 (2): 153–173.

Peltzman, Sam (1976). "Toward a More General Theory of Regulation." *Journal of Law and Economics* 19 (2): 211–240.

Persson, Torsten, and Guido Tabellini (2003). *The Economic Effects of Constitutions.* Cambridge, MA: MIT Press.

Peterson, Paul E. (2007). *Saving Schools: From Horace Mann to Virtual Learning.* Cambridge, MA: Harvard University Press.

Pfeffer, Jeffrey (2015). *Leadership BS.* New York: Harper Collins.

Pharr, Susan J., and Robert D. Putnam (2000). *Disaffected Democracies: What's Troubling the Trilateral Countries?* Princeton, NJ: Princeton University Press.

Pigou, Arthur C. (1932). *The Economics of Welfare, 4th ed.* London: Macmillan.

Piketty, Thomas (2014). *Capital in the Twenty-First Century.* Cambridge, MA: Harvard University Press.

Pink, Daniel H. (2011). *Drive: The Surprising Truth About What Motivates Us.* New York: Penguin Press.

Pinker, Steven Arthur (2011). *The Better Angels of Our Nature: Why Violence has Declined.* New York: Penguin Press.

Polsby, Nelson (1968). "The Institutionalization of the U.S. House of Representatives." *The American Political Science Review* 41 (1): 144–168.

Posner, Richard A. (1974). "Theories of Economic Regulation." *Bell Journal of Economics and Management Science* 5 (2): 335–358.

(1977). *Economic Analysis of Law.* Boston: Little-Brown.

Primo, David M. (2007). *Rules and Restraints: Government Spending and the Design of Institutions.* Chicago: University of Chicago Press.

(2014). "*Making Budget Rules Work: 2014 Edition.*" Fairfax, VA: George Mason University, Mercatus Center.

Pritchett, Lant, and Lawrence H. Summers (2014). "Asiaphoria Meets Regression to the Mean." Cambridge, MA: National Bureau of Economic Research, Working Paper 20573.

Pritchett, Lant, and Michael Woolcock (2002). *Solutions When the Solution is the Problem: Arraying the Disarray in Development.* Center for Global Development Working Paper No. 10.

Putti, Joseph M., Samuel Aryee, and Tan Kim Liang (1989). "Work Values and Organizational Commitment: A Study in the Asian Context." *Human Relations* 42: 275–288.

Querebin, Pablo (2016). Family and Politics: Dynastic Persistence in the Philippines. *Quarterly Journal of Political Science* 11 (2): 151–181.

Reading, Brian (1992). *Japan: The Coming Collapse.* London: Orion Books.

Ridley, Matt W. (2010). *The Rational Optimist: How Prosperity Evolves.* New York: HarperCollins.

(2015). *The Evolution of Everything.* New York: HarperCollins.

Rivkin, Steven, G., Eric A. Hanushek, and John F. Kain (2005). "Teachers, Schools and Academic Achievement." *Econometrica* 73 (2): 417–458.

Rodrik, Dani (2014). "When Ideas Trump Interests: Preferences, Worldviews, and Policy Innovations." *Journal of Economic Perspectives* 28 (1): 189–208.

Rose-Ackerman, Susan (1978). *Corruption: A Study in Political Economy*. New York: Academic Press.

(1986). Editor. *The Economics of Nonprofit Institutions: Studies in Structure and Policy*. New York: Oxford University Press.

Roser, Max (2015). "Democratization." www.OurWorldInData.org.

Roth, Alvin E. (2015). *Who Gets What – and Why: The New Economics of Matchmaking and Market Design*. New York: Houghton Mifflin Harcourt.

Russakoff, Dale (2015). *The Prize*. New York: Houghton Mifflin Harcourt.

Sachs, Jeffrey D. (2006). *The End of Poverty: Economic Possibilities for Our Time*. New York: Penguin Press.

Sachs, Jeffrey D., and Andrew M. Warner (2001). "The Curse of Natural Resources." *European Economic Review* 45: 827–838.

Sandel, Michael J. (2009). *Justice: What's the Right Thing to Do?* New York: Farrar, Straus and Giroux.

(2012). *What Money Can't Buy: The Moral Limit of Markets*. New York: Farrar, Straus and Giroux.

Schama, Simon (1989). *Citizens: A Chronicle of the French Revolution*. New York: Alfred A. Knopf.

Schuck, Peter H. (2014). *Why Government Fails So Often: And How it can do Better*. Princeton, NJ: Princeton University Press.

Schweizer, Peter F. (2011). *Throw Them All Out: How Politicians and Their Friends Get Rich Off Insider Stock Tips, Land Deals, and Cronyism That Would Send the Rest of Us to Prison*. New York: Houghton Mifflin Harcourt.

(2013). *Extortion: How Politicians Extract Your Money, Buy Votes, and Line Their Own Pockets*. New York: Houghton Mifflin Harcourt.

(2015). *Clinton Cash: The Untold Story of How and Why Foreign Governments and Businesses Helped Make Bill and Hillary Rich*. New York: Harper Collins.

Scully, Gerald W. (1988). "The Institutional Framework and Economic Development." *Journal of Political Economy* 96 (3): 652–662.

(1994). *What Is the Optimal Size of Government in the United States?* Dallas, TX: National Center for Policy Analysis.

Shambaugh, David (2016). *China's Future*. Cambridge, UK: Polity Press.

Shaw, Ian (2003). *The Oxford History of Ancient Egypt*. New York: Oxford University Press.

Shelley, Mary (2013). *The Complete Poems of Percy Bysshe Shelley*. New York: Modern Library/Random House.

Shepsle, Kenneth A. (1980). "The Private Use of Public Interest." *Society* 17 (4): 35–41.

Shleifer, Andrei, and Robert W. Vishny (1993). "Corruption." *Quarterly Journal of Economics* 108 (3): 599–617.

(1998). *The Grabbing Hand: Government Pathologies and Their Cures*. Cambridge, MA: Harvard University Press.

Silverstein, Michael J., Abheek Singhi, Carol Liao, and David Michael (2012). *The $10 Trillion Prize: Captivating the Newly Affluent in China and India*. Boston: Harvard Business Review Press.

Simon, Herbert A. (1978). "Rationality as Process and as Product of Thought." *American Economic Review* 68 (2): 1–16.

Sinn, Hans-Werner (2014). *The Euro-Trap: On Bursting Bubbles, Budgets, and Beliefs.* New York: Oxford University Press.

Smith, Adam ([1776] 1937). *An Inquiry Into the Nature and Causes of the Wealth of Nations.* Edited by Edwin Cannan. New York: Random House.

Smith, Noah (2015). "Japan's Debt Dilemma." *The Milken Institute Review*, 2nd Quarter: 46–54.

Smith, Richard Norton (2014). *On His Own Terms: A Life of Nelson Rockefeller.* New York: Random House.

Solow, Robert M. (1956). "A Contribution to the Theory of Economic Growth." *Quarterly Journal of Economics* 70 (1): 65–94.

Sowell, Thomas (1975). *Race and Economics.* New York: David McKey Co.

Spencer, Herbert (1896). *The Study of Sociology.* New York: D. Appleton and Company.

Stansel, Dean (2005). "Local Decentralization and Local Economic Growth: A Cross-Sectional Examination of U.S. Metropolitan Areas." *Journal of Urban Economics* 57 (1): 55–72.

(2006). "Jurisdictional Competition and Local Government Spending in U.S. Metropolitan Areas." *Public Finance Review* 34 (2): 173–194.

Stewart, Whitney (2001). *Deng Xiaoping: Leader in a Changing China.* Minneapolis, MN: Lerner Publications Company.

Stigler, George J. (1971). "The Economic Theory of Regulation." *Bell Journal of Economics and Management Science* 2 (1): 3–21.

Strouse, Jean (1999). *Morgan: American Financier.* New York: Random House.

Surowiecki, James (2004). *The Wisdom of Crowds.* New York: Doubleday/Anchor Books.

Svensson, Jakob (2005). "Eight Questions about Corruption." *Journal of Economic Perspectives* 19 (3): 19–42.

Tax Foundation (Annual). *Facts & Figures: How Does Your State Compare?* Washington, DC: Tax Foundation.

Telser, Lester G. (1980). "A Theory of Self-Enforcing Agreements." *Journal of Business* 53 (1): 27–44.

Thomas, Melissa A. (2015). *Govern Like Us: U.S. Expectations of Poor Countries.* New York: Cambridge University Press.

Tiebout, Charles M. (1956). "A Pure Theory of Local Expenditures." *Journal of Political Economy* 64 (5): 416–424.

Tocqueville, Alexis ([1835–1840] 2003). *Democracy in America.* Edited by Isaac Kramick. New York: Penguin Press.

Tolstoy, Leo (2010). *War and Peace.* New York: Oxford University Press.

Toynbee, Albert Joseph ([1934–1961] 1989). *A Study of History.* Edited by Jane Caplan. New York: Gramercy.

Tullock, Gordon (1967). "The Welfare Costs of Tariffs, Monopolies, and Theft." *Western Economic Journal* 5 (3): 224–232.

Tullock, Gordon, Arthur Seldon, and Gordon L. Brady (2002). *Government Failure: A Primer in Public Choice.* Washington, DC: Cato Institute.

UNESCO (2014). *Higher Education in Asia.* Montreal: UNESCO Institute for Statistics.

United Nations Office on Drugs and Crime. *Global Study on Homicide 2013.* Vienna, Austria: United Nations.

Wagner, Adolph (1958). "Three Extracts on Public Finance." In *Classics in the Theory of Public Finance* 1–15. Edited by Richard A. Musgrave and Alan Peacock. New York: Macmillan.

Wallis, W. Allen (1976). *An Overgoverned Society.* New York: Free Press.

Walters, Stephen J. K. (2014). *Boom Towns: Restoring the Urban American Dream.* Stanford, CA: Stanford University Press.

Wang, Xuanhui (1998). *Taxation in China, 1997/1998.* Hong Kong: FT Law and Tax, Asia Pacific.

Weber, Max ([1905] 2002). *The Protestant Ethic and the Spirit of Capitalism.* New York: Penguin Press.

Weitzman, Martin L. (1974). "Prices vs. Quantities." *Review of Economic Studies* 41 (4): 472–491.

Welch, Finis (1966). "Measurement of the Quality of Schooling." *American Economic Review* 56 (2): 379–392.

Williamson, Oliver E. (1975). *Markets and Hierarchies.* New York: Free Press.

(1976). "Franchise Bidding for Natural Monopolies-In General with Respect to CATV." *Bell Journal of Economics* 1 (1): 73–104.

Wilson, James Q. (1989). *Bureaucracy: What Government Agencies Do and Why They Do It.* New York: Basic Books.

Winter, Jay (2003). Editor. *America and the Armenian Genocide of 1915.* New York: Cambridge University Press.

Wittman, Donald (1989). "Why Democracies Produce Efficient Results." *Journal of Political Economy* 97 (6): 1395–1424.

Wolf, Charles J. (2003). *Markets or Governments: Choosing Between Imperfect Alternatives.* Cambridge, MA: MIT Press.

Woods, Frederick A. (1913). *The Influence of Monarchs: Steps in a New Science of History.* New York: Macmillan.

Workman, Samuel (2015). *The Dynamics of Bureaucracy in the U.S. Government: How Congress and Federal Agencies Process Information and Solve Problems.* New York: Cambridge University Press.

World Factbook (2015). Central Intelligence Agency. www.cia.gov/library/publica tions/the-world-factbook/index.html February 2, 2016.

Zhang, Weiying (2015). "The Power of Ideas and Leadership in China's Transition to a Liberal Society." *Cato Journal* 35 (1): 1–40.

Zimbardo, Philip G. (2007). *The Lucifer Effect: Understanding How Good People Turn Evil.* New York: Random House.

Ziobrowski, Alan J., James W. Boyd, Ping X. Cheng, and Brigitte J. Ziobrowski (2004). "Abnormal Returns from the Common Stock Investments of Members of the United States Senate." *Journal of Financial and Quantitative Analysis* 39 (4): 661–676.

(2011). "Abnormal Returns from the Common Stock Investments of Members of the U.S. House of Representatives." *Business and Politics* 13 (1): 1–24.

Zingales, Luigi G. (2012). *A Capitalism for the People: Recapturing the Lost Genius of American Prosperity.* New York: Basic Books.

Zucman, Gabriel (2015). *The Hidden Wealth of Nations*. Chicago: University of Chicago Press.

Zupan, Mark A. (1989). "The Efficacy of Franchise Bidding Schemes in the Case of Cable Television: Some Systematic Evidence." *Journal of Law and Economics* 32 (2): 401–456.

(1991a). "Paradigms and Cultures: Some Economic Reasons for Their Stickiness." *American Journal of Economics and Sociology* 50 (1): 99–103.

(1991b). "An Economic Explanation for the Existence and Nature of Political Ticket Splitting." *Journal of Law and Economics* 34 (2): 343–369.

Zupan, M.A. (2011). "The Virtues of Free Markets." *Cato Journal* 31 (2): 36.

Zupan, Mark A. (2015a). "Government Self-Capture and the Decline of Nations." Unpublished working paper, Simon Business School, University of Rochester

(2015b). "The Duration and Motivation of Autocracies." Unpublished working paper, Simon Business School, University of Rochester.

(2015c). "The Road to Virtue." *Schweizer Monat*, Issue 1030.

Index